Logic and Programming in Logic

Ramin Yasdi

Translated by Chris. Bowerman

immediate publishing

While every precaution has been taken in the preparation of this book, the publisher assumes no responsibility for errors or omissions, or for damages resulting from the use of the information contained herein.

Immediate Publishing is an imprint of Afterhurst Limited, Publishers
27 Church Road
Hove
East Sussex
BN3 2FA

British Library Cataloguing in Publication Data

A catalogue record for this book is available from the British Library

ISBN 1-898931-02-X

Printed by Biddles Ltd., Guildford and King's Lynn

Contents

FOREWORD 7

1 LOGIC-PROGRAMMING SYSTEMS 10

Origins 11
Topic 1 13
Overview 13
Outlook 23

2 PROLOG 24

From Logic to Prolog 24
Topic 2 26
Overview 26
Facts 26
Rules 27
Queries 28
Topic 3 35
Syntax and Semantics of Prolog Programs 35
Objects and Predicates 35
Symbols 36
Atoms 36
Constants 36
Variables 36
Structure 37
Terms 38
Lists 38
Operators 38
Matching 38
Assignments of Values (explicit) 40
Topic 4 42
Recursive Rules 42
Topic 5 50
Lists 50
Operations on Lists 53
Sorting Procedures with Lists 59
Topic 6 75
Fail and Cut Operator 75
Topic 7 91
Built-in Predicates 91

3 LOGIC 112

Foundations 112
Topic 8 112
Syntax 112
Semantics 112
Alphabet 113
Calculus 113
Logical Formulae 113
Relationship between Syntax and Semantics 113
Proof Procedure 114

4 PROPOSITIONAL LOGIC 118

Propositions 118
Propositional Form 119
Propositional Connections 119
Topic 9 121
Axiom Systems in Propositional Logic 121
Topic 10 135
Proof Procedures in Propositional Logic 135

5 PREDICATE LOGIC 142
Topic 11 144
Topic 12 158
Converting a Formula into Clausal Form 158

6 HERBRAND PROOF PROCEDURE 162
Topic 13 164
Herbrand Domains 164

7 RESOLUTION METHODS 176

Resolution in Propositional Logic 176
Resolution in Predicate Logic 177
Topic 14 179
Substitution 179
Composition 179
Topic 15 182
Unification 182
Problems of Unification 182
Example for Unification 182
Unification Procedure 184

Topic 16 188
Consistency Checking with Resolution 188
The Proof of a Theorem with Resolution 188

8 RESOLUTION STRATEGIES 192

Disadvantages of the Resolution Principle 192
Elimination of Tautologies 192
"Set-of-support" Resolution 192
P_1 and N_1 Resolution 193
Hyper-resolution 193
Input resolution 193
Linear resolution 194
Entity resolution 194
Subsumption resolution 194
Topic 17 196
SLD Resolution 196
SLD Derivation 196
Remarks 198

9 NEGATION IN LOGIC PROGRAMMING 208
Topic 18 210
The not Procedure 210
Remarks on the not Predicate 211
Topic 19 215
Closed World Assumption 215
Topic 20 218
Negation as Failure 218

10 SEARCH 236
Topic 21 238
Search Strategies 238

APPENDIX A 244

APPENDIX B 271

BIBLIOGRAPHY 274

INDEX 277

Foreword

This book came into being during the course of the author's teaching duties at a number of high schools, where he found it necessary to produce this presentation.

Since many books on Prolog and mathematical logic are on sale, it is pertinent to ask: "Why then, produce another book in these areas?"

When looking at the existing books it becomes apparent that they are concerned with the problems of either the programming language or mathematics. On the one hand the beginner is confronted with the technical details of how to solve a problem by programming in this language, and on the other hand feels out of depth with the formal description of the logic. As yet there is no introductory presentation of these two viewpoints.

Students are offered courses in "mathematical logic" but often without any practical experience. Prolog constitutes a most fascinating programming language. The language enables mathematically logical sentences' soundness and completeness to be proved and translated into commands which the computer is able to execute at least in part. However, the user makes little use of these capabilities. Prolog courses, as generally offered in universities, are mostly in the form of short courses, in which there simply is no room to discuss the theoretical basis of the language. Even a good Prolog programmer would not be able to produce efficient programs or explain an unexpected or false result of the Prolog system, if he were not familiar with the mathematical basis of the system. How, for example, would he understand "occurs check", in Prolog, if he did not know about unification or predicate logic.

Another problem is that students generally learn Prolog in later stages of their course, when they have got used to at least one procedural language, are comfortable with the sequential processing which a "von Neumann machine" provides. At the beginning there are enormous problems in moving over from a procedural to a declarative approach. For this reason it seems advisable to adapt the teaching of declarative programming to that of procedural languages from the beginning, in order to make oneself feel more familiar with the alternative.

This book aims to overcome these disadvantages. It takes an easy-to-read style and presumes no prior knowledge of formal logic. In order to make the subject more comprehensible and in order to deepen knowledge, several exercises are provided; the solutions to the exercises are given in a separate appendix.

In this sense, the book is suited to being used as a course textbook as well as for self-study. It should not be seen as removing the need for students to take an active part in lectures.

I would like to thank the anonymous reviewer for the useful comments and suggestions. I thank my translator, Chris. Bowerman.

Despite all this help, no doubt some errors remain. People who wish to report errors are welcome to do so.

Ramin Yasdi
Chemnitz, 1996

Above all, my dear friend I recommend
to you collegium logicum.
This will doubtless break the spirit in,
laced into its boots,
so that thereafter it carefully
treads a train of thought
and not roundabout
erroneous tos and fros ...
The philosopher who enters there
and shows you that it must be so:
The first was this, the second that
and therefore the third and forth was that,
and if the first and second be not true
The third and fourth were not at all.

- Johann Wolfgang von Goethe -

> A logic program is a set of axioms, or rules, defining relationships between objects. A computation of a logic program is a deduction consequence of the program. A program defines a set of consequences, which is its meaning. The Art of Logic Programming is constructing concise and elegant programs that have the desired meaning.
>
> - L. Sterling,
> E. Shapiro, 1986 -

1 LOGIC-PROGRAMMING SYSTEMS

The ability to reason logically is a major facet of intelligent behaviour. The intelligent behaviour of individuals is determined by the knowledge that they have of their environment. A person can, on the basis of his experience of the world around him, use certain logical rules to make conclusions that determine his behaviour when faced with unknown problems. Much of this knowledge is descriptive and can be written in a declarative form. It has been shown that the most flexible forms of intelligence depend, to a great extent, on the use of declarative knowledge.

The wish to automate the process of logical inference and to build machines which can think like people goes right back to R. Descartes and G.W. Leibnitz in the seventeenth century. Descartes' discovery that classical Euclidian geometry could be created by algebraic methods alone was an insight which not only strongly influenced mathematics but was also important for deductive systems, i.e., the dream of being able to produce logical human thought on a machine.

Leibnitz's idea was to develop a universal logical language, the "lingua characteristica", in which every truth could be formulated and a corresponding calculus for the language, the so-called "calculus ratiocinator". He wanted to make it possible to translate natural language conditions and also meaning, which could not be handled by number theory. He had the impression that such a calculus - if developed - would be able to be automated (rather like a calculator) and that in this way human thinking could avoid the drudgery of tedious work. This view can be seen most clearly in the wonderful description of two well-meaning people who, in the midst of a good philosophical debate in search of truth, translate their arguments into "lingua characteristica" and then cease to argue as two philosophers but say, rather like two computer experts: "calculemus: we'll just compute it."

ORIGINS

Logic is a discipline that has occupied Man for centuries. Aristotle (384-322 BC) defined logic. He taught logic at the University of Athens and placed the principles of logic on a sound foundation. Euclid (300 BC) played a similar role. He taught and made geometry and number theory systematic.

Modern logic (symbolic or mathematical) was developed by Gottlob Frege most notably in the production of his *Begriffsschrift* (a paper in which expressions are represented as symbols). This contained the complete development of the area of mathematical logic which we now call *first order predicate calculus*. The use, on the one hand of Boolean logical connectives and quantifiers, and relations and functions on the other, constituted the first description of a complete functional logic such as would be familiar to us today. He used *Modus Ponens* as an inference rule. The *Begriffsschrift* is relevant not just because in it a logical calculus was developed and fully constructed but also due to the methodical approach by which the syntax and semantics of a formal language were separated and explicitly defined. The *Begriffsschrift* is not, therefore, just the precursor of today's mathematical logic but also the model for all formal and programming languages.

Future impetus came through the work of Theoralf Skolem in which he developed a systematic method which made it possible to prove the completeness of any set. In two works, which appeared in 1920 and 1928, he introduced the elimination of quantifiers (by Skolem functions) and a construction which is known to us today under the slightly erroneous name of *Herbrand universes*.

Similarly, in 1928 the book "*Foundations of Theoretical Logic*" by D. Hilbert and W. Ackerman appeared. In this book the ideas important to the automation of logic were presented, for the first time, to a broad mathematically-interested audience. In this book, the *decidability* problem was, amongst other things introduced: the problem of deciding whether or not there is an algorithm which can decide for any given proposition of predicate logic if it is true or false.

In 1930 Herbrand provided the proof in his doctorate that for a well-formed mathematical proposition, soundness can not be proved. This semi-decidability of predicate calculus is the formal proof of all deduction systems, i.e., if a theorem is true then it can be proved in a finite number of steps. If this does not succeed then there are two possibilities: either, a proof of incorrectness can succeed in special cases, or the program keeps running without terminating and it is impossible to say.

Alfred Tarski (1934) introduced a complete semantic theory for predicate logic in which he provided a more precise definition of soundness correctness, logical consequence and other related terms.

A little later, Alan Turing and Alonzo Church independently showed that there is no general proof procedure which can determine whether or not a proposition is true in predicate calculus. A proof procedure means a deterministic process which always terminates and delivers a decision. In his 1936 publication, in which he described his eponymously named abstract machine, Turing related the decidability problem back to the halting problem and showed that the question of whether or not such a machine halts is undecidable.

In 1950 the development of the computer had progressed and the first program for checking propositions the "*logic theory machine program*" was developed.

In the year 1954 J. A. Robinson [48] published his treatise on the proof of theorems and clausal-form logic: "the resolution principle". He defined expressions such as clause, literal and unification.

Under the direction of G. Robinson, a group of scientists at the Argonne National Lab, near Chicago, were occupied with proving mathematical propositions by computer. In this group, in which J. A. Robinson and L. Woos worked, the weakness of programming with the Herbrand method [30] was recognised very quickly: namely the undifferentiated use of Herbrand-Instances. A general, machine-oriented, logical principle was sought which could unify these thoughts into a single inference rule. This so-called "resolution" method was developed from 1963-4 by J. A. Robinson in the article "A machine-oriented logic, based on the resolution principle", published in the *Journal of the Association for Computing Machinery.*

After the publication of this article, people in many places began to program resolution-based proof procedures as efficiently as possible in order to see how they performed. Over the next few years, many research groups in Edinburgh and the United States began to look at a variety of resolution methods and approaches for logic programming. These ranged from procedurally-oriented approaches at MIT to improvements of the unification algorithm at Stanford. In the end, Kowalski [40] showed the way, by using procedurally-based work with his SLD-system, in which he showed how Horn clauses, which are organised procedurally as well as declaratively, could be used for storing knowledge.

The first logic programming-based interpreter was implemented by Roussel in Marseille. Further, more efficient interpreters and a compiler were developed in Edinburgh, as well as elsewhere. This culminated in 1972 when Alan Colmerauer presented a logic programming system in 1972 [16] which was to form the basis for programming in logic.

In 1981 the Japanese announced that this programming language was to become the basis for research into their fifth generation computers.

Topic 1

Overview

1.1 Definitions

This section gives an overview of the logic-related expressions used in this book. Some of the expressions used are only examined fully later.

"Logic" is called the study of the logical consequence of reasoning and argument. "Yes, that's logical" or "That's not logical!" are everyday criteria that we use or hear said colloquially. What we mean by that is that something is true or false, right or wrong: either way it can not be denied.

The expression comes from the Greek and refers to the procedures used to draw correct conclusions from facts and events. Like Logos the "thinking spirit" in ancient Greek philosophy, it plays a central role. The learned scholar Aristotle defined scientific logic as a distinct part of philosophy which he called "analysis": the basic form of all scientific reasoning.

In the Age of Enlightenment efforts were made, in particular by the philosopher Leibniz, to create a universal science by linking logic to mathematics. Immanuel Kant made initial steps in the direction of transcendental logic and categories: a metaphysical logic which mirrored "German idealism" and lead Hegel to dialectic logic.

Formal Logic

Logic is a formal system in which inexact, everyday expressions can be approximated in a mathematically exact manner. A formalist would say that, *formal* logic is a formal language in which certain expressions can be assigned truth values.

Logic can profit enormously from the area of information technology (IT), since IT makes much use of case studies and experimental results. The "brain" of the computer is based on the study of formal logic. Logic plays a similar role in IT to differential calculus in physics.

Mathematical Logic

Mathematical logic is a theory in which models of the mathematical language and naive logic are formulated and, in time, developed into reasoning. As a subarea of mathematics, mathematical logic is formulated in terms of the language of mathematics. Mathematical methods are, therefore, used. Typical of this is the manner in which new expressions are posited, definitions given and arguments developed, for example in the formula: $(x+y)z = xz + yz$. The product of the sum of the two numbers and the third is identical to the sum of the products of the first and the third and the product of the second and the third.

Mathematical logic constitutes the basis for the investigation of all logical languages such as: propositional logic, predicate logic, modal logic, temporal logic, fuzzy Logic, 3-valued logic.

Predicate Logic

The most common form of mathematical logic is the extended form of propositional logic, predicate logic. It is used to formalise and prove aspects of programs. The "relational structure", indeed the concept behind predicate logic, is that of the set of objects, relations and functions.

As in propositional logic, formulae are constructed by means of atoms and other formulae. Atoms, however, may be not just literals but also predicates with arguments. Terms themselves can be constructed from constants, variables, function terms and formulae quantified with quantifiers, such as "for all",$\forall$ and "there exists a", $\exists$. In predicate calculus all sentences are strings of letters which are organised according to the precise rules of a grammar. These words, whose entirety constitutes the whole of the formal language of predicate calculus, are called formulae. A reason for predicate logic's expressive power lies in the fact that it is possible to use logical operators, with which complex sentences can be built, without having to state the truth or falsity of the constituent sentences. Further flexibility stems from the use of quantifiers and variables. With quantifiers it is possible to express facts about all the objects in a universe. The existential quantifier makes it possible to assume the existence of an object with particular characteristics without actually defining the object. Variables are place-holders, which can be replaced by any value in the permitted range for the variable.

When defining relations between objects, the order in which the objects are given plays an important role: `father(Peter,Max)` can just as well mean "Peter is the father of Max" as "Max is the father of Peter". The programmer must make an irreversible decision about which interpretation to select. In the relation above, relations for the objects and the associated relations would be used. The relation name `father` is called a "predicate"; the objects which the relation describes are called "arguments".

Clausal Form

The representation of knowledge in the form of clauses has proved to be very powerful for building knowledge-bases, consisting of facts and rules. Predicate logic formulae can, to a certain extent, be simplified and reduced to the elementary connectives "and", "or" and "not" and quantifiers can be removed. In the resulting clausal form all the variables are universally quantified and the connectives "AND", "OR" and "NOT" arranged from the outside in, that is in conjunctive normal form (CNF).

Horn Clauses

Whilst general clausal form is always produced directly from the predicate logic form, a restricted form is used in logic programming, with at the most one literal on the left side of the clause. This type of clause is called a Horn clause. This type of restriction to one consequent has been shown to be the most practical. The simple construction of Horn clauses make it much easier to automate resolution because Horn clauses can be viewed and processed as procedures.

The left side of the Horn clause is called the head and the right side, if it exists, is called the tail of the clause. A Horn clause without a head is a statement to be proved. For example:

Fact	`king(henry) :-`
Rule	`king(X):- married(Y, X), king(Y)`
Query	`:- king(henry)`

It should be noted that programming in logic is not necessarily the same as programming in Horn logic clauses.

Resolution

The resolution procedure enables the propositions of predicate logic, which are in clausal form, to be proved. The procedure used consists of the following steps:
The clauses are ordered so that the non-negated literals are on the left and the negated literals on the right. If the same literal occurs on opposing sides then a new clause can be formed by dropping the entire literal and adding it to a new clause. In this way larger, similarly sized or smaller formulae can be produced. If two single element clauses [K] and [¬K] meet then the empty clause, or contradiction, [], is produced and the procedure terminates. Although no clauses can be derived in this way, contradictions within a set of clauses can be found. This suffices for a proof of the original theorem and is not demonstrated by deriving clauses from the set of clauses but through the presumption of the opposite which leads to contradiction. For example:

An axiom system contains the following two clauses in which the first is not a Horn clause and ";" means "OR".

```
nice(Ollie);merry(Ollie) ←
      friday(today),wages(yesterday)
      sings(Ollie) ← drinks(Ollie), merry(Ollie)
```

New clause

```
nice(Ollie); sings(Ollie) ← friday(today),
      wages(yesterday), drinks(Ollie)
```

Axiom System

Logic is a subarea of mathematics in which fundamental questions such as the freedom from contradiction of mathematical theories and mathematical expressions such as "proof" and "definition" are defined and treated. To this end, a language (calculus) is created in which the logical relations can be more readily and more exactly seen and overviewed. The process of logic calculus is to represent the collection of logical elements by means of symbolic signs and to perform computations on these, in accordance with mathematical procedure. In addition, rules are introduced which transform given formulae and strings of symbols into other formulae or strings of symbols. In this fashion, the process of drawing logical conclusions is rendered more precise.

A calculus thus defines, foremost, a set of true logical propositions and facts (so-called axioms). Also, a set of rules are made available with which new facts can be derived from old facts. In evaluating such a calculus the expressions *soundness* and *completeness* play a central role.

Such a positive, deductive calculus is correct if every formula *F* from the set of formulae *T* can be derived by means of inference rules *A*, as a logical consequence of *T*. A calculus is sound when every logical consequence *F* of the set of formulae *T* can be derived by means of inference rules *A*.

In this way mathematical logic lays the foundations for knowledge-based programming. It is a tool used in order to be able to represent information in formal mathematics and in order to be able to reduce "logical thought" to the formal search for symbols.

1.2 Logic Programming

What is logic Programming?

Logic programming is often also called knowledge-based programming. In the language of logic, knowledge consists of a set of true propositions. When the user enters an assertion to a logic program the system attempts to show whether or not it is true or false on the basis of the knowledge. This type of programming method aims to draw conclusions based on the knowledge of a given domain of application which is stored in the computer.

Based on this, logic programming can be said to be a computational formalism which brings together the following principles:

- it uses logic as a language to formalise facts (knowledge)
- it uses derivation procedures (inference procedures) in order to use and manipulate the knowledge.

Starting Point

Whenever we wish to describe some fact about the world around us, we normally use the declarative sentences of a natural language, e.g.:

1. Every mother loves her children.
2. Martha is a mother and Thomas her child.

By applying a given rule of derivation we can use such descriptions in order to draw conclusions. If we know that propositions 1 and 2 are true then it is possible to draw from that the conclusion:

3. Martha loves Thomas.

On closer examination of propositions 1 and 2 we see that they describe the universe, that is, the entire knowledge about the persons and relationships between them, e.g.:

... is a mother ...
... is a child ...
... loves ...

This example reflects the main ideas of logic programming, namely the description of actual relationships between objects and the use of a programming system in order to be able to draw conclusions such as 3.

Logic programming is, thus, programming by describing.

Logic on the Computer

A machine can store information about the world around it in two basic ways. There are, thus, two basic ways of using computers:

a. Conventional method: procedural
The user states what the problem is and the user controls how it is solved.

b. Alternative method: declarative
The user states what the problem is and the system controls how it is solved.

For example, in a computer program for matrix conversion, coded knowledge is defined as implicit knowledge which is stored during the sequence of operations to be carried out. It would be very difficult to extract this knowledge from the code for alternatives. This knowledge is called procedural knowledge since it is inseparably linked to the procedures which make use of it.

Let us look at this from the perspective of a table-based database of personal data which is used by a program in order to extract certain data. In this the data are separated from the program code, and are used and manipulated by it on demand. Knowledge expressed in this manner is known as declarative knowledge because it embodies a description of a world. In general, such propositions are stored in symbolic structures which the procedures which use the knowledge can access. The knowledge stored in this way is known as explicit knowledge. Programs which represent knowledge explicitly have proven themselves to be more flexible because in them data is separately stored from the actual program.

In logic programming, the declarative representation of knowledge is preferred because it has the great advantage that the knowledge can be changed without needing to change the program which uses that data. Knowledge represented in such a way can also be used for other purposes which may not even have been foreseen at the time that the knowledge was compiled. The knowledge base needs to be neither repeated nor extended nor developed specially from scratch for each application. In some instances, it is also possible to add to declarative knowledge by inference procedures which can then, in turn, be used to derive further new knowledge.

The use of declarative knowledge is more resource intensive and slower than when directly using procedural knowledge. In procedural programming this problem is solved by defining a function or procedure to search the data structures defined and return the result. In logic programming the question is posed in the form of a statement. In order to prove this proposition, the knowledge available is searched in a series of steps. The existence of such a statement is proved when an object is found which matches the proposition given above. In this way, efficiency is sacrificed to flexibility.

Logic Programming

Now we come to the question of how to formalise the functions and relations so that standard methods of deduction can be carried out on the logical formulae that are produced in this way. As already described above, predicate logic proves to be a good basis for a universal form of representation since it allows knowledge to be formulated for any number of application domains. Logic programming is, therefore, the use of the formulae of predicate logic as the instructions of a programming language.

In a logic program, predicate logic is used to represent the knowledge by means of Horn clauses. The programmer codes the facts and rules, which are a form of declarative sentence, as predicate logic clauses. The resulting program is thus a set of logical formulae.

When a problem has to be solved the program is asked to draw conclusions, based on facts and rules, according to an inference strategy, which produces the logical connections between premises and conclusions, according to the second principle, mentioned above. This occurs according to certain inference rules, such as Resolution or Modus Ponens. Inference rules are used to derive a new, true proposition from a set of propositions.

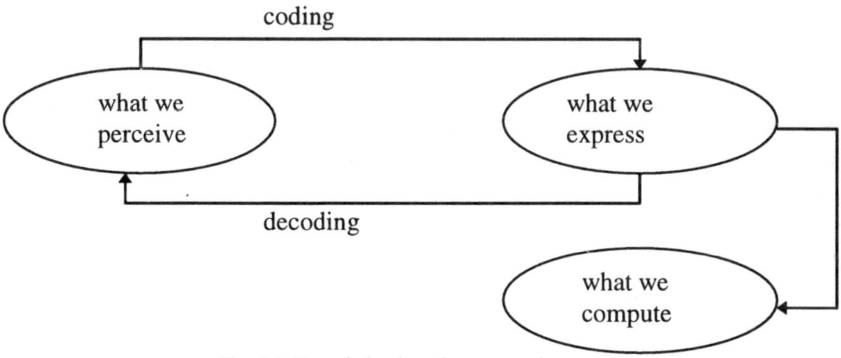

Fig. 1.1: Knowledge-based programming

The logical formulae stored in the program are the only items of information available to the computer for solving problems. This means that these also constitute the contents or semantics of the program. The entire knowledge of this special domain is made up of nothing more and nothing less than what is stored there. The consequence of this is that the only conclusions that can be made are those that can be derived from this knowledge. On the one hand this means that only the true and satisfiable propositions and formulae should be available (to the system, anyway), in order to guarantee the termination of the system. On the other hand, such a program can only have the "meaning" or sense that its stored propositions have.

In summary here is the definition of a logic program according to L. Sterling and E. Shapiro:

"A logic program is a set of axioms or rules which defines the relationship between objects. The computation of a logic program is a deductive consequence of the program. A program defines a set of consequences which is also its contents. The art of logic programming lies in building short and elegant programs which have the intended meaning."

1.3 Architecture and Function of a Logic Programming System

As we saw above, by logic programming it is possible, with the aid of predicate logic, to create an environment which is can solve problems in a specific domain of knowledge. This environment is known as a logic-programming system (LPS).

A logic-programming system is made up of three components: the user, the inference engine, the knowledge-base and an agreed semantics, i.e., a description of how the facts in the knowledge base are interpreted. The basic architecture of such a system is shown in Fig. 1.1.

Knowledge base

The foundation for an LPS is the knowledge base, which holds the knowledge as a set of facts and relations of a certain subarea (universe). This information is stored, for example, in the form of Horn clauses and can be accessed in order to solve a query by the inference engine. This knowledge base can be extended by means of further facts, rules and inferences.

Inference Engine

The inference engine constitutes the central component of an LPS. This virtual machine is an "inference procedure" which:

a. looks through the knowledge base, according to a given search strategy, in order to draw conclusions about a query, by means of deduction

b. determines the inference method to use for determining the truth or falsehood of the query.

Well-known inference rules are resolution or Modus Ponens. Breadth-first and depth-first searches are examples of search strategies.

If the query is a logical consequence of the facts and rules which are stored then a correct solution (answer) can be found. If the query can not be answered from the knowledge in the knowledge base then the answer is considered to be insoluble. This insolubility should always be seen in relation to the knowledge base and search strategy (inference rule). An extension of the knowledge-base or modification of the search strategy can enable solutions to previously-insoluble problems to be found.

User

The user queries the LPS in order to determine the truth of given propositions or relations. This, of course, presumes that the user or the programmer either already has the knowledge of this particular problem area or has stored them.

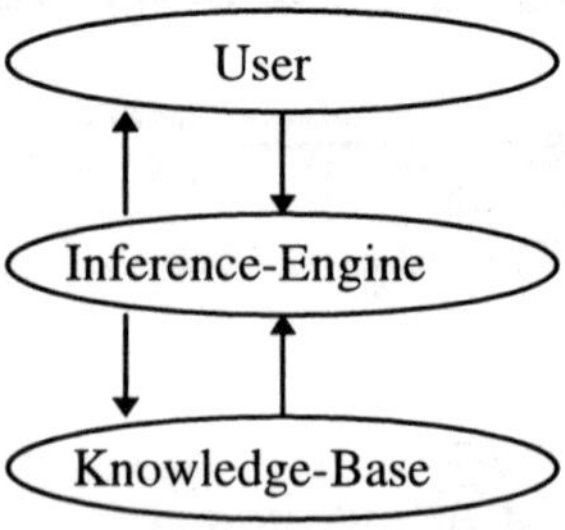

Fig. 1.2 Logic Programming System

The following example may clarify the mode of operation of an LPS:

```
man(socrates)                 Fact
mortal(X) if man(X)           Rule
? mortal(socrates)            Query
yes                           Answer
```

If a problem such as "Is Socrates mortal?" should need to be solved then a natural language query needs to be formulated, converted into clausal form and entered into the machine:

```
? mortal(socrates)
```

This query is passed by the system to the inference procedure. In order to solve the problem it attempts to prove the proposition, by making inferences using knowledge which supports the proposition. The information recorded in our case is:

```
man(socrates)                 Socrates is a man
mortal(X) if man(X)           all men are mortal
```

The inference machine now tries to make inferences based on the facts and rules. In the above example: if socrates is a man and all men are mortal then Socrates is mortal. The answer is correct because it is a logical consequence of the facts and rules and the system accordingly replies `yes`. If the user wishes to view the facts and rules which contributed to the solution or if the user does not understand it then he can use the explain function in order to list all the facts and rules which contributed to the answer.

Application Areas

Expert systems are an important applications area. Here too knowledge of a specific domain is collected and used by a specialist to answer given questions. The basic architecture and function of such a system is as per Fig. 1.2.

- if the user knows something then he passes it on to the computer:

facts and rules

- if the user does not know something then he asks the computer:

queries

- if the computer knows then it delivers an answer:

answers

- if the user does not understand then he requests an explanation: explanation

1.4 Logic-orientated Programming Languages

The best known is Prolog, of which more in the following chapters. Further programming languages in which logical relations can be represented are PL/1 (programming language one) and LISP [55].

Two logic-programming languages which are not based on resolution are Haridis LPL and MacLennans Relational Programming. The Haridis system is based on natural deduction proof procedures and supports the negation and if-and-only-if which is difficult to express with Horn clauses. In relational programming systems whole relations are computed simultaneously and operations are only performed on whole relations instead of the tuples (data elements) of a relation.

1.5 Pros and Cons of Logic Programming

Pros

The basic advantage of logic programming lies in the fact that knowledge can be represented in a machine-independent manner. This permits more flexible and intelligent programs than is currently possible with procedural systems.

Indeed logic programming can be considered to be the cornerstone of knowledge based programming and of artificial intelligence. Formal expressiveness makes it possible to code the assumptions of the problem in a direct and machine-independent manner in order to expose implicit assumptions.

Inferences, made as a result of these formulations, constitute the new knowledge which can now be incorporated into the previous knowledge.

A further plus point lies in the use of mathematical principles in order to describe precise and simple characterisations of the relations between programs, their results and their specifications as well as to describe other programs.

Knowledge is thus separated from its use and this enables different types of implementation to be produced without affecting the logical capacity and integrity of the data. This means that the control mechanism or the architecture of the system can be changed without having to modify the knowledge base. In this way a universal foundation for the standardisation of software technology has been realised. Knowledge can therefore be modified and extended in order to support higher forms of knowledge representation. Further advantages are:

- good expressiveness
- well-defined semantics and syntax (close to natural language)
- criteria for soundness and completeness
- incremental program development
- direct creation of the prototype from the specification
- why and why-not explanations

Disadvantages

Logic programming necessitates a different style of thinking from procedural programming (which is not an absolute disadvantage) and it is unfamiliar to someone who does not know the methodology.

Furthermore, computer technology is not yet able to deliver the right environment for programming such complex systems. The development and use of parallel architectures will probably offer improved scope in the future.

Related to this is the problem with the language itself. No really satisfactory method has been found by which to implement these computational ideas in a conventional language.

The use of meta-logical operators such as `assert` and `retract` for data manipulation leads to the possibility of a discrepancy between the declarative and procedural semantics.

The order of the clauses and the literals within the clauses has a great effect on the flow of the program in Prolog.

In implementing negation by means of *negation by failure*, the commutativity of the premises of the clauses can no longer be guaranteed. This rule, along with Prolog's search strategy, can lead to incorrect derivations.

A further criticism comes from the side of the logic programmers whose main concern lies in the current predilection in logic programming for the use of predicate logic.

Outlook

Even if Leibnitz's inspirational vision of a general "lingua characteristica" has not been realised and no politician has to send his arguments to an authority equipped with a mechanical "calculus ratiocinator" for checking, it is true that logic-oriented, knowledge-based systems, such as, for example, expert systems, are a core part of modern technology and are becoming an increasingly common element of computer technology.

> Even from stones which lie in the way
> something beautiful can be built
> - Johann Wolfgang von Goethe -

2 PROLOG

FROM LOGIC TO PROLOG

Prolog is derived from the words "PROgramming in LOGic" and uses symbolic logic as a programming language.

Being the most common form of mathematical logic, first-order predicate logic constitutes the basis of Prolog. In predicate logic formulae are built up of atoms (literals, predicates with arguments) and other forms, with the help of "and", "or", "not", "if" and "if and only if". The formulae can be quantifed by means of the quantifiers "for all" and "there exists". The formulae of predicate logic are simplified in that the multiplicity of logical connectives is restricted to the elementary connectives "and", "or" and "not" and the quantifiers removed. By means of these transformations the formulae of predicate logic are converted into clausal form.

LOGic programming is restricted to Horn clauses. This restricted clausal form has at most one literal or proposition on the left hand side.

At the heart of Prolog is the inference mechanism: under what conditions can the validity of the conclusion be drawn from the validity of the premises? Prolog attempts to prove the validity of the left hand side from the validity (provability) of the right hand side. Prolog can, therefore, be considered to be a "prover" for Horn-clause logic.

A Horn clause with head and tail is a proposition (rule) whose validity is to be proved. A Horn clause without tail is a piece of data (a fact) which does not need to be proved. A Horn clause without a head is a proposition to be proved (a query).

The idea behind the Prolog language is, on the one hand to describe the characteristics of objects and the relationships between objects as relational facts and, on the other, to formulate the logical relationships between these facts as rules. Prolog is a declarative language, that is, Prolog uses axioms instead of procedures. Prolog programs consist of propositions and facts and not of the algorithms, data types, branches, iterations, assignments etc. familiar in imperative languages (PASCAL, COBOL, FORTRAN). In conventional programming languages a program consists of:

program = algorithm + data structures

A precondition for the implementation of a program is that the programmer knows the solution procedure (algorithm) for the problem to solve. This must be known because the execution of the program is exclusively controlled by the algorithm by means of the corresponding control structures.

For Prolog the following schema applies:

program = logic + control

Facts and rules which contribute to the solution are formulated in logic.

This means that Prolog does not make any distinction between the "program" and the "data". The data structures are not considered to be explicit components of a program as they are inseparably linked to the subject of logic. This quasi-equality initially makes understanding harder, for those used to structured programming.

What still remains is control. This is taken on by the Prolog compiler/interpreter. The programmer does not have any control structures, as such, at his disposal. He can just use the sequence of the facts and rules that he has declared in order to influence or cut the search for a solution. It should be pointed out that, apart from a few exceptions to be mentioned shortly, the order of declaration of the facts and rules has no effect on program execution. The remark refers not to the "how" but to the "what".

A Prolog program can be regarded as a knowledge base which can be used to answer questions. A knowledge base consists of a set of propositions (facts) as well as propositions about propositions (rules). Programming, or program execution, takes place by proving propositions about a knowledge base - the inference of logical conclusions from a knowledge base. In order to carry out this checking, Prolog systems contain an inference engine. The system uses this component to determine, with respect to the query, whether or not one or more of the facts are held in the knowledge base is true or whether or not they can be derived from rules held within the knowledge base. The procedure according to which this verification is carried out is known as the "inference algorithm". This algorithm is based on the resolution principle. The resolution principle makes it possible to prove propositions in clausal form mechanically. It specifies how a proposition can follow from another.

In contrast to a conventional, imperative language Prolog can undo all calculations on the failure or success of a query and search for an alternative, in order to find another or indeed any solution. This means that the Prolog system tries to find all possible values which answer the query. In this way the Prolog system can work out, by means of the inference component, whether or not a proposition, contained in a query, is held within the knowledge base, that is, whether or not it is derivable from the knowledge base. In this connection the expression "closed world assumption" is important. This expression means that facts which are not known to be true is taken to be false; if a query can not be derived then this just means that it can not be derived from the knowledge base. This does not mean that that the proposition is "false".

Topic 2

Overview

Prolog programs consist of:
facts: about objects and their relationships,
rules: relationships between propositions,
queries: with which the objects, described in the facts and rules, can be called up.

Facts

Let us look at the family tree in Fig. 2.1. From the diagram we can read off the following proposition:

<Henry is the grandfather of Peter's child Anne>

Within the proposition the facts of the form:

<grandfather of ...'s child ... >

describe a relationship between the objects "Henry", "Peter" and "Anne". This relationship is called a predicate and is represented in a short form as: `grandfather(henry,peter,anne).` In this formalised representation the predicate is represented by the predicate name `grandfather-of` and the objects `henry`, `peter`, `anne` as arguments of the predicate.

The meaning of the names of the predicates and arguments is determined by the programmer. They must be used consistently throughout the program. The names can be chosen freely as the logical structure of the relation is all that is important. For this reason meaningful names should be used. The following guidelines should be observed when formulating predicates:

- The names of the predicates and constants must begin with a small letter.
- The names of variable arguments are indicated with an initial capital letter.
- The first part of a fact is the predicate name; followed by the arguments in round brackets.
- The number of arguments is not fixed and can, therefore, also be zero.
- The individual arguments are separated from each other by commas.
- The order of the arguments within a predicate is important and should not be varied.
- Predicates of the same name but different arity (number of arguments) represent different facts.
- Every fact must be terminated with a full stop.

These guidelines apply to all dialects, for which individual particularities should be observed.

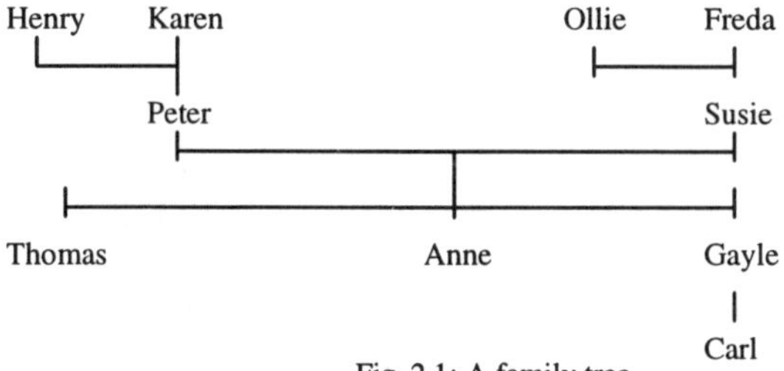

Fig. 2.1: A family tree

Rules

Prolog can derive new facts from existing facts by means of rules. A rule is an expression whose effect is that the truth value of a given fact is dependent on one or more facts. Thus, for example, the fact:
`grandparent(henry,anne)` is derivable from the knowledge base according to the rule:

then a person "is grandparent" of their grandchild
if the person "is parent" of the child
and the child "is parent" of the grandchild

because the knowledge base contains the facts:
`parent(henry, peter)` and `parent(peter, anne)`. This rule is formalised as:

```
grandparent(henry, anne):-
      parent(henry, peter),
      parent(peter, anne).
```

In this the "if ... then" relationship is indicated in the rule by the ":-" symbol. The derived fact is on the left of the ":-". The comma "," on the right hand side, between the two facts, indicates a logical "AND" connection.

The actual sense of the rule does not lie in representing a concrete meaning. Rather, the rule permits a general, regular form of description for representing many different relationships between predicates. Therefore, place keepers or variables must be used in place of constants, in their respective positions, within the formal representation.

If we choose to use the names "Person", "Child" and "Grandchild" to represent variables then the above rule can be given as:

```
grandparent(Person, Grandchild):-
        parent(Person, Child),
        parent(Child, Grandchild).
```

The formalised rule is interpreted as follows:

The rule head `grandparent(Person, Grandchild)` can have its variables, `Person` (e.g., by `henry`) and `Grandchild` (e.g., by `anne`), replaced concretely when either of the predicates in the rule tail, linked by ",", `parent(Person, Child)` and `parent(Child, Grandchild)`, are derived from the knowledge base. This means that for there to be an instantiation of the variable "Child", facts must exist in the knowledge base for the chosen constants for `parent(Person, Child)` and `parent(Child, Grandchild)`.

The rule outlined above, along with the facts, results in the following Prolog program:

```
parent(henry, peter).
parent(karen, peter).
parent(ollie, susie).
parent(freda, susie).
parent(peter, thomas).
parent(peter, gayle).
parent(susie, thomas).
parent(susie, anne).
parent(susie, gayle).
parent(gayle, carl).
grandparent(Person, Grandchild):-
        parent(Person, Child),
        parent(Child, Grandchild).
```

Queries

When we have entered the above program into the Prolog system as a knowledge base, we can then make queries. Queries begin with the "?-" symbol. The query acts as a goal to prove and is called a "goal". A goal is entered with a terminating period. A simple query could be:

```
?- parent(susie, gayle).
```

The inference component then looks through the knowledge base in order to see if the predicate is known to the Prolog system or can be derived. That is, a similarly-named predicate is searched for in the knowledge base. If this is found then the individual objects (arguments) of the goal predicate as well as the number of them are compared with the one just found. This form of comparison is called *pattern-matching*. If the arguments are identical, as in our example, then the answer "yes" is returned. This means that query can be derived (proved) from the current knowledge base. If, on the other hand, the query:

```
?- parent(henry, susie).
```

is asked then the answer "no" is returned, which indicates that the query can not be derived from the current knowledge base.

If we wanted to query the relationship as to whether `henry` is a parent of `peter` AND if `ollie` is a parent of `susie`, then the following query would be used:

```
?- parent(henry, peter), parent(ollie, susie).
```

In this query (goal), a comma is used between the predicates in order to indicate a logical AND. This means that this goal can only be derived when both the `parent(henry, peter)` and `parent(ollie, susie)` can be derived. If the query is as to whether `henry` is a parent of `susie` OR whether `ollie` is a parent of `susie`, then the goal is of the form:

```
?- parent(henry, susie); parent(ollie, susie).
```

In this example the semicolon ";" indicates the logical OR connection. This means that the goal can only be derived when at least one of the predicates `parent(henry, susie)` OR `parent(ollie, susie)` is derived. In our example the answer "yes" is returned as the second predicate, `parent(ollie, susie)`, can be derived from the knowledge base.

These examples show the first, simple use of the knowledge base in which the system is asked about the knowledge it contains. These queries are also called qualified questions. In contrast there is a second use of the knowledge base in which several answers are possible and are returned. How does this come about? For example let us display `anne`'s parents. It would be possible to proceed, as below:

```
?- parent(peter, anne).
yes
?- parent(ollie, anne).
no
?- parent(susie, anne).
yes
?- parent(freda, anne).
no
```

It would clearly be easier to use variables. The query then looks as below:

```
?- parent(Person, anne).
```

The answer would then be:

```
Person = peter
Person = susie
```

In this case Person is a variable. The query has the effect that all objects in the knowledge base in which parent is the first argument and anne is the second argument are returned.

The process of replacing variables, i.e., the matching of terms by replacing variables by other arguments (objects, terms) is called *unification.*

It is also possible to return all the possible parent-child relationships with the query:

```
?- parent(Person_1, Person_2).
```

The answers are then:

```
Person_1 = henry        Person_2 = peter
Person_1 = karen        Person_2 = peter
Person_1 = ollie        Person_2 = susie
Person_1 = freda        Person_2 = susie
Person_1 = peter        Person_2 = thomas
Person_1 = peter        Person_2 = anne
Person_1 = peter        Person_2 = gayle
Person_1 = susie        Person_2 = thomas
Person_1 = susie        Person_2 = gayle
Person_1 = susie        Person_2 = carl
```

If the queries are just composed of variables then these are, therefore, called "unqualified queries". Queries that are composed of at least one constant are called "semi-qualified queries".

An "anonymous variable" is represented by an underscore "_". These variables are used when a given position in a rule or query can take any object and when it is not important for further processing what that object is.

At this point, we shall now explain how a goal is evaluated. We shall use the knowledge base for kinship relations, above. We shall establish if there is a person who is a child of peter and whose child is carl, so that peter is the grandfather of carl. The following goal is given to Prolog:

```
?- parent(peter, Person), parent(Person, carl).
```

The inference component searches the knowledge base for a predicate which matches the first part of the above query: ?- `parent(peter, Person)`. A further constraint is, the first argument `peter`. The variable `Person` can stand for any argument. If the inference component finds a pattern which matches the first part of the query - which is the case for:

```
parent(peter, thomas).
```

then the variable `Person` is replaced by the object `thomas`, or alternatively, the variable `Person` is bound to the object `thomas`. This process is known as *instantiation*, i.e., the variable `Person` is instantiated to the object `thomas`.

If a variable appears more than once within a query or clause then each occurrence of the variable can only be replaced by the same object. As the goal consists of two subgoals, the inference component now tries to evaluate the second subgoal, as the Prolog system searches the knowledge base from beginning to end for `parent(thomas, carl)`. As this subgoal is not derivable the Prolog system sets a mechanism in motion known as *backtracking*. The inference component of the Prolog system takes a step back in the series of subgoals to process and attempts to prove `parent(peter, Person)` in a different way. The binding of the variable `Person` to `thomas` is thus undone. A new pattern is now sought. The next one found is:

```
parent(peter, anne).
```

The variable `Person` is instantiated to `anne`. Now the inference component derives the second subgoal `parent(anne, carl)` from the knowledge base, with a similar lack of success. Backtracking takes place again. Now

```
parent(peter, gayle)
```

is found and the variable `Person` instantiated to `gayle`. Given this binding searching continues and

```
parent(gayle, carl)
```

is found. Since both subgoals could be proved the goal

```
parent(peter, Person), parent(Person, carl)
```

is satisfied.

```
parent(karen, peter).
parent(henry, peter).
parent(ollie, susie).
```

```
parent(freda, susie).
parent(peter, anne).
parent(peter, gayle).
parent(susie, anne).
parent(susie, gayle).
parent(susie, thomas).
parent(peter, thomas).
parent(gayle, carl).

female(karen).
female(freda).
female(susie).
female(anne).
female(gayle).

male(henry).
male(ollie).
male(peter).
male(thomas).
male(carl).

grandparent(Pers_1, Pers_2):-
      parent(Pers_1, Child),
      parent(Child, Pers_2).
mother(Person, Child):-
      parent(Person, Child),
      female(Person).
unequal(Person_1, Person_2):-
      Person_1 \== Person2.
sister(Pers_1, Pers_2):-
      parent(Parents, Pers_1),
      parent(Parents, Pers_2),
      female(Pers_1),
      unequal(Pers_1, Pers_2).
descendant(Pers_1, Pers_2):- parent(Pers_2, Pers_1).
descendant(Pers_1, Pers_2):-
      parent(Pers_2, Child),
      descendant(Pers_1, Child).
ancestor(Pers_1, Pers_2):- parent(Pers_1, Pers_2).
ancestor(Pers_1, Pers_2):-
      parent(Pers_1, Child),
      ancestor(Child, Pers_2).
```

The rules for ancestor and descendant are special in one respect compared to the other rules. Whilst the other rules only refer to further facts or rules, the `ancestor` and `descendant` rules contain facts that refer to themselves. This use of facts is called *recursive*. The procedure is defined recursively. More about recursion can be found in topic 4.

2.1 Exercises for Topic 2

1. The knowledge base is the family program, above.

a. Which answers does the Prolog system return to the following queries?

i. `?- parent(anne, Person).`
ii. `?- parent(Person, susie).`
iii. `?- parent(henry, Person), parent(Person,susie).`
iv. `?- parent(ollie, Pers_1), parent(Pers_1, Pers_2), parent(Pers_2, Carl).`

b. Formalise the following in Prolog:
i. Who is the parent of `peter`?
ii. Does `anne` have a child?
iii. Which grandparents does `thomas` have?

c. Translate the following sentences into Prolog rules:
i. Everyone who has a child is happy.
ii. It is true for all persons that: if the person has a child and that child has a sister then the person has two children.

d. Define the following relations as rule:
i. Grandchild `grandchild(Pers_1, Pers_2)`
ii. `aunt(Pers_1, Pers_2)`

2. There is a company whose board of directors is made up of the chairman, treasurer, apprentice supervisor, organising committee, and departmental heads.

a. Write a Prolog program about the period of office of the board members. For example, Henry was apprentice supervisor from 1990 until 1992.
b. Add the following rule to the knowledge base:
Whoever is head of section and apprentice supervisor asks to take on new staff.
c. Enable the following queries to be made:
i. From when to when was Henry apprentice supervisor?
ii. Were Henry and Ollie on the board at the same time?

3. Given the following flights network:

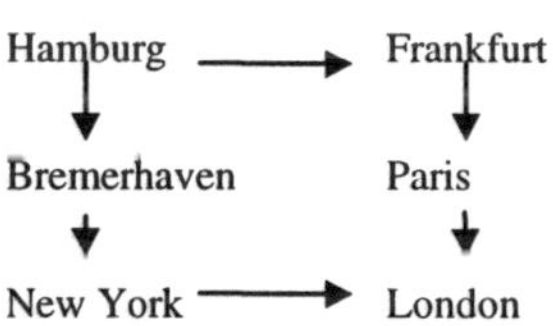

Develop a Prolog program. The following questions should be possible:
b. Questions about direct connections (Hamburg - Paris)

c. Questions about connections via a given town (one or many, e.g., Hamburg via Frankfurt to Paris).
d. Questions/Rules about whether towns have multiple routes (e.g., Paris).

Topic 3

Syntax and Semantics of Prolog Programs

By syntax we mean the study of sentence construction. The word syntax comes from the Greek (syntaxis) and means order or "composition". Grammatically syntax is the totality of rules for the construction of sentences from words. In a language the correct combination of symbols and expressions is studied without reference to their meaning.

Semantics means the study of the elements of symbolic systems with respect to what is meant by the symbols. Whilst syntax is concerned with the combination of symbols, semantics is concerned with the meaning of the symbols used.

In this section we shall look at the syntax and semantics of Prolog.

Objects and Predicates

The result of the process of representing the real world in a Prolog program is objects and predicates. Prolog provides a data object according to the nature of the real world objects.

The expression Data Type is avoided in Prolog because there are no type conversion errors in Prolog. Similarly there are objects which exist by name only (individuals such as father, money) and have no "content" (assigned or constant content). Therefore data objects are not spoken of.

If an object has a simple structure which is directly derivable from a constant or variable then it is called a *simple object*. More complex objects are represented by a structure which is made of a collection individual, elementary objects. The structures include lists, simple trees and nested trees: they are called *terms* and enable the programmer to define structured data types.

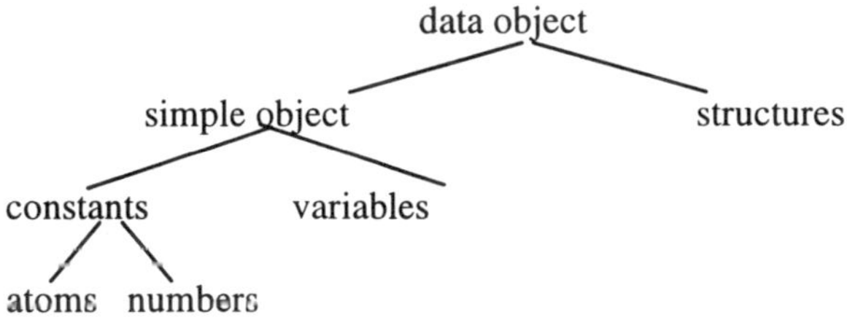

Fig. 2.2: Abstraction of the real world

Only by converting the relationships between individual objects into a program can propositions be formulated which express facts or rules about the world being represented.

The predicates are clearly indicated by their *functor* (predicate name). The precise way in which Prolog neatly differentiates one predicate by the functor and *arity* of the predicate (number of arguments) gives users a clear choice of powerful representation.

Names as functors of predicates are to be avoided, if possible, unless the predicate defines an independent object with the meaning "consists of".

Symbols

The following symbols are defined in Prolog:

- capital letters A, B, ... Z
- lower case letters a, b, ... z
- numbers 0, 1,2, ... 9
- special symbols +, -, *, /, <, >, :-, ?, $, _, %
- AND-operator ",", OR-operator ";"

Atoms

Atoms indicate predicates, operators or other individuals. Atoms are composed of numbers, letters, hyphen and underscore. They begin with a small letter. It is also possible to define atoms within single quotation marks. If single quotation marks are used then the atoms can be made up of any characters desired. Another syntactic form in which atoms can appear is in special symbols. This results in operators and meta-syntactic symbols being atoms. Examples of atoms are:

```
fred, lenny-14, lenny_14, 256, '20.April.1993', ==,
!, ?
```

Note

Numbers are only considered as atoms because of their unchangeable nature. In general they are not considered to be atoms in the Prolog sense. The built-in predicate `atom(X)` produces a negative answer to the query `?- atom(256).` Another, built-in predicate includes numbers and returns the appropriate positive answer.

Constants

In contrast to variables, constants have a fixed value. They behave as atoms or numbers.

Variables

Variables are used to indicate uninstantiated arguments of predicates or functors. They are constructed similarly to atoms but differ in the following respects:

- They begin with either a capital letter or with the underscore "_" character, e.g., `Lenny`, `Lenny_14`

- The hyphen is interpreted as subtraction in arithmetical expression *is*, e.g., `4 is 6-2.`
  The hyphen can also be used to separate variables, e.g., `six(eight-two).`

  The query: ?- `six(Y-two).`
  Returns `Y=eight`
  The query: `?- six(Z).`
  Returns: `Z=eight-two.`

- A variable can also consist of just an underscore. This is known as the anonymous variable or place-holder. It does not get instantiated as a "normal" variable during the process of searching for a solution, i.e., no temporary value is assigned. If more than one place-holder is used then they are each handled separately, e.g.,

```
has-parents(Person):-    has-mother(Person,_);
                         has-father(Person,_).
```

- Variables are held to be *bound* when the same variables are used in a conjoined clause. If a variable is used more than once without being assigned a value then this occurs during the proof procedure under the control of the system (*instantiation*), in order to provide reference values for other propositions. In the example:

```
proposition(X):- proposition1(X),
                 proposition2(X).
```

  In concrete terms it means that the variable "X" within the clause must always have the same value (*unification*). In the example:

```
propositions(X): proposition1(X);
                 proposition2(X).
```

  if X is not bound then it may not be subsequently unified.

Structure

The expression structure is ambiguous. On the one hand it describes data objects which can not be constructed from the variables and constants which are available. In this sense structures express lists, simple trees and nested trees.

On the other hand, the Prolog system manages the predicates and considers the predicates to be structures. An examination of the syntax of a fact reveals that a fact is a structure. The differentiation between data objects and predicates is irrelevant to Prolog as it does not see any meaning in a structure.

A structure begins with an atom, followed by an open bracket. In this bracket one or more comma-separated arguments are placed. A structure ends with a closing bracket. For example:

```
author(harry).
author(harry, address).
author(harry, address(Street, Town)).
```

Terms

The language constructs of Prolog are built up from terms. The following constructs are possible:

- constants
- variables
- structures
- lists

A term with specific variables is known as a *ground term.*

Lists

The list is a special form of structure. They are a topic in themselves and will be treated later.

Operators

Prolog also allows various operators to be used in order to change, equate or compare the values or contents of variables. The important operators are:

$$=, \neq, >, <, \leq, \geq$$

Apart from the operators for equality or inequality, the other comparison operators can only be used on numbers, text constants or variables to which a value has been assigned.

Matching

The equality relation does not just perform its usual mathematical task but also begins to check whether or not terms can actually be made equal (*unified*). This is true when the *free* (unassigned) variables of a term take values (*instantiate*) such that the terms match and the Prolog system can continue or end the proof of the proposition (subgoal or actual query). This understanding of equality is called matching.

Two terms can be matched and are considered by the system to be identical if they are equal (in the usual sense) or unified (can be made equal by instantiation).

- The equality of terms in Prolog is:
  Constants are equal when they are identical, i.e., constants are only equal to

themselves.
- individuals (atoms):
  harry= harry
  harry≠susie
- text constants
  'Harry'='Harry'
  'Harry'≠'HARRY'
- numeric constants
  1993=1993
  1994≠1993
- individual/text constants, numeric constants
  May.92 ≠ 'May.92'

- Variables are equal if:
  - they are identical (given the same name), e.g., *X*=*X*;
  - both are assigned the same value, e.g., *X*=12, *Y*=12 ⇒ *X*=*Y*;
  - both have no value assigned, thus, in Prolog: *X*=_, *Y*=_ ⇒ *X*=*Y*;
  - only one has an assigned value and the free variable can be unified with the assigned variable.

- A variable is equal to a constant (and the converse) if:
  - the variable contains the constant;
  - the variable can be unified with the constant.

- Structures are equal if they have the same functor and number of arguments (arity) and the arguments of the structures are equal (that is, match). Note: The objects of structures are either simple objects (variables or constants) or also structures which can be reduced to simple objects. The equality of the objects can be judged by means of the above rules.

Matching (proof of equality) changes the values of variables if, during unification (equating terms), they are instantiated (temporarily assigned). For example:

1. *X*=12.
   X=12 can only be unified if *X* is instantiated to 12. No value is assigned as the whole expression is true.
2. *X*=2, *Y*=2.
   The "X=2" part of the expression can only succeed with the instantiation of "*X*" to 2. Similarly, "*Y*" must take the contents of *X* in order to satisfy the query.
3. *X*=12, *X*=*Y*; *Y*=10
   X is instantiated to 12 ("*X*=12" becomes true);
   Y is unified with *X* (instantiated to 12, "*X*=*Y*" becomes true);
   the last part of the expression fails (*X* and *Y* are bound variables);
   the current instantiations are undone;

no other unification is possible;
the query can not be proved → no solution → no assignments.

4. `date(day, december, 1993) = date(31, Month, Year).`
   These propositions are unified by the instantiation of day to 31, Month to december and Year to 1993.
5. `date(31, 12) = date(31, 12, year).`
   These propositions can not be matched because the number of the arguments (arity) is different → no solution → no assignment.
6. `triangle(point(1,1), A, point(2,3))=`
   `triangle(X, point(4,Y), point(2,Z)).`
   `triangle = triangle (functors are identical);`
   Arity (number of arguments) is 3 in both cases.

The instantiation	leads to matching of
X=point(1,1)	point(1,1)=*X*
A=point(4,*Y*)	*A*=point(4,*Y*)
Z=3	point(2,3)=point(2,*Z*)

The "=" operator therefore assigns the values with which the system attempts to prove the query, to the variables during run-time. This is also the case for qualified queries such as ?- `p(2,2)` if the predicate `p` stands for a rule which uses variables. If a proof is found then the variables are reset.

Assignments of Values (explicit)

As well as the assignment of values by the system as a means to find a solution (instantiation), there is also the explicit assignment of values by the programmer or user:

```
?- Result is father(henry, june).
?- Result is 10*2-3.
```

The built-in predicate *is* can store a variable, individual, text constant or number. This does not cause the result to be stored but the predicate which leads to the result. The system answers the query `?- X=4+5` with `X=4+5` because `X` is directly instantiated to `4+4` and not with `9`. Only the formulation `?- X is 2+3` receives the answer `X=5`.

Exercises for Topic 3

1. Name the following types of objects:
   a. Diana
   b. diana
   c. 'Diana'
   d. _diana
   e. 'Diana goes home'
   f. goes(diana, Home)
   g. 45

h. 5(*X*, *Y*)
i. +(north, west)
j. three(black(cards))

2. Do the following matching operations succeed? What values are assigned to the variables?
   a. point(*A*,*B*)=point(1,2)
   b. point(*A*,*B*)=point(*X*,*Y*,*Z*)
   c. plus(2,2)=4
   d. +(2,*D*)= +(*E*,2).
   e. triangle(point(-1,0),*P*2,*P*3)=triangle(*P*1,point(1,0),point(0,*Y*))

3. a. Write a term that describes a line segment at *X*=5.
   b. A square is described by the relation rightangle(*P*1,*P*2,*P*3,*P*4) in which *P* is a line segment. Define the relation "regular(*R*)" for a right angle.

4. Define the following family relations for the facts given.
   uncle(*X*,*Y*):-
   parents(*X*,*Y*):-
   wife(*X*,a):-
   husband(*X*,b):-
   aunt(*X*,*Y*):-

Topic 4

Recursive Rules

A recursion is the definition of a function by means of itself. In programming this can be seen as a form of loop. This loop needs a termination condition because it would otherwise (theoretically) be endless. In Prolog, a procedure is recursive if, within a rule, the predicate which defines the procedure is called again.

Recursive problem solutions eventually enable more efficient programming, as can be seen from many examples which operate with dynamic data structures (linear lists, trees, graphs).

We shall consider recursive rules by means of the "Ancestor Program":

Helen has a son called Robert. Robert, similarly, has a daughter called Anna. Anna is the grandchild of Helen. It therefore follows that Helen is a direct ancestor of Robert and an indirect ancestor of Anna.

For all X and Z, it is true that: X is an ancestor of Z if X is a parent of Z.

We translate this into Prolog and produce the following short program:

```
parent(helen, robert).
parent(robert, anna).
ancestor(X, Z):- parent(X,Z).
```

We would now like to ask the system who Helen's descendants are. As we already know Helen is an ancestor of Robert and also Anna[1] .

```
?- ancestor(helen, Z).
```

The system answers: `Z=robert`

The answer is not totally correct since Helen is actually also an ancestor of Anna. This means that we need to extend the program. Figure 2.3 illustrates this graphically.

In order to be able to achieve the desired result we must add the following rule to our previous program:

```
ancestor(X,Z):- parent(X,Y), parent(Y,Z).
```

Informally this means:

---

[1] The symbols "?" and ":-" are synonyms.

if *X* is the parent of *Y* and *Y* the parent of *Z* then *X* is an ancestor of *Z*.

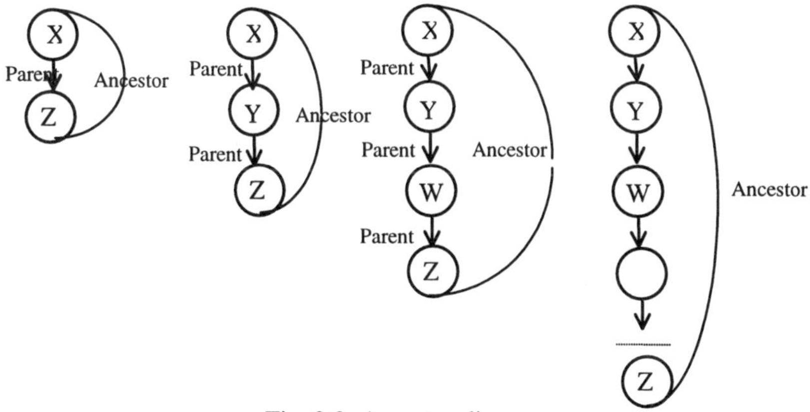

Fig. 2.3: Ancestor diagram

With this extension, the answer to the query:

```
? ancestor(helen, Z)
```
is returned as `Z=robert` and `Z=anna`.

The correct result would, however, have been reached if we had added two rules such as:

```
ancestor(X,Z):- parent(X,Z).
ancestor(X,Z):- parent(X,Y), parent(Y,Z).
```

If "Anna" should also be a parent then a further rule would need to be added so that we arrive at the right answer:

```
ancestor(X,Z):- parent(X,Y), parent(Y,W),
parent(W,Z).
```

The whole program would get longer but what is more important is that it only works to a certain extent. It only discovers ancestors up to a specific depth in the family tree because the length of the chain of persons between the ancestor and the descendant is limited by the length of the ancestor clause. A better and more elegant formulation of the ancestor relation is to define the relation using itself. This type of call is known as recursion. This means that the program will function correctly to any arbitrary depth.

Formally, it can be described as follows:
For all *X* and *Z* it is true that:
X is ancestor of *Z*

if there is a *Y* with the following characteristics
- *X* is a parent of *Y* and
- *Y* is an ancestor of *Z*

In Prolog form this is:

```
ancestor(X,Z):- parent(X,Y), ancestor(Y,Z).
```

If we add into our program the following two lines then we are in the position to establish all direct and indirect ancestors.

```
ancestor(X,Z):- parent(X,Z).
ancestor(X,Z):- parent(X,Y), ancestor(Y,Z).
```

In order to prove this we'll extend the knowledge-base with the following predicates:

```
parent(helen, robert).
parent(thomas, robert).
parent(thomas, lisa).
parent(robert, anna).
parent(robert, val).
parent(val, jacob).
```

We ask for Helen's ancestors: `?- ancestor(helen, Z).`

1. Solution: Helen is the parent of Robert. This means that Robert is a descendant.
   `Z=robert`
2. Solution Helen is the parent of Robert. Robert is the ancestor of Anna. This means that Anna is a descendant.
   `Z=anna`
3. Solution: Helen is a parent of Robert. Robert is an ancestor of Val. This means that Val is a descendant.
   `Z=val`
4. Solution: Helen is a parent of Robert. Robert is an ancestor of Val. Val is an ancestor of Jacob. This means that Jacob is a descendant.
   `Z=jacob`

Further queries are:

```
?- ancestor(thomas, val).
yes
```

Proof
Matching of the Goals with the first rule:

```
ancestor(X,Z):- parent(X,Z).
```

```
X=thomas, Z=val

?- parent(thomas, val).
no
```

Matching the goals with the second rule:

```
ancestor(X,Z):- parent(X,Y), ancestor(Y,Z).
X=thomas, Z=val, Y=free
```

Two new goals:

a) `parent(thomas, Y)`
b) `ancestor(Y, val).`
Matching a) with the predicate from the knowledge base gives:

```
Y=robert
```

b) becomes `ancestor(robert, val)` matching b) with the first rule

```
ancestor(X,Z):- parent(X,Z).
X=robert, Z=val
```

4.1 Changing the Ordering

The "procedural meaning" of a Prolog program is determined during the execution of the derivability proof. As the inference algorithm often runs in a different way if the clauses are differently ordered, the procedural meaning of a Prolog program can similarly change. Under certain circumstances the procedural meaning can lead to the program executing an endless loop.

The procedural meaning should be distinguished from the "declarative meaning" of a Prolog program, which is determined by the predicates in the clauses and is independent of the order in which the clauses are given. Declarative meaning is about "if" and not "how" a goal is derivable. The declarative meaning of the ancestor program, for example, therefore resides in the knowledge about the family in the knowledge base. This knowledge is not changed if the order of the clauses are changed.

In order to establish whether or not a modified form of the rules in the ancestor program has an effect on the execution of the derivability proof, we shall test the following four variants. Here is the program once more:

```
parent(helen, robert).
parent(thomas, robert).
parent(thomas, lisa).
parent(robert, anna).
```

```
parent(robert, val).
parent(val, jacob).
ancestor(X,Z):- parent(X,Z).  *** Rule 1 ***
ancestor(X,Z):-  parent(X,Y),  ancestor(Y,Z).   ***  Rule
2 ***
```

1. We query the original form with:
`ancestor(thomas, val).`

As can be seen from Fig. 2.4 we receive the answer "yes". This means that Thomas is a direct ancestor of Val.

2. We swap rule 1 with rule 2 so that we run the following program with the same goal as in the first program.

```
ancestor(X,Z):- parent(X,Y), ancestor(Y,Z).
ancestor(X,Z):- parent(X,Z).
```

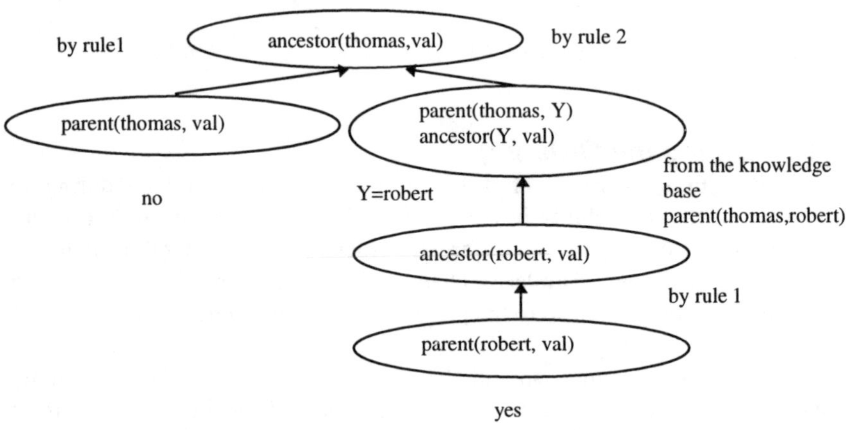

Fig. 2.4: changing the ordering of a program

On inspection of the previously given form it can be seen that we have not made any changes to the declarative meaning, i.e., the inherent logic of both of the rules is unchanged, as before. We therefore expect the goal:

```
?- ancestor(thomas, val).
```

to be answered with "yes" by the derivability proof. This is the case, even though in this version a somewhat larger derivation tree results, which means that the inference mechanism is a program-independent component whose mode of operation is directly affected by modified clause ordering.

3. We change the ordering of the predicates in the tail of rule 2 so that it looks as below:

```
ancestor(X,Z):- parent(X,Z).
ancestor(X,Z):- ancestor(Y,Z), parent(Y,Z).
```

Compared to the previous form we have, once again, made a declarative change. Therefore we also expect a positive answer to the query:

```
?- ancestor(thomas, val).
```

Although there is, in comparison to the original form and the first variant, an additional cost in the execution of the derivability proof, imposed by the procedural modification, we also obtain the correct answer in this case.

4. As a final variant we shall investigate changes in the order of the rules along with changes to the ordering of the predicates in the tail of the rule of the original second rule. This produces the following program:

```
ancestor(X,Z):- ancestor(Y,Z), parent(Y,Z).
ancestor(X,Z):- parent(X,Z).
```

This program is also given the same query to answer:

```
?- ancestor(thomas, val).
```

Although the declarative meaning of the clauses is unchanged, as before, the procedural changes lead to a program execution which never ends. This means that the derivability proof can not be completed because the inference algorithm is stuck in a never-ending loop. How this happens is described in more detail below.

After the comparison of the goal with the head of the first rule, the derivability of the tail of the rule must be proved. This leads to the subgoal `ancestor(Y', val)`. This subgoal must be compared with a rule head from the knowledge base, in order to find a suitable assignment for Y'. This succeeds on the first rule head, giving the assignments:

```
Y":=:Y'
Z:=: val.
```

In comparison with earlier assignments, this is different, since now, in contrast, one variable has been assigned to another. This form of assignment is known as a *pact* which is made between the variables. This is indicated by the symbol ":=:". This symbol is read as meaning:

- that no constants have been bound to the variables Y' and Y" and
- that an assignment to variable Y' produces an assignment of the same value to variable Y", and the converse.

According to the assignments given, the subgoal `ancestor(Y", val)` must be derived next in order to derive the tail of rule 1. This means: it must be compared to a rule head in the knowledge base.

It can be seen that this subgoal is, with the exception of the name of the first arguments (Y', Y", Y''', ...), totally identical to the goal given above. This means that the task of deriving the subgoal arises continuously. This causes the procedural execution to get stuck in a never-ending loop. We can therefore establish that whilst the declaration of the rules in this form does not have any declarative consequences, it does have procedural ramifications which lead to a never-ending loop.

This illustrates a problem of logic programming in Prolog:

When using recursive rules it is insufficient just to consider the declarative meaning of the clauses, indeed attention must, instead, be given to the procedural meaning with respect to execution by the inference algorithm. This means that the order of the rules within the knowledge base and the order of the predicates within the rule tail must be attended to.

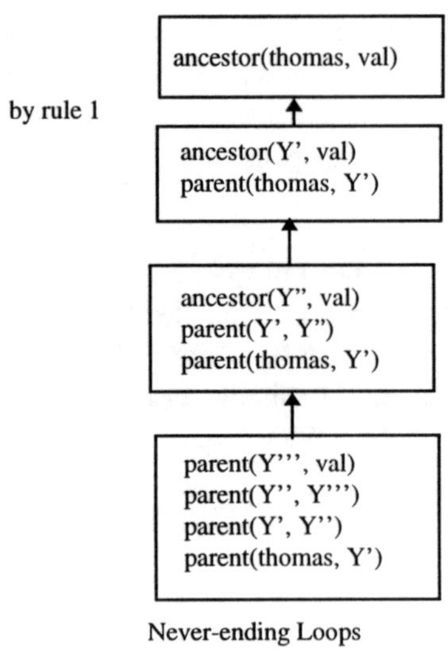

Fig. 2.5: Changing the ordering of the program

Because when processing a logical AND connective, the comparison is always attempted from left to right there is always the concern until the final subgoal is fully derived that (unlike in the last variation) branching of the derivation tree does not take place in the same continuously recurring manner. On the contrary, such a search should be halted by a termination condition, after a certain number of steps. This is normally achieved by introducing a similarly named, non-recursive, first clause as a termination condition of a rule.

4.2 Program Cycles

We have seen that through the correct sequence of predicates in the rule tail and through the termination condition of recursive rules, it is possible to prevent the program from getting into a never-ending loop during execution. These precautions do not suffice if the description of the facts or their order is "inappropriate" for procedural execution. In such situations there may be situations in which a query leads to a program looping, i.e., being caught in a never-ending loop. This behaviour can be explained by the order of the facts within the program which means that it is necessary to ensure that the program does not loop by ensuring the most appropriate arrangement of facts.

Exercises for Topic 4

1. Write a program for the calculation of Fibonacci numbers.
   Rules of generation:
   fibonacci(0)=1
   fibonacci(1)=1
   fibonacci(*N*)=fibonacci(*N*-1) + fibonacci(*N*-2)

2. Write a program which defines the natural numbers, as follows:
   - 0 is a natural number
   - The successor of a natural number is a natural number

3. Draw up a database of your (or another) family and define the following relations:
   a. Husband
   b. Wife
   c. Parents
   d. Uncle
   e. Aunt
   f. Father in law
   g. Mother in law
   h. Cousin
   i. Parents(Child, Father, Mother)
   j. Parents in law(Child, Father in law, Mother in law)
   k. Stepchild(Child, Parents)
   l. Step brother
   m. Step sister
   Avoid answers appearing more than once in backtracking.

Topic 5

Lists

A list is a finite, ordered sequence of objects of a given datatype. The elements of a list can be any terms (atoms, structures and also lists). The length of a list is not prescribed and can freely develop without limitation (other than memory). Lists are used when it is not obvious beforehand how many elements a datatype will need. Lists are ideal for implementing higher datatypes such as trees and graphs.

5.1 Construction and Representation of Lists

In Prolog, as opposed to conventional languages, there is a relationship between elements and components of a list definition. The list elements are objects which are grouped into a list, like elements of an array in Pascal.

List components are made up of: the list head (= first element) and list tail (= rest of the list) in which the list tail is once again a list. The list is therefore composed of a head and tail. The tail can be an empty list. The separation of the two parts is performed by the list separator which is represented by a vertical bar "|".

There are various representation schemes for lists. We shall just look at one:

Bracket Notation

In bracket notation the elements of the list are placed in square brackets, separated by commas. For example:

- Four independent elements:
  [*a*, *b*, *c*, *d*]
- A list with four variables:
  [*A*, *B*, *C*, *D*]
- An empty list with no contents:
  [ ]
- A list with one element "Apple":
  [apple | []]
- A list with several elements separated into head and tail:
  [*H*|*T*]
  [apple, pear, cherry, pineapple]
  [apple, pear, cherry | [pineapple]]
  [apple, pear | [cherry | [pineapple]]
  [apple | [pear | [cherry | [pineapple]]]
  [apple | [pear | [cherry [pineapple | [ ]]]]]
  [apple | [pear | [cherry | [pineapple | [ ]]]]]

Dot Notation

In dot notation, the elements of the list are separated by "." and terminated by the symbol "nil". By means of dot notation, it can be seen that lists are linear structures. For example:

- Four independent elements:
  *a.b.c.d.*nil
- A list with four variables:
  *A.B.C.D.*nil
- An empty list without content:
  nil
- A list with one element, apple:
  apple.nil

Functor Notation

In functor notation, the functor symbol "." stands before the round brackets. The elements of the list are separated by comma and terminated with [ ]. For example:

- Four independent elements:
  .(a, .(b, .(c, .(d, [ ]))))
- A list with four variables:
  .(A, .(B, .(C, .(D, [ ]))))
- An empty list without content:
  [ ]
- A list with one element, apple:
  .(apple, [])
- A list with several elements separated into head and tail: .(H, T):
  .(apple, .(pear, .(cherry, .(pineapple, [ ]))))

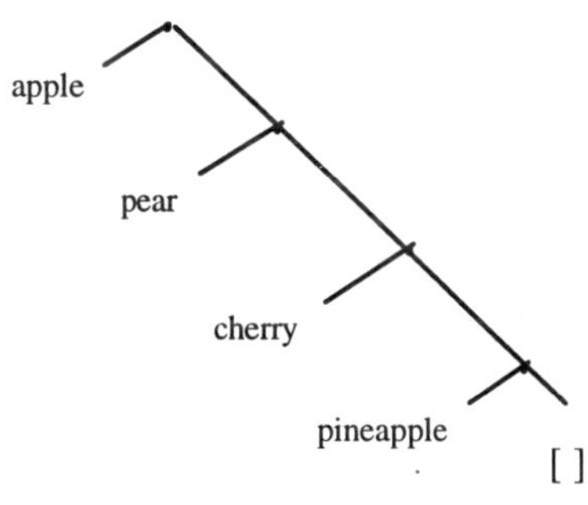

Processing Lists

In Prolog, it is only possible to access the first element (head) and remainder (tail) of the list, i.e., direct access to individual list elements is not possible. In order to get a list element which is not the first element, it is necessary to make successive attempts. This definition corresponds to the recursive definition of lists in Prolog.

The processing of lists, therefore, takes place in an essentially recursive manner. This means that in order to use a list head for instantiation it must first be split off. This splitting takes place repeatedly until the list tail consists only of the empty list. From this we can see that the empty list is the termination condition for recursion.

A list-based algorithm therefore stops when the list tail just contains the empty list as a final element.

We shall consider the processing (splitting off) of the four element list:
[apple, pear, cherry, pineapple]

1. Split [apple | [pear, cherry, pineapple]]
2. Split [pear | [cherry, pineapple]]
3. Split [cherry | [pineapple]]
4. Split [pineapple | [ ]]

Unification of Lists

During matching variables in the list are replaced with constants. The following table shows how the list components can be unified and if unification is possible.

List 1	List 2	Equivalences
[*a*]	[*X*|*Y*]	*X*=*a*, *Y*=[]
[*a*|*x*]	[*a*,*b*]	*X*=*b*
[*X*,[*Y*|*Z*]]	[*a*,*b*,*c*]	*X*=*a*, *Y*=*b*, *Z*=*c*
[*a*,[*X*]|*Z*]	[*Y*,[*b*]|[*c*,d]]	*Y*=*a*, *X*=*b*, *Z*=[*c*,d]
[*a*|*X*]	[*Y*|*b*]	*X*=*b*, *Y*=*a*
[]	*X*	*X*=[]
[*a*,*b*,*c*]	[*X*|*Y*]	*X*=*a*, *Y*=[*b*,*c*]
[*a*,*b*]	[*X*|[*Y*|*Z*]	*X*=*a*, *Y*=*b*, *Z*=[]
[*a*,*b*]	*X*	*X*=[*a*,*b*]
[*X*,*a*]	[*a*,*b*]	not possible
[]	[*X*|*Y*]	not possible
[*a*]	[*X*|[*Y*]]	not possible
[*a*,*b*]	[*X*,*Y*,*Z*]	not possible
[*a*,*b*]	[*X*]	not possible

5.2 Membership

Membership is a predicate which serves to determine whether or not an element is contained in a list. This is the case when an element is either contained in the list head or in the list tail.

Membership is expressed in Prolog by means of a fact and a rule.

```
member(X, [X|Tail]).
member(X, [Head|Tail]):- member(X, Tail).
```

These clauses should be understood as follows:

If *X* occurs in the list then it is either in the head of the list (this corresponds to the fact) or it is a component of the tail of the list (this corresponds to the rule given). If we wish to prove if *X* is in the tail of the list then both clauses are used. In this way the tail of the list is gradually reduced.

After processing the list *X* is either unified or it can be shown not to be a member of the list. The recursive nature of list processing is important, as can be seen from the following examples.

```
?- member(cherry, [apple, pear, cherry, pineapple]).
```

1. Split (apple is split off)
   `X=cherry, Tail=[pear, cherry, pineapple]`
   The new query now reads:
   `?- member(cherry, [pear, cherry, pineapple]).`
2. Split (cherry is split off)
   `X=cherry, Tail=[cherry, pineapple]`
   The new query would then be:
   `?-  member(cherry, [cherry, pineapple]).`
   This query succeeds and we receive a “yes”.

A further example.

```
?- member([pear, cherry, pineapple],[apple,[pear,
cherry, pineapple]]).
```

In this case splitting off occurs only once with `apple` and the tail of the list:

```
        [pear, cherry, pineapple]
```

moves to the list head and therefore is successfully unified. We receive the answer “yes”.

Yet another example.

```
?- member(pineapple,[apple,[cherry, pineapple,
plum]]).
```

In this case the element `apple` is split off first and the tail:

```
        [cherry, pineapple, plum]
```

moves into the head of the list. The element pineapple does not match the head of the list, resulting in the empty list. The algorithm terminates. We receive the answer “no”.

Operations on Lists

In the text below some of the most common list operations used in programming are explained. Most of the operations are in the form of built-in functions which are supplied by the manufacturer. For this reason our presentation here is short and we point the reader to the relevant documentation.

5.3 Joining of lists (append or concatenate)

These operations join two lists together. This therefore creates the list with the contents [*a*,*b*,*c*,*d*] from the lists [*a*,*b*] and [*c*,*d*]. Many compiler dialects define this function as append and we use that here:

```
append(List1, List2, Wholelist)
```

This predicate can be similarly used as a query, as the following examples show.

- `?- append([a,b],[c,d],[a,b,c,d]).`
  `yes`
  The first and second list together produce the third list.
- `?- append([a,b],[c,d],[a,b,a,c,d]).`
  `no`
  The first and second list do not both together produce the third list.
- `?- append([a,b],[c,d],Wholelist)`
  `Wholelist=[a,b,c,d]`
  The variable `Wholelist` is instantiated to the resulting list.
- `?- append([],[a,b,c,d],Wholelist).`
  `Wholelist=[a,b,c,d]`
  If the first list is empty then the resultant Wholelist is the contents of the second list.
- `?- append([X|[a,b,c,d]],[d],Wholelist).`
  `Wholelist=[X,a,b,c,d]`
  The whole list is made up of the chaining together of List 1 and List 2.

The append predicate can be written in Prolog as follows:

```
append([], List, List).
append([Head|Tail], List, [Head|Wholelist]):-
append(Tail, List, Wholelist).
```

The termination in line one occurs if the first list is empty, in which case, the second list becomes the Wholelist. In the second line, the head and tail of the list are determined as the call recursively executes. In this way, the result list is produced `[Head|Wholelist]` in which the Wholelist is the chaining together of `[Head|Tail]` and `List`.

The way in which Prolog works on chaining together lists can be clarified with the query:

```
?- append([apple,pear,cherry],[pineapple],Fruit).
```

First of all the second clause is used and unified with the query:

```
append([apple|pear,cherry],[pineapple],[apple|Fruit])
```

These recursive steps are repeated until the first list is empty.

```
append([],[pineapple],Fruit)
```

The head of the list of the variables takes the values “apple”, “pear”, “cherry” one after the other. Then, with the aid of the first clause, “Fruit” is made identical with the list, here, “[pineapple]” and then Prolog takes a step back through the calls of append. Here the head of the list is still bound to “cherry”, i.e., fruit is now bound, with the help of rule two again, to the element “cherry”.

Prolog’s further processing would be:
Present position:

```
append([],[pineapple],[pineapple]).
```

This produces:

```
apple([pear,
cherry],[pineapple],[pear,cherry,pineapple]).
append([apple([apple,pear,cherry],[pineapple],[apple,
pear,cherry,pineapple]).
```

Thus the result of the variable “Fruit” = [apple,pear,cherry,pineapple].

Membership can also be defined with the help of chaining, as follows:

```
member(X,List):- append(List1, [X|List2],List).
```

This should be interpreted as meaning that *X* is a member of a list “List” if “List” can be so divided up that the second list has *X* at its head.

append can additionally be used to transform a list into other lists.

```
?- append(List1, List2, [apple, pear, cherry]).
List1 = []          List2 = [apple, pear, cherry]
      = [apple]                 = [pear, cherry]
      = [apple, pear]                 = [cherry]
      = [apple, pear, cherry]         = []
```

5.4 Adding an Element

The simplest way to add an element *X* to a list "List" is to put the element at the start of the list so that it becomes the new list head.

```
[X|List]
```

Another possibility would be to use a procedure that looked as follows:

```
add(X, List, [X|List]).
```

Example:

```
List = [apple, pear, cherry]
X= pineapple
?- add(pineapple, [apple, pear, cherry], List).
List = [pineapple, apple, pear, cherry]
```

5.5 Deleting an element

The first occurrence of a specific element *X*, only, is deleted.

Call: ?- `delete(Element, List-old, List-new).`

Program:

```
delete(_,[],[]).
delete(X,[X|Tail],Tail).
delete(X,[Y|Tail],[Y|Tail1]):- delete(X, Tail,Tail1).
```

The first line is for termination when the old list is empty.

In the second line deletion, occurs when *X* is found in the head of the list. The program then terminates.

The third line moves on recursively if an element other than the one to be deleted is found. For example:

```
?- delete(cherry, [apple, pear, cherry, pineapple,
cherry], L).
```

Prolog begins with the rule and spawns two goals:

```
delete(cherry, [pear, cherry, pineapple, cherry], L).
delete(cherry, [cherry, pineapple, cherry],L).
```

Now, by means of the first clause *L* becomes instantiated to the list "[cherry, pineapple, cherry]" and the program jumps back to the call in the second clause. The head of the list, containing "cherry" is split off. This is shown in the following steps:

1. delete(cherry,[cherry,pineapple,cherry],[pineapple, cherry]).
2. delete(cherry,[pear,cherry,pineapple,cherry],[pear, pineapple,cherry]).
3. delete(cherry,[apple,pear,cherry,pineapple,cherry], [apple,pear,pineapple,cherry]).

The final *L* now contains the elements "[apple, pear, pineapple, cherry]".

Hint
If all specified elements are to be deleted then the second clause should not terminate but call up the list again. The second clause needs to be modified as follows:

```
delete(X, [X|Tail], L1):- delete(X, Tail, L1),!.
```

The cut operator "!" is used in this example. More details of the cut operator are provided, later. In order to get a good, intuitive feel for the cut operator we shall, for the moment, think of the cut as a one-way switch which prevents backtracking. What we are really telling Prolog is "No backtracking". The cut is written as an exclamation mark "!" and is placed between goals as a pseudo-goal.

5.6 Sublist

A sublist is understood to mean a list which occurs within another, e.g.:

```
?- sublist([c,d,e],[a,b,c,d,e,f]).
yes
?- sublist([c,e],[a,b,c,d,e,f]).
no
```

The second query is false because the order of the elements is not correct.

The `sublist` predicate can be defined as:
`S` is a sublist of `L` if
- in two lists `List1` and `List2` can be separated out.
- `List2` can be separated out into two lists `S` and `List3`

The form of this definition in Prolog is:

```
sublist(S,L):-
        append(List1,List2,L),
        append(S,List3,List2)
```

The algorithm uses the previously defined predicate `append`.

For example: the production of all the sublists of a list.

```
?- sublist(S, [a,b,c]).
S=[];
S=[a];
S=[a,b];
S=[a,b,c];
S=[b];          etc.
```

5.7 Reversing a List

This function reverses the order of the elements of a list. The function is described by means of the predicate:

```
reverse(Original_list,Inverted_list).
```

such that the query:

```
?- reverse([a,b,c],Inv_list]).
```

produces the answer list: `Inv_list = [c,b,a].`

The list inverting proceeds according to the following steps:

1. Splitting off the head of the list,
2. Inverting the tail of the list,
3. The list held in the head of the list is added to the inverted list.

This is continued by means of recursion, until the list is inverted and the termination condition ([]) is met.

The implementation of the algorithm in Prolog is:

```
reverse([],[]).
reverse([First|Rest],List):-
reverse(Rest,Temporary_list), append(Temporary_list,
[First],List).
```

This program requires the use of the `append` predicate which has already been described.

Example: The list [*a*,*b*,*c*] should result in the reversed list [*c*,*b*,*a*].

Firstly the sequence is cut off at the first element:

```
reverse([a,b,c],List)
reverse([a,b],List)
reverse([c],List)
```

```
reverse([],List)
reverse([],[])
```

In the next steps the last element of the list "c" is added to the list "List" and returned as a temporary result in the "reverse" relation.

```
append(c,[],List)
append(c,[],[c])
reverse([c],[c])
```

The steps just given are necessary for the next temporary result in which the additional element "b" is then added by recursion, as described above.

```
append(b,[c],List)
append(b,[],List)
append(b,[],[b])
append(b,[c],[c,b])
append([b,c],[c,b])
```

The last step works as those above.

```
append(a,[c,b],List)
append(a,[b],List)
append(a,[],List)
append(a,[],[a])
append(a,[b],[b,a])
append(a,[c,b],[c,b,a])
reverse([a,b,c],[b,c,a])
```

The result of the reversed list is therefore: `List=[b,c,a]`

Sorting Procedures with Lists

5.8 Bubblesort

Bubblesort is a simple procedure for the sorting of a linear field. It involves comparing the neighbouring elements of the list to be sorted and swapping them according to a chosen sort criterion (≥).

The procedure is explained by means a number game with five numbers and the sort criterion "greater".

The linear list contains the values 53, 79, 10, 89 and 16

Here, the order of the first two neighbour numbers is examined. If the second is larger then the two numbers are swapped. If not then both the next neighbouring numbers are compared until a greater number is encountered and just one element remains in the left over list.

1. Iteration: 53, 10, 79, 16, 89
   The index i begins at number 53 and swaps number 53 with number 10, as 53 is greater than 10. At the next step the comparison determined whether or not 53 is greater than 79. This is not the case. 53 is thus left in the second position and then number 79 is compared to 16 as these two numbers are the next neighbouring pair. These are swapped again. This is the last swap for this iteration, the number 79 remains at fourth position and the number 89 as the last element of the list. Now the second iteration can begin.
2. Iteration: 10, 53, 16, 79, 89
   In this iteration the index starts again with the first numbers in the series. In this instance only the numbers 53 and 16 are swapped.
3. Iteration: 10,16,53,79,89
   In this list nothing more can be swapped. However, the algorithm keeps running until only one element is left in the list. For completeness we shall note the two remaining iterations.
4. Iteration: 10,16,53,79,89
5. Iteration: 10,16,53,79,89

We can see that in the last two iterations nothing has changed. The algorithm now terminates as the number 89 is reached as a last element.

From this example we can now define the algorithm in Prolog. We use the cut operator in this example. We shall come back to the cut concept in much more detail in the following topic but, for now, the easiest way to get a good intuitive feel for the cut is to think of it as a one-way switch that prevents futile backtracking. At this point we tell Prolog explicitly not to backtrack by means of the cut mechanism. The cut is written as "!" and is inserted between goals as a kind of pseudo-goal. The bubblesort algorithm is given below:

```
bubblesort([],[]).
bubblesort(List,Sorted_list):-
swap(List,List1),!,bubblesort(List1,Sorted_list).
bubblesort(Sorted_list,Sorted_list).

swap([X,Y|Tail],[Y,X|Tail]):- greater(X,Y).
swap([Z|Tail],[Z|Tail1]):- swap(Tail,Tail1).

greater(X,Y):- X > Y.
```

With the aid of this algorithm we shall demonstrate the operation of the Prolog system with the example of the series of numbers 53, 79, 10. The call to the program is:

```
?- bubblesort([53,79,10],Sorted_list).
```

This initially produces the following calls:

```
?- swap([53,79,10],List1).
?- greater(53,79).
```

This pair of numbers is not to be swapped, as 53 is not greater than 79.

The head of the list (the number 53) is now split off and the next pair of elements, 79 and 10, compared with each other. The next call of the two pairs of elements is:

```
?- swap([79,10]).
?- greater(79,10).
```

As 79 is greater than 10, the pair of numbers are swapped with each other and the first iteration is therefore complete. The temporary result is:

```
swap([53,79,10],[53,10,79]).
```

The next call relates to the temporary result:

```
?- bubblesort([53,10,79],Sorted_list).
```

The following calls are now made:

```
?- swap([53,10,70],List).
?- greater(53,10).
```

This pair of numbers is now swapped as 53 is greater than 10. The temporary result is then:

```
swap([53,10,79], [10,53,79]).
```

The final call would then be:

```
?- bubblesort([10,53,79],Sorted_list).
```

The result obtained is:

```
Sorted_list = [10,53,79]
```

5.9 Quicksort

Quicksort is, like bubblesort, a fast and simple sort procedure for a list. In contrast to bubblesort, it never directly swaps neighbouring elements but those which may be far apart. For this to be carried out the list to be sorted must be split into two sublists. In this sort procedure a random element is needed, e.g., the first or last element. In one list are placed the elements which are less than the randomly chosen element and in the other those greater. This process continues via recursion until it is not possible to make any further subdivisions into sublists, i.e., until the termination condition is reached ([]). After the subdividing the sublists must be assembled, once again, into a sorted list.

Two rules should be observed:

1. If the first list is empty then there is nothing to sort therefore the second list is also empty.
2. If the list is not empty then an element of the list is chosen and the list subdivided into two lists. All elements greater than the chosen element are placed in the list "greater" and all other elements in the list "lesser". Both these lists are sorted, once again. The sorted list is assembled from the "greater" and the "lesser" list by "joining".

In order to facilitate understanding we shall give an example of a list to be sorted in which the chosen element is the first element of the list.

[6,3,8,1,5,10,4,7,11,2,9]

We select number 6 and divide the remainder of the list into two further lists which are lesser or greater than this number.

[3,1,5,4,2] 6 [8,10,11,7,9]

We again choose the first element of both of these lists (the 3 and the 8) and respectively subdivide them into two further lists of greater and lesser numbers.

[1,2] 3 [5,4] 6 [7] 8 [10,11,9]

The same process is repeated again, during this, the empty list is added into the lesser list.

[] 1 [2] 3 [4] 5 [] 6 [7] 8 [9] 10 11

We now just join the lists together and achieve the result:

[1,2,3,4,5,6,7,8,9,10,11]

From this the quicksort algorithm can be formulated for Prolog.

```
quicksort([],[]).
quicksort([X|Tail],Sorted_list):-
      divide(X,Tail,Lesser,Greater),
      quicksort(Lesser,Sorted_lesser_list),
      quicksort(Greater, Sorter_greater_list),
      join(Sorted_lesser_list,[X|Sorted_greater_list]
,Sorted_list).
divide(X,[],[],[]).
divide(X,[Y|Tail],[Y|Lesser],Greater):-
      greater(X,Y),!,divide(X,Tail,Lesser,Greater).
divide(X,[Y|Tail],Lesser,[Y|Greater]):-
      divide(,Tail,Lesser,Greater),
      join([],List,List]).
join([X|List1],List2,[X|List3]):-
```

```
      join(List1,List2,List3).
greater(X,Y):- X > Y.
```

Prolog's operation is shown with the example of the number series 4,1,3,2. From the algorithm it can be seen that we take the first element as the marker.

The quicksort query reads:
?- quicksort([4,1,3,2],S).

The first steps of processing by the Prolog system are to divide the list into two further lists and the second to compare the elements:

```
divide(4,[1,3,2],_,_)
greater(4,[1])
divide(4,[3,2],_,_)
greater(4,3)
divide(4,[2],_,_)
greater(4,2)
divide(4,[],_,_)
divide(4,[],[],[])
divide(4,[2],[2],[])
divide(4,[3,2],[3,2],[]).
divide(4,[1,3,2],[1,3,2],[])
```

Above the numbers 1,3,2 have been placed into the list "lesser" and the empty list in the list "greater".

[1,3,2] 4 []

The next marked element is the number 1.

The next query reads:

```
?- quicksort([1,3,2],_)

divide(1,[3,2],_,_)
greater(1,3)
divide(1,[2],_,_)
greater(1,2)
divide(1,[],_,_)
divide(1,[],[],[])
divide(1,[2],[],[2])
divide(1,[3,2],[],[3,2])
```

After this subdivision and the greater comparison, we achieve the following interim result:

[] 1 [3,2] 4 []

The next query reads:

```
?- quicksort([3,2],_)

divide(3,[2],_,_)
greater(3,2)
divide(3,[],[],[])
divide(3,[2],[2],[])
```

The interim result is: [] 1 [2] 3 [] 4 []

The final query is:

```
?- quicksort([2],_).

divide(2,[],_,_)
divide(2,[],[],[])
```

The final division gives: [] 1 [] 2 [] 3 [] 4 []

The final query leads to the termination of further subdivision because only the empty list remains to subdivide:

```
?- quicksort([],_).
```

After we have subdivided all the elements in the list, checked them and divided them into their respective “greater” or “lesser” lists, they are reassembled again at the end by recursion, i.e., joined with each other again.

As a solution we get: S=[1,2,3,4]

5.10 Sorting by Insertion

When sorting by insertion, the last pair of elements of a list are compared, for example, with each other, according to a sort criterion (< or >) and placed in the correct order. Then, the next element from the remainder list is inserted into the previously sorted list, until the termination condition is met ([]).

Two rules should be observed:

1. If the first list is empty then there is nothing to sort, hence, the second list is empty.
2. If the second list is not empty, the tail of the list is sorted and the remaining elements of the head are inserted into the already existing, sorted list.

For example: we have the following numbers in a list: 27,57,22,16.

Firstly, 22 and 16 are compared with each other. Since 22 is greater than 16, 22 is placed into the sorted list.

After the first iteration: 27,57,16   22

Now 57 is compared to 16. Since 57 is greater than 16 the 57 is placed into the sorted list in the right place, obviously by comparison with the pre-existing number, 22.

After the second iteration: 37,26   22,57

This process is repeated with both of the last elements.

After the this iteration we therefore get: 16   22,27,57

The final iteration now just compares the 16 with the 22 and adds it in the first position since 16 is smaller than 22.

The result is therefore: 16,22,27,57

We implement the algorithm in Prolog as:

```
insertionsort([],[]).    /* Termination condition */
/* The list is continually added to until the last
element is reached. A new list is produced which
inserts the elements correctly */
insertionsort([X|Tail],Sorted_list):-
       insertionsort(Tail,Sorted_tail),
       insert(X,Sorted_tail,Sorted_list).
/* Move all elements right until this allows a new
list to be built. */
insert(X,[Y|Sorted_list],[Y|Sorted_list1]):-
       greater(X,Y),!,
       insert(X,Sorted_list,Sorted_list1).
insert(X,Sorted_list,[X|Sorted_list]).

greater(X,Y):- X > Y.
```

The operation of the Prolog system is shown with the example of the series of numbers: 4,1,3,2.

The query for the insertion sort reads:

?- insertionsort([4,1,3,2],S).

The first steps the Prolog system takes are:

```
insertionsort([1,3,2],_)
insertionsort([3,2],_)
insertionsort([2],_)
insertionsort([],_)
insertionsort([],[])
```

By recursion the two last elements are processed and compared with each other.

```
insert(2,[]_)
insert(2,[],[2])
insertionsort([2],[2],_)
insert(3,[2|_],_)
greater(3,2)
```

Since 3 is greater than 2 the 3 is inserted first and then the 2.

```
insert(3,[],_)
insert(2,[],[3])
insert(3,[2],[2,3])
insertionsort([3,2],[2,3])
```

The next element that is read is the 1. This is compared to the first element of the already sorted list. As 1 is not greater than 2 it is inserted at the correct position, here, in front of the 2.

```
insert(1,[2,3],_)
greater(1,2)
insert(1,[2,3|_],[1|_])
insertionsort([1,3,2],[1|_])
```

Now the 4 is compared, by means of the sort criteria (< >), with the already sorted elements (numbers). This results in the 4 having to be inserted after the numbers 1,2,3.

```
insert(4,[1,2,3],_)
```

As a result we get the following, sorted list: S=[1,2,3,4]

5.11 Merge Sort

As far as understanding goes, merge sort is relatively simple. A list to be sorted is repeatedly subdivided into two large lists until only two elements remain to be sorted. By recursion, at the end, these lists are joined together and it is during this merging that sorting takes place.

To aid understanding we shall choose, as a list to sort, the list with the same numbers as for quicksort: [6,5,8,7,3,4,1,2]

1. Step:
   Subdivide the list into two identically large lists, by means of alternating insertions:
   [6,8,3,1]   [5,7,4,2]
2. Step:
   These two lists are once again respectively subdivided into two further sublists, by means of alternating insertions:
   [6,3] [8,1]   [5,4]   [7,2]
3. Step:
   A similar subdivision as in steps 1 and 2:
   [6] [3]   [8][1]   [5] [4]   [7][2]
4. Step:
   After there is just one element in each list the lists are reassembled in pairs, by sorting:
   [3,6] [1,8]   [4,5]   [2,7]
5. Step:
   As in step 4 the next lists are reassembled:
   [1,3,6,8]   [2,4,5,7]
6. Step:
   Final joining produces the sorted list:
   [1,2,3,4,5,6,7,8]

We translate this algorithm into Prolog code:

```
merge([],L,L).
merge(L,[],L).
/* Move over the head of both lists into the results
list */
merge([X|Rest1],[Y|Rest2],[X|list]):-
      smaller(X,Y),
      merge(Rest1,[Y|Rest2],List).
merge([X|Rest1],[Y|Rest2],[Y|list]):-
      not(smaller(X,Y)),
      merge([X|Rest1],Rest2,List).
/* Subdivide the lists into further lists*/
divide([],[],[]).
divide([X],[X],[]).
divide([X,Y|Rest],[X|List1],[Y|List2]):-
      divide(Rest,List1,List2).
/* The actual merge sort algorithm */
mergesort([],[]).
mergesort([X],[X]).
mergesort([X,Y|List],Sorted_list):-
```

```
        divide([X,Y|List],Part1,Part2),
        mergesort(Part1,Sorted_part1),
        mergesort(Part2,Sorted_part2),
        merge(Sorted_part1,Sorted_part2,Sorted_list).
merge[X|Rest1],[Y|Rest2],[Y|List]):-
        merge(Sorted_part1,Sorted_part2,Sorted_list).
smaller(X,Y):- X < Y.
```

We shall test the algorithm with the query:

```
?- mergesort([4,1,3,2],Sorted_list).
```

The first steps Prolog takes are:

```
divide([4,1,3,2],_,_).
divide([3,2],_,_).
divide([],_,_).
divide([],[],[]).
divide([3,2],[3],[2]).
divide([4,1,3,2],[4,3],[1,2]).
```

The subdivision into two further lists produces the interim result of:

[4,3]   [1,2]

The next call with the elements 4 and 3 reads:

```
?- mergesort([4,3],_).
divide([4,3],_,_).
divide([],_,_).
divide([],[],[]).
divide([4,3],[4],[3]).
```

The next interim result reads:

[4][3]   [1,2]

The Prolog system, of course, works differently from our example. In the Prolog system, the empty list is also processed as it is used as a termination condition.

The next call is then:

```
?- mergesort([4],_).
mergesort([4],[4]).
mergesort([3],_).
mergesort([3],[3]).
merge([4],[3],_).
smaller(4,3).
```

```
merge([4],[],[4]).
merge([4],[3],[3,4]).
mergesort([4,3],[3,4]).
```

Both elements 4 and 3 are now correctly sorted and the right part, above, is now processed:

```
?- mergesort([1,2],_).
```

At this call, the process repeats itself, as described before. The steps start by sorting pair-wise:

```
merge([3,4],[1,2],_).
smaller(3,1).
```

As 3 is not smaller than 1 the next element (=2) of the second list is compared with 3.

```
merge([3,4],[2],_).
smaller(3,2).
merge([3,4],[],_).
merge([3,4],[],[3,4]).
merge([3,4],[2],[2,3,4]).
merge([3,4],[1,2],[1,2,3,4]).
mergesort([4,1,3,2],[1,2,3,4]).
```

As a result we get the sorted list:

```
Sorted_list = [1,2,3,4]
```

5.12 Naïve Sort (Slowsort)

Naïve sorting is a very inefficient sorting algorithm. At the start, a permutation of the list to be sorted has to be built. This permutation then needs to be checked in order to see whether or not it is sorted. If the permutation is not sorted then the sorting process is carried on for as long as is necessary for the list to be sorted.

Call:

```
?- naivesort(Unsorted_list,Sorted_list).
```

The algorithm for naïve sorting in Prolog looks as below:

```
sort([]).
sort([_]).
sort([X,X|Rest]):- sort([X|Rest]).
```

```
sort([X1,X2|Rest]):-
      smaller(X1,X2),
      sort([X2|Rest]).

insert(X,List,[X|List]).
insert(X,[Head|Rest1], [Head|Rest2]):-
insert(X,Rest1,Rest2).

join([],[]).
join([X|Rest],Joined):-
      join(Rest,Restjoined),
      insert(X,Restjoined,Joined).

naivesort(List,Sorted_list):-
      join(List,Sorted_list),
      sort(Sorted_list).

smaller(X,Y):- X < Y.
```

Since the algorithm produces *n*-factor different permutations, the naïve sorting algorithm needs a large number of possible permutations and, therefore, a hopelessly long time, which means that it is seldom used. We therefore shall just use the two numbers 1 and 2 in our example of two numbers to sort. The call reads:

```
?- naivesort([2,1],Sorted_list).
```

The first steps are:

```
join([2,1],_).
join([1],_).
join([],_).
join([],[]).
insert(1,[],[1]).
join([1],[1]).
insert(2,[1],_).
insert(2,[1],[2,1]).
sort([2,1]).
smaller(2,1).
```

Here the permutation steps are described by the insertion of single elements. This process consumes much time until, eventually, the sort criterion is met.

Since 2 is greater than 1 a new join is called:

```
join([2,1],[2,1]).
insert(2,[1],[2,1]).
insert(2,[],2).
insert(2,[1],[1,2]).
```

```
join([2,1],[1,2]).
sort([1,2]).
smaller(1,2).
```

By permutation the 1 is placed in the correct position and we can put both elements in the sorted list. As a result we get:

```
naivesort([2,1],[1,2]).
```

5.13 Summary

The list is a commonly used structure. We have tried to present lists in an easy-to-understand manner and have tried, along the way, to show in detail how lists are constructed, processed and sorted. Lists are employed on the one hand to collect instantiations of one or more variables and, on the other hand, to indicate orderings between two or more values.

As list processing is always recursive, it is sometimes difficult to comprehend how an algorithm is processed. This, therefore, makes it important to keep the algorithms relatively short in order to be able to make it easier to carry out subsequent maintenance.

Similarly, problem descriptions should always be developed such that a relationship is created between two predicates (with lists as arguments). In this, one of the predicates should hold the original list as an argument and the other predicate the list which has been created from the tail of the original list, as an argument. The corresponding rule should contain one of these predicates in the head of the rule and the other in the tail. In addition, it is always important to define a suitable termination condition, so that the algorithm does indeed stop. Sometimes, it is possible that an algorithm which meets these desiderata runs very slowly or consumes much memory.

Exercises for Topic 5

1. Write the following lists as terms with "." as a functor and including the empty list.
   a. [*a*,*b*]
   b. [*a*|*b*]
   c. [*a*|*b*,*c*],[*d*]
   d. [*a*,*b*,|*X*]
   e. [*a*|[*b*,*c*]]
   f. [*a*,*b*,|[]]
   g. [[]|[]]
   h. [*a*|[*b*,*c*|[]]]

2. Which pairs of list are unifiable?

a. [*a*,*b*|[]]	and	[*X*|*Y*]
b. [*a*,*b*|[*c*,*d*]]	and	[*X*,*Y*|*Z*]
c. []	and	[*X*]
d. [1,2,3]	and	[*X*|-]
e. [1,2,3]	and	[-|*X*]

3. What are the answers to the following queries?
   a. *f*([*a*,*b*,*c*]).
      ?- f([_|[*X*|_]]).
   b. *f*(*X*,[*X*|_]).
      ?- *f*(*Y*,[*a*,*b*,*c*]).
   c. *t*(*X*,[_,_,*X*|_]).
      ?- *t*(*Y*,[*a*,*b*,*c*]).
   d. *l*(*X*,[*X*]).
      l(*X*,[_|Tail]):- *l*(*X*,[Tail]).
      ?- *l*(*Y*,[*a*,*b*,*c*]).
   e. *n*(*X*,[Head|_]).
      n(*X*,[_|Tail]):- *n*(*X*,Tail).
      ?- *n*(*a*,[*a*,*b*,*c*,*d*]).

4. What are the answers to the following "member" queries?
   a. `?- member(c, [a,b]).`
   b. `?- member(X, [a,b,c]).`

5. Detail how the "member" predicate processes the following queries. Give the answer.
   a. `?- member(b, [a,b,c]).`
   b. `?- member(b, [a, [b,c]]).`
   c. `?- member([b,c], [a, [b,c]]).`

6. Write a program which accepts a list of whole-number values and then produces the sum of these values.

7. Develop a program which accepts a list and shows (or produces) the last element.

8. Develop a predicate which accepts a two-element list and proves if two elements are next to each other in a list.

9. Develop a predicate which makes a new list from two lists. This new list should contain all elements which do not occur in the other list. Skip this exercise if you are not familiar with the cut "!" operator.

10. This relation should be defined so that "Element" is the last element of the list "List".
    Relation: `last(Element,List)`
    a. using "append"
    b. without using "append"

11. Define the relation "length" which counts the number of elements in a list.

12. Develop two predicates:

    `even_length(List)` and `uneven_length(List)`

13. Develop a relation which reverses lists.

    ```
    reverse_list(List,Reversed_list).
    ```

14. Define the predicate "palindrome"(List). A list is a palindrome if it reads the same both forwards and backwards. For example:

    [m,a,d,a,m,i,m,a,d,a,m]

15. Develop a relation
    `rotate(List1,List2)`
    so that `List2` is like `List1` but with all elements shifted one place to the left. For example:
    ```
    ?- rotate([1,2,3,4,5],List1), rotate(List1,List2).
    List1=[2,3,4,5,1]
    List2=[3,4,5,1,2]
    ```

16. Develop the relation

    ```
    subset(Set,Subset)
    ```

    in which Set and Subset are two lists which represent sets. For example:

    ```
    ?- subset([a,b,c],Subset).
    ```

```
Subset=[a,b,c];
Subset=[b,c];
Subset=[c];
Subset=[];
Subset=[a,c];
Subset=[a]; etc.
```

17. Develop a relation

```
divide_list(List,List1,List2)
```

such that the number of elements in both `List1` and `List2` are divided approximately equally in number.

18. Write a predicate `dividelist` that tests to see if all the elements of one list are contained in another.

19. Write a predicate `mix` that takes elements from two lists in alternation and writes them to a new list.

20. Write a program which, from a list of numbers, produces the greatest common denominator.

21. Develop the following sort procedure:
Divide a list into two lists: List1 and List2, of roughly the same length. Sort List1 and List2 to result in Sorted1 and Sorted2. Mix Sorted1 and Sorted2 to produce the sorted list.

22. Define the predicate `ordered(List)`
which is true if a list consists of an ordered list of numbers. For example, the following list is not an ordered list:

```
ordered([1,7,9,9,11,18,25]).
```

Topic 6

Fail and Cut Operator

The operators "fail" and "cut" belong to the execution control operators. The existence of these operators makes it possible to control the flow of a Prolog program. With the fail operator it is possible to force backtracking. In order to explain the functioning of the operators in more detail the backtracking process is first explained.

6.1 Backtracking

The backtracking procedure is a proof procedure in which it is attempted to extend a partial solution to a problem to a complete solution. It is attempted to extend the partial solution that has been found step by step. If this extension does not succeed then the solution is in a dead-end. In order to get out of the dead-end it is necessary to undo one or more of the partial steps. Attempts are then made to extend the resulting partial solution in new ways.

The undoing of steps and the extending in new directions is repeated until a solution to the problem is found or until it becomes evident that there is no solution. The possibility of running into dead-ends and then finding a way out is characteristic of backtracking procedures. Prolog's attempts to find a solution are based on this procedure. Because the time to compute increases exponentially with the depth of the search, attempts should be made to avoid dead-ends as much as possible, by means of constraints.

Principal Strategy of Solution Search

- Prolog seeks to satisfy goals from left to right. Only when a subgoal is satisfied is the next goal considered.
- If a variable is instantiated by answering a subgoal then the variable is also bound in the rest of the subgoal.
- The search for an individual subgoal takes place from the top to the bottom of the knowledge base.
- If a subgoal can not be answered with "yes" then the backtracking procedure is invoked. This means that Prolog retreats to the previous goal, returns the values of any variables instantiated in this subgoal to their previous values and searches for another solution to the subgoal. If this exists then the next subgoal is attempted again; if this does not work then a further step of backtracking is invoked.
- On many Prolog systems, the search for a solution often begins a further search after returning variable instantiations for a query with variables. This corresponds to backtracking initiated from the final goal of the query. On many Prolog systems the user can achieve the same effect by entering semicolons.

This procedure will be clarified by means of examples.

The following facts constitute the knowledge base. Numbers are only used to number rules for the purposes of explanation.

```
1. student(harry).
2. student(tina).
3. student(mark).
4. lives(tina,london).
5. lives(harry,sunderland).
6. lives(mark,sunderland).

?- student(X), lives(X,sunderland).
```

An attempt is made to derive the first subgoal `student(X).` The first fact found is `1. student(harry).` This satisfies the first subgoal; "X" is instantiated to "harry". Prolog marks this spot.

Now an attempt is made to confirm the second subgoal. The first fact with the same name and arity is
`5. lives(harry,sunderland).`

With this Prolog can answer the question.

```
1. student(harry).
2. student(tina).
3. student(mark).
4. lives(tina,london).
5. lives(harry,sunderland).     <==
6. lives(mark,sunderland).

?- student(X), lives(X,sunderland).
X=harry
```

Now a further solution is sought. This can be initiated by a ";". Prolog now looks for other ways of satisfying the second subgoal, in order, perhaps, to return an alternative solution. The knowledge base is searched for this from the marked spot at 5. No solution is found. The system backtracks to the first goal again, which leads to the variable being uninstantiated and unbound. In this step the first subgoal is now resolved with fact `2. student(tina)`; "X" is instantiated to "tina". On attempting to satisfy the second subgoal too, Prolog fails as there is no corresponding fact `lives(tina,sunderland)` in the knowledge base. Backtracking to the first subgoal then follows.

```
1. student(harry).
2. student(tina).          <==
3. student(mark).
4. lives(tina,london).
```

```
5. lives(harry,sunderland).
6. lives(mark,sunderland).

?- student(X), lives(X,sunderland).
```

An attempt is again made to find a solution for the first subgoal from the mark. During this process `student(X)` is resolved with `3. student(mark).` and "X" is instantiated to "mark". The attempt to derive the second subgoal is also, now, successful as a corresponding solution is available in the knowledge base with the fact `6. lives(mark,sunderland).`

Output is produced and we obtain a second valid answer. Further backtracking does not deliver any more solutions; the search ends.

Representing the Solution Search by means of an AND-OR Tree

Prolog's search for a solution is represented below by means of an AND-OR tree. This method will be clarified by using an example.

```
1. likes(harry,computing).
2. likes(harry,animals).
3. likes(tina,animals).
4. likes(tina,biology).
5. enjoys(Someone,biology):- likes(Someone,animals),
   likes(Someone,biology).
?- enjoys(Someone,biology)
```

For this example the solution tree is represented as below:

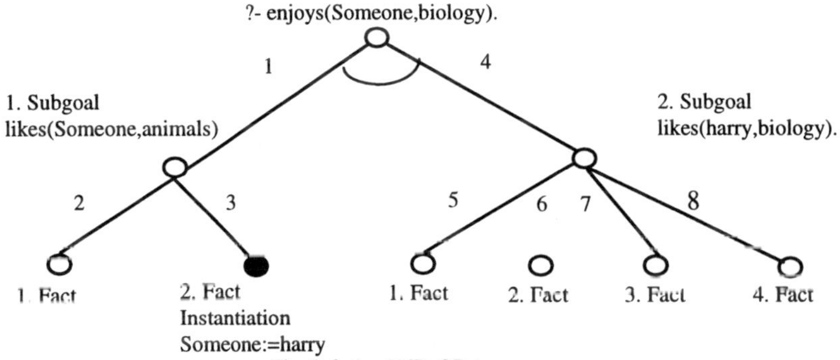

Fig. 2.6: An AND-OR tree

In order to derive the goal or query with the system both subgoals must be possible, As both of these subgoals must be derivable for an instantiation of "Someone", the above branches are linked together and indicate an AND connection.

The facts from 1 to 4 are shown as OR nodes as they should be regarded as constituting alternative unifications for both subgoals.
In the solution tree, the steps of the solution procedure are numbered in order. The nodes indicate the places at which unification should succeed. The filled nodes indicate the places at which unification was successful. In our example, the first subgoal after the second step is satisfied in this way, by instantiating the variable "Someone" with the constant "harry". The attempt is now made to derive the second subgoal. The variable "Someone" is still instantiated to "harry". As the derivability of the second subgoal

```
likes(harry,biology)
```

is not met backtracking is initiated after step 8.

The further development of the solution tree is shown in the following solution tree.

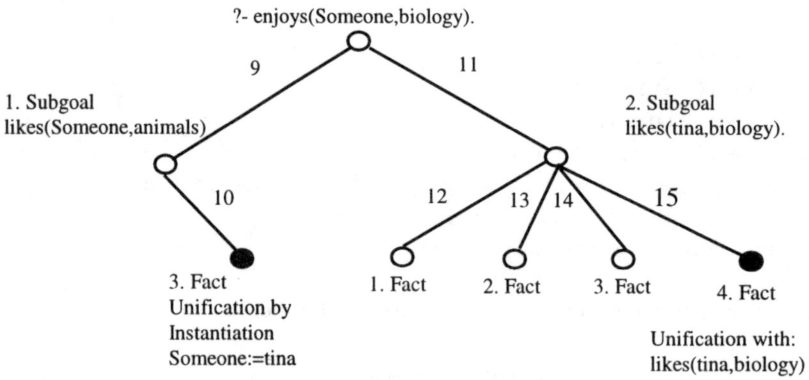

Fig. 2.7: An AND-OR tree (continued)

In the 9th step the instantiation of "Someone" is undone again. Then, an attempt is made to derive the first subgoal with fact 3. This succeeds and the variable "Someone" is instantiated to "tina". In the 11th step the task of deriving the second subgoal in the form "likes(tina,biology)" arises again. The unification then succeeds finally in step 15. In this "Someone" is instantiated to "tina", the first and second subgoals, and thus, the derivability of the query is proved. Prolog answers the query: `Someone=tina`.

6.2 The Fail Operator

With the help of this operator backtracking can be forced. This technique is explained by means of an example. Let us use the following knowledge base:

```
1. likes(harry,computing).
2. likes(mark,sport).
```

```
3. likes(tina,animals).
4. likes(henry,biology).
5. enjoys:-  likes(Person,Fact),
             write('Student: '),display(Person),
             write('enjoys: '),display(Fact).

?- enjoys.
Student: harry enjoys: computing
```

The query

```
?- enjoys
```

produces

```
Student: harry enjoys: computing.
```

The output of the rest of the knowledge base does not occur as the predicate "enjoys" is seen to be "true" after the call. If the predicate "enjoys" was set back to "false" during matching, Prolog would then attempt to instantiate the variable "Person" and "Fact", on the right hand side of the rule, to one of the other constants available in the knowledge base. In accordance with backtracking, Prolog would attempt to insert new variables until all had been matched. The result is that all combinations are produced. If it were possible to influence the matching of the predicate such that the result is always "false", then it would make backtracking manipulable.

This technique is made possible in Prolog by the fail operator. By hanging the operator at the end of the right side of the rule the manipulation of control is perfect. Matching of the "enjoys" predicate now terminates with "false". Prolog is therefore forced to search for further solutions. This has the consequence that all combinations are produced. If the built-in operator "fail" is added to the right side of a rule then this is declared to be "false". Each attempt to unify then results in a miss. For example:

```
1. likes(harry,computing).
2. likes(mark,sport).
3. likes(tina,animals).
4. likes(henry,biology).
5. likes(liz,maths).
6. enjoys:-  likes(Person,Fact),
             write('Student: '),display(Person),nl,
             write('enjoys: '),display(Fact),nl,fail.

?- enjoys.
Student: harry enjoys: computing
```

```
Student: marc enjoys: sport
Student: tina enjoys: animals
Student: henry enjoys: biology
Student: liz enjoys: maths
NO
```

On the first attempt to derive the predicate “enjoys”, Prolog finds fact 1. It is immediately possible to derive the predicate with fact 1. Although the derivation is possible, the fail operator renders the result “false” and, therefore, initiates new backtracking. The fail operator can also be added to the query. Dependent on the Prolog system it is written `FAIL` or `fail`. The form of the query is as below:

```
?- enjoys, fail.
```

The output would be as above.

In many Prolog systems there is a feature whereby exhaustive backtracking is also initiated when the fail operator is not used. If the operator in our example is modified so that it has the following form: `enjoys(Person,Fact)`, i.e., is given two additional arguments, then all the possible instantiations of the variables “Person” and “Fact” are shown.

```
Student: harry enjoys: computing
Student: marc enjoys: sport
Student: tina enjoys: animals
Student: henry enjoys: biology
Student: liz enjoys: maths
5. Solutions
```

Output in the above form can also be achieved by directly giving Prolog a so-called internal goal of the form:

```
goal enjoys, fail.
```

With this extension of the program querying by means of an external goal is no longer necessary.

6.3 The Cut Operator

An important operator for the specification of control is the cut operator. It is represented by a “!” and appears in a logic program as a premise but is not regarded as a logical component of the program.

The cut operator belongs, like the fail operator, to the execution control operators. With this operator it is also possible to directly influence backtracking. With the cut operator it is possible to force the termination of backtracking. This form of influence is the most common control mechanism in Prolog.

The procedural semantics of the cut operator are as below:

When the cut operator is met for the first time, as a subgoal to be proved, then it always succeeds but leaves an execution remark on the control stack, along with a pointer to the subgoal which leads to the activation of the clause in which the cut operator appeared. If, later, when backtracking, the propagation of failure comes across this remark then this leads to the goal marked by the cut operator being failed.

The system can, therefore, become committed to all that was selected since firing the subgoal which activated the cut. Alternatives for this subgoal are given as little consideration as those for the subgoal which lie before the cut in the cut clause.

The inclusion of the cut operator makes it possible to turn backtracking on or off. It can be said that the cut enables certain decisions to be frozen. It can be incorporated in different positions of the rule tail. This can be broken down into three cases:

1. The cut is placed at the end of the query or rule. In this case the variables are instantiated only once and the search for a solution terminates - no further backtracking takes place. For example:

```
1. likes(harry,computing).
2. likes(mark,sport).
3. likes(tina,animals).
4. likes(henry,biology).
5. likes(liz,maths).
?- likes(Person,Fact),!.
```

Prolog answers this query with: Person=harry, Fact=computing

The search for other alternatives is successfully halted. Without the cut all five combinations would have been given.

In the next example the cut also appears at the end of the query. The query is now formulated as a conjunction. Both subgoals must be met. For example:

```
1. student(harry).
2. student(tina).
3. student(mark).
4. lives(tina,london).
5. lives(harry,sunderland).
```

```
6. lives(mark,sunderland).

?- student(X), lives(X,Y),!.
X=harry Y=sunderland
```

The output is produced as expected; one solution is given. Had the cut not been employed then Prolog would have produced all three answers. The cut prevents the first variable instantiations from being undone and forces termination.

For reasons of completeness the cut operator is also shown along with a rule. For example:

```
1. likes(harry,computing).
2. likes(mark,sport).
3. likes(tina,animals).
4. likes(henry,biology).
5. likes(liz,maths).
6. enjoys(Person,Fact):-
            likes(Person,Fact),
            write('Student: '),display(Person),
            write('enjoys: '),display(Fact),nl,!.
?- enjoys(Person,Fact).
Student: harry enjoys: computing
```

In this instance the system delivers just one solution. The search for alternative solutions is halted.

2. The cut is placed at the beginning of a rule's premise. If the cut clause is met for one instantiation of the variables then no further alternatives are sought. For example:

```
1. likes(harry,computing).
2. likes(mark,sport).
3. likes(tina,animals).
4. likes(henry,biology).
5. likes(liz,maths).
6. enjoys(Person,Fact):-
   !,likes(Person,Fact),young(Person).
7. enjoys(Person,Fact):- likes(Person,Fact).
8. young(harry).
9. young(mark).
10.young(henry).

?- enjoys(Person,Fact).
```

In this example all facts should, theoretically, be shown. The following combinations should be shown by the first rule:

```
Person: harry enjoys: computing
Person: marc enjoys: sport
Person: henry enjoys: biology
```

The existence of the second rule also adds the combinations:

```
Person: tina enjoys: animals
Person: liz enjoys: maths
```

in the next iterations. This result is not produced because the cut in the first rule completely prevents the calling of rule 2.

3. The cut is placed between the premises of a query or rule. In this case backtracking only takes place within the query or rule up to the cut. In addition, the decision as to which fact should be matched against the predicate is frozen. Alternative rules or facts are not checked. This style of usage of the cut operator is shown in the following example:

```
1. student(harry).
2. student(tina).
3. likes(animals).
4. likes(biology).

?- student(X),!,likes(Y).
student=harry      likes=animals
student=henry      likes=biology
```

In this case the mode of operation of the cut can be understood as follows:

The query to the system causes Prolog to attempt to answer the two subgoals. Fact 1 in the knowledge base causes variable *X* to be instantiated to “harry”. Further processing causes the knowledge base to be searched in order to instantiate the variable *Y*. This event is possible with fact 3, Instantiating *Y* to “animals”. Prolog tries to derive the query in alternative ways. In this the instantiation of *Y* is undone during backtracking and instantiated to “biology”. This leads to the two answers, above, being produced. The normal subsequent backtracking step is prevented by the backtracking operator. It acts like a wall against which there is a ladder on only one side. Once the proof procedure has gone past the cut there is no going back. Backtracking can only now occur after the cut. That means that the variable instantiation of *X* to “harry” can not be undone. The instantiation to “tina” is, therefore, no longer possible.

In order to demonstrate the mode of operation of the cut operator, we shall look at another example:

The following rule represents the development of the graph in Fig. 2.8. A query giving the *X* value should return the corresponding *Y* value of the graph.

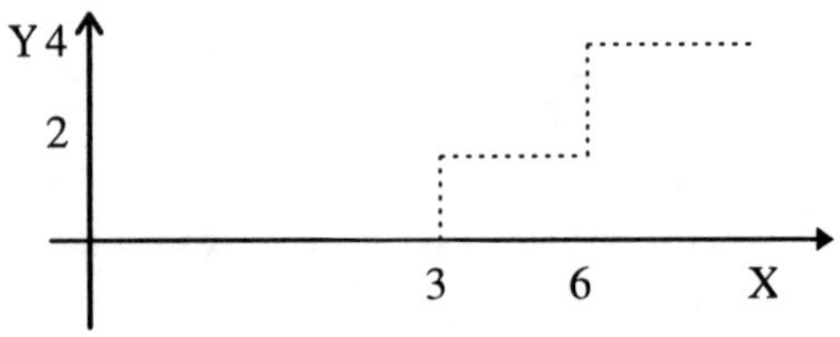

Fig. 2.8: The step function

if $X < 3$ then $Y=0$
if $3 \leq X$ and $X < 6$ then $Y=2$
if $6 \leq X$ then $Y=4$

We shall transform these rules into Prolog notation:

```
1. f(X,0):- X < 3,!.
2. f(X,2):- 2 =< X, X < 6,!.
3. f(X,4):- 6 =< X.
```

1. Query

```
?- f(1,Y), 2<Y.
NO
```

In this query Prolog goes to rule 1, in order to fulfill the first subgoal. This action is successful. By that action *X* is instantiated to 1 and *Y* to 0. The second subgoal can not be fulfilled, as 2 is not smaller than 1. The cut produces a termination and the alternative rules are not searched.

2. Query

```
?- f(7,Y).
Y=4
```

In this case an attempt is made to meet the goal by rule 1. The attempt fails as 7 < 3 is false. Backtracking ensues, as the cut has not been reached. The variable instantiations are undone. The second rule does not lead to the goal, either. The instantiation of *X* to "7" can satisfy the goal but the second condition of the rule is not met, as 7 < 6 is a false proposition. As, once again, the cut has not been reached backtracking ensues. The third rule is successful: the goal can be derived from this rule.

A more efficient solution in Prolog looks as below:

```
f(X,0):- X < 3,!.
f(X,2):- X < 6,!.
f(X,4).
```

The system gives the correct answer, *Y*=0, to the query `?- f(1,Y).`

If the cut operators were removed from these examples then we would get three incorrect answers, namely: *Y*=0, *Y*=2, *Y*=4. Prolog would search through all alternative rules, in this case. The meaning of the program would be false.

Summary of the Functions of the Cut Operators

- The cut operator appears only in the premise part of the rule.
- A cut operator between the premises of a rule serves to cut the proposition (before and after the cut operator), i.e., if the cut appears within a conjunction and it is followed by a further predicate, whose derivability proof fails, then backtracking is possible only as far as the cut. Backtracking to a predicate left of the cut is not possible.
- The cut operator always succeeds as a built-in operator, i.e., if the clause up to the cut succeeds then the clause is seen to be proved. It follows that no alternative rules for the instantiation of the variables are sought if variables of a rule satisfy the cut clause.

Possible uses of the Cut Operator

- The cut serves to terminate possibly infinite backtracking during search. This is particularly necessary if:
  a. the correct rule has already been found
  b. a negative termination condition has been met (in conjunction with the use of fail)
  c. the single possible solution has been found and no further alternative rules can be attempted
- Cut can be used to construct termination conditions and therefore guide recursive processes.
- Cut serves to make programs more efficient as no alternatives are checked. It must be ensured that no solutions are missed and that the query is so formulated that a single solution to the problem is satisfactory.
- When using cut it is necessary to ensure that no unexpected answers are produced. These can be produced when answers are produced as closely as possible to the cut operator. To combat this the operator is moved as far forward as possible.

Problems with the use of the Cut Operator

By the use of the cut operator the relative meaning of the Prolog program can be changed. The cut operator trivially strengthens Prolog's tendency to incompleteness since successful paths, which occur in a partial construction of the proof tree when cut protects against searching for alternatives, are hidden from the search procedures. The problem can be demonstrated by means of the following predicate logic examples:

```
p:- a,b.
p:- c.
```

The proposition means that from `p` either `a`, `b` or `c` can be derived. The existence of an alternative is shown in logic by means of disjunction.

$$p \Leftrightarrow (a \wedge b) \vee c$$

If the order of the clauses is now reversed then the declarative meaning is preserved, What happens, however, when a cut is introduced and the order of the clauses is swapped around?

```
p:- a, !, b.
p:- c.
```

The proposition is changed as below:

$$p \Leftrightarrow (a \wedge b) \vee (\neg a \wedge c)$$

As can be seen the proposition has totally changed. According to this the predicate *p* is derivable if *a* and *b* are derivable or *a* can not be derived and *c* can be. This change arises from the cut in clause 1 preventing clause 2 being called. Only when *a* is not derivable can the second clause be considered. If the clauses are reordered then the declarative meaning of the clauses is restored.

```
p:- c.
p:- a,!,b.
```

The logic notation is:
$$p \Leftrightarrow c \vee (a \wedge b)$$

As this illustration shows the cut should be used with care. Incorrect usage can produce unexpected side effects or may cause the program to deliver incorrect results. When formulating the rules tests should be made to determine how the program behaves with and without cut. If unexpected incorrect answers are produced then the formulation of the rules needs modification or the cut may need to be moved. This proposal is demonstrated by a small example:

```
max(X,Y,Y):- X =< Y,!.
max(X,Y,X):- Y =< X.
```

```
?- max(5,10,Maximum).
```

```
Maximum=10
```

The query can be successfully derived immediately with the first rule so that the variable “Maximum” or Y respectively, is instantiated to the greater of the two values. The condition in the first rule is fulfilled, $X \leq Y$; the cut is reached and the second rule is not tested. If the cut is removed then the second rule is definitely called but the derivation fails as the condition $Y \leq X$ is not met. The cut can, therefore, increase efficiency without changing either the meaning or the correctness of the program. The opposite is shown in the next example:

```
max(X,Y,Y):- X =< Y,!.
max(X,Y,X).

?-max(5,10, Maximum).
Maximum=10
```

In this case the result is as above. If the cut is removed then the answer is false. We get the result Maximum=5, which is not correct. In this case the rule would need tweaking, if not then we are aware of the result.

6.4 Cut and Fail Combined

The use of both these operators in the order “!, fail” has the effect that a proof is not just terminated but fails under all circumstances. If this combination of operators appears during the derivability proof of a rule then the predicate’s head is immediately seen to be underivable. This behaviour can be explained from the familiar modes of operation of the operators.

If the cut operator is encountered during variable instantiation, whilst undergoing derivability proof, then the clause is considered to be satisfied and no further alternative instantiations of the variables are investigated. If, at the end, the fail operator is encountered, the result of the derivability proof for the operator is always false. These characteristics of the operators are what gives rise to the ability to initiate exhaustive backtracking.

In this example the knowledge base is made up of living things and flowers. Animals which are living things but not flowers are what are being dealt with.

```
1. living(rose).
2. living(dog).
3. flower(rose).
4. animals(X):- flower(X),!,fail.
5. animals(X):- living(X).

?- animals(rose).
No
?- animals(X).
```

```
No
animals(dog).
Yes
```

The workings will be explained in brief, by means of the three queries.

When the first query is asked Prolog tries to derive the first goal by means of the first rule. In this way the variable *X* is instantiated to "rose". Prolog also finds a fact in the knowledge base which makes this derivation of the goal possible. After this the cut operator is passed, which makes it impossible to derive the goal by other rules. The final fail operator negates the fact, which had been true up to then. This means that the goal can not be derived. On the second query the procedure for finding a solution is similar, as Prolog tries to derive the goal "animals(*X*)" by means of the first goal. Only the third query gives us a solution since the cut was not passed in the first rule, and the goal can be derived from an alternative rule.

Exercises for the Topic

1. Given the following program:

```
action(1):- write('You entered one').
action(2):- write('You entered two').
action(3):- write('You entered three').
action(X):- X =\=1,X=\=2,X=\=3,
    write('I do not know this number').
:- write('Type a number from 1 to 3'),
read(Choice),action(Choice).
```

Modify the program so that only one action is carried out.

2. Given the following program:

```
1. father(X,Y):-parent(X,Y),male(X).
2. parent(ben,tom).
3. parent(mary,tom).
4. parent(sam,ben).
5. parent(alice,ben).
6. male(ben).
7. male(sam).
```

a. Draw the tree for the goals

```
    ?- father(X,tom).
    ?- father(X,Y).
```

b. Replace 1. with 1':

```
father(X,Y):- parent(X,Y), male(X),!.
```

Show in the tree which branches are removed by the cut.

3. Given the following program:

```
1. proud(X):- father(X,Y),newborn(Y).
2. father(X,Y):- parent(X,Y), male(X).
3. parent(john,mary).
4. parent(john,chris).
5. male(john).
6. newborn(chris).
Goal: ?- proud(john).
```

a. What is the answer for the goal: `?- proud(john).`

b. Replace 2. by 2':

```
father(X,Y):- parent(X,Y), male(X),!.
```

What is the answer?

4. Given the following program.

```
1. proud(X):- father(X,Y),newborn(Y).
2. father(john,simon).
3. father(john,mary)
4. newborn(simon).
5. newborn(mary).
Goal: ?- proud(X).
```

a. What is the answer for the goal?
b. Add a cut in so that only one answer is given.

5. Given the following program:

```
top(X,Y):- p(X,Y).
top(X,X):- s(X).
p(X,Y):- true(1),q(X),true(2),r(Y).
p(X,Y):- s(X),r(Y).
q(a).
q(b).
r(c).
r(d).
s(e).
```

Draw the tree for the goal: `?- top(X,Y)` and show which branches are removed by the cut:
a. when true(1) is replaced by cut;
b. when true(2) is replaced by cut.

Topic 7

Built-in Predicates

Prolog makes some pre-defined, standard predicates available which can be used by the programmer in the same way as those which he has defined himself. The use of these predicates, for input and output for example, is the same on all Prolog systems regardless of the hardware used.

Often these predicates are not describable in terms of pure logic, e.g., mathematical predicates can not be described without knowledge of the numbers. The numbers are, again, often dependent (value ranges) on the system, hardware. Numbers can not therefore be described in Prolog.

The built-in predicates relate to many areas of the Prolog system. They can be divided into classes according to their function:

- *Input/output predicates*
  By means of the input/output predicates Prolog can access the peripherals. This enables, for example, input from the keyboard or access to the disks.
- *Mathematical predicates*
  These predicates can be used for arithmetical operations in Prolog, such as the carrying out of basic types of calculation.
- *Knowledge base predicates*
  This group of predicates enables the Prolog knowledge base to be changed at run time by adding or removing facts, for example.
- *Structure predicates*
  This sort of predicate enables Prolog datastructures to be investigated. Structure predicates allow the testing of atoms, for example.
- *Execution control predicates*
  These predicates enable the execution of the program to be modified from within the program, e.g., "cut" and "fail".
- *Miscellaneous predicates*
  Predicates with various other functions such as comparison predicates.

These predicates constitute quasi-standards for Prolog systems but can differ between dialects in syntax and semantics. This makes it important to refer to the Prolog system's documentation. The predicates mentioned here constitute just a small selection of the predicates available on Prolog systems today. They constitute, as it were, the smallest common denominator. In this exposition greater emphasis is placed on their function.

7.1 Input/Output Predicates

Two groups of I/O predicates can be distinguished. One group, terminal-i/o, enables input by means of the keyboard. The second group, file-i/o, is intended for data handling.

Terminal I/O

These predicates read in or display single characters or whole terms.

read(Term)

Semantics: **read** gets the next complete **term** from the current input medium. The term must be terminated with a period "." which is not part of the term. The period is removed from the input stream.

Examples:
```
?- read(T),write(T).
non plus ultra amore est
T=non plus ultra amore est
yes
```

Remark: In the case of failure **read** is ignored by backtracking. **Term** is instantiated anew to the next term.

write(Term)

Semantics: **write** writes the argument **Term** to the current output medium. Unbound variables in the **Term** are shown as uniquely numbered variables prefixed with underscore. Operator declarations are observed.

Examples:
```
?- Z is 5+6, write(Z).
Z=1
yes
write(Z).
_245
yes
```

Remark: In the case of failure the output predicate is ignored. The output is not repeated.

display(Term)

Semantics: This predicate functions exactly as **write** but does not observe any operator declarations. All structures are shown in the same manner: first the functor and then the arguments (in brackets).

nl

Semantics: **nl** sends a control sequence to the current output medium in which a line feed takes place. **nl** can only be satisfied once.

get(Char)

Semantics: **get** reads in an uninstantiated argument **Char** which is the ASCII equivalent of the next character from the current input stream. If the argument **Char** is already instantiated to a number when called then it is placed in the output stream for the next character with this ASCII equivalent.

Examples:
```
?- write('Please enter your
```

```
age:'), get(A),get(B).
Please enter your age: 26
A=50
B=54 (corresponds to ASCII codes
for 2 and 6)
yes
?- get(B).
A
B=65
yes
```

Remark

In the case of failure **get** is ignored in backtracking. **Char** is instantiated to the next character. **get0** is an extended version. This predicate works like **get** but does not ignore control characters and spaces.

put(Number)

Semantics

put returns the ASCII equivalent character of the **Number** in the current output stream. The number can be a whole number expression.

Examples

```
?- put(49).
1
yes
?- number(0,[Null]),put(Null+1).
!
Null=48
yes
```

Example: Menu control in Prolog

```
start:- menu(start,'mainmenu:').
menu_line(start,q,'point 1',true).
menu_line(start,w,'(start, w, 'point 2')',fail).
menu_line(start,e,'point 3',fail).
menu_line(start,r,'point 4',fail).
menu_line(start,t,'point 5', true).

menu(Type,Title):- repeat,
            Insert=20,
            menu_display(Type, Insert, Title),
            choice(Type,Insert,Option,Status),nl,
            execute(Option),
            Status.
menu_display(Type, Insert,Title):- new_menu
            write(Title),nl,
            picklist(Insert,Type).
choice(Type,Insert,Option,Title):- repeat,
            write('Please choose: '),
            character_read(Choice),
            menu_line(Type,Choice,Option,Status), !.
character_read(C):- get(C),!.
execute(Option):- Option,!.
picklist(Insert,                            Type):-
menu_line(Type,Choice,Option,_),
            tab(Insert),write(Choice),write('-'),
            write(Option),nl,fail.
picklist(_,_):- nl.
new_menu:- nl,nl.
```

Example: Converting Umlauts

```
go:-        repeat,get0(C),deal_with(C),fail.
deal_with(132):-  !,    /*  ä */
            put(97),
            put(101).
deal_with(142):-  !     /* Ä */
            put(65),
            put(101).
deal_with(129):-  !     /* ü */
            put(117),
            put(101).
deal_with(154):-  !     /* Ü */
            put(85),
            put(101).
deal_with(148):-  !     /* ö */
            put(117),
```

```
              put(108).
deal_with(153):-  !       /* Ö */
              put(79),
              put(101).
deal_with(225):-  !       /* β */
              put(115),
              put(115).
deal_with(X):-     put(X).
```

File I/O

The file Input/ouput predicates are divided in two groups. One group serves to write to a file and the other to read from a file. The members of this group of predicates are highly interrelated.

The output of data to a file is achieved over an output stream to the given file. The standard output stream goes to the pseudo file *user*. This is not a file in the conventional sense but the user's terminal. If the data are to be output not just on the screen then the output stream for the *user* file needs to be diverted to a particular file, e.g., *demodat*. This happens with the assistance of predicates such as:

tell(file)

Semantics — **tell** links the file indicated to the current output stream. If this is not yet open then it is opened.

Examples — `?- tell(demodat)`
`yes`

Remark — All subsequent output predicates now output their information to demodat and no longer to the screen. The predicate `tell(user)` redirects the output stream to the terminal. An output file is closed with the predicate `told`. An end of file marker is placed in the file. The terminal is used for output.

telling(X)

Semantics — If the user does not know which output stream he has currently chosen then he can discover this with the predicate **telling**. It instantiates the argument to the name of the current output file.

Examples — `?- telling(X).`
`X=demodat`
`yes`

see(File)

Semantics — Just as the output of data to a file takes place by diverting the output stream the input of data from a file takes place by diverting the input stream to the corresponding file. This happens with the help

		of the predicate **see**. It links the file given to the current input stream. if it is not yet open then it is opened.
	Examples	`?- see(demodat).` `yes`
seeing(X)		
	Semantics	If the user does not know which input stream he has currently chosen then this can be found out with the help of the **seeing** predicate.

	Examples	`?- seeing(X).`
		`X=demodat`
		`yes`

seen		
	Semantics	**seen** closes the current input medium and return it to the terminal.

Example: Storing and Reading Data from a File

```
?- tell(file1), write('Logic_Programming'), told.
yes
?- see(file1), read(X), seen.
X=Logic_Programming
yes
?- tell(file2),
write('Logic.'),nl,write('Programming'),told.
yes.
?- see(file2),read(X),read(Y), seen.
X=Logic
Y=Programming
yes
?- tell(file3), put(65),told.
yes
?- see(file3),get(Y),seen.
Y=65
yes
```

Example: Displaying the contents of a file on the screen

```
showfile(Filename):-
            see(Filename),
            repeat,
            readAndShow(Text),
            Text=end_of_file,
            seen.
readAndShow(Text):- read(Text),show(Text),!.
show(end_of_file).
show(Text):- write(Text),nl.
```

7.2 Mathematical Predicates

Computers are very commonly used for the processing of numbers and calculation. To this end mathematics, or more accurately, arithmetic is used. In the following we shall have a closer look at Prolog's built-in arithmetic capability.

For Prolog, every arithmetic operator is a predicate, which means it takes a functor and an argument list. We usually write our arithmetic expressions in infix notation, i.e., *Operand*, *Operator*, *Operand*, e.g., (a+b). Prolog supports this form of notation and thinking. Internally, however, it transforms the arithmetical expressions into prefix notation, i.e., *Operator*, *Operand*, *Operand*, (+ a b). The operator is placed before both the operands to which it shall be applied. Prolog processes this prefix notation in as natural a manner as we do our infix notation. In order to clarify this a few examples of prefix and corresponding Prolog, infix notation follow:

Infix	**Prefix**
4+5	+(4,5)
4+5+6	+(4,+(5,6))
3×4	×(3,4)
3×4+6	+(6×,(3,4))
3× (4+6)	×(3,+(4,6))
A is 4+5	is(*A*,+(4,5))
10 mod 2	mod(10,2)

This transformation enables Prolog to treat arithmetic expressions as normal Prolog.

Definition of Operators

In Prolog it is possible to define operators. This often leads to a simplification of the function. In Prolog syntax operators always have three characteristics: a priority class, a certain associativity and a name. The priority class refers to the hierarchy of operators (e.g., point calculation before subtraction). The introduction of these classes takes place on a scale from 1 to 1200. By associativity is understood the ordering of the operators and its arguments.

There are three possibilities: infix, postfix and prefix notations. The possible specifications for infix operators are *xfx*, *xfy*, *yfx*, *yfy*; for postfix operators are *xf*, *yf* and for prefix operators are *fx*, *fy*. The Prolog programmer can now define his own operators and give them a suitable priority class, associativity and name. This is achieved by means of the predicate:

op(Priorityclass, Associativity,Name).

Name	Associativity	Priority Class
:-	*xfx*	1200
?-	*xfx*	1200
;	*xfy*	1100
,	*xfy*	1000
not	*fy*	900
=	*xfx*	700
is	*xfx*	700
=	*xfx*	700
\=	*xfx*	700
==	*xfx*	700
\==	*xfx*	700
<	*xfx*	700
>	*xfx*	700
≤	*xfx*	700
≥	*xfx*	700
+	*fx*	500
-	*fx*	500
x	*yfx*	400
/	*yfx*	400
mod	*xfx*	300

Table 2.1: Pre-defined Operators

is

Syntax: *Z* is <arithmetic expression>; is(*Z*,<arithmetic expression>)

Semantics: **is** evaluates the arithmetic expression according to the usual rules and returns the result in variable *Z* or compares it with the numerical value to which this is instantiated.
The arithmetic expressions can contain the usual two place operators (+, -, x, ÷, mod) as well as the unary operators (+ and -). Each term *X* and *Y* in the arithmetic expression must be instantiated to a numeric value or arithmetic expression.

Examples:

```
?- R is 10 mod 4.
R=2
```

```
yes
?- A is 1+2+3*4+5/6.
A=15.8333
yes
A is 4.
A=4
yes
```

+

Syntax: Expression1 + Expression2;
+(Expression1,Expression2)

Semantics: The result is produced by the addition of **Expression1** to **Expression2**. In this the expression can be a number, variable or expression.

Examples:

```
?- A is 3+4.
A=7
yes
?-A is 3+4+5.
A=12
yes
?- A is +(3,4).
A=7
yes
```

-

Syntax: Expression1-Expression2;
-(Expression1,Expression2)

Semantics: The result is produced by the subtraction of **Expression2** from **Expression1**.

Examples:

```
A is 4-3.
A=1
yes
?- A is 3-4+2.
A=1
yes
?- X is 6, is(Y,-(X,5)).
X=6
Y=1
yes
```

*

Syntax: Expression1 * Expression2;
*(Expression1,Expression2)

Semantics: The result is produced by multiplying **Expression1** with **Expression2**

Examples:

```
?- A is 4*3.
A=12
yes
```

```
?- A is 4*3+2.
A=14
yes
?- X is 4, is(Y,(-
(*(X,3),*(2,3)))).
X=4
Y=6
yes
```

/

Syntax: Expression1/Expression2; /(Expression1,Expression2)

Semantics: The result is produced from the division of **Expression1** by **Expression2**.

Examples:

```
?- A is 12/3.
A=4
yes
?- A is 11/3.
A=3.667
yes
```

mod

Syntax: **Expression1** mod **Expression2**; mod(Expression1,Expression2)

Semantics: The result is the remainder of the integer division of **Expression1** by **Expression2**.

Examples:

```
?- A is 10 mod 2.
A=0
yes
?- A is 10 mod 3.
A=1
yes
```

Example: For an Arithmetic Function

```
fac(0,1):- !.
fac(N,E):- N1 is N-1,fac(N1,E1),E is E1*N,!.
```

7.3 Comparison Operators

Prolog offers six predicates with which integer predicates can be compared. Here too infix notation is supported in Prolog

<

Syntax: Expression1 < Expression2; <(Expression1,Expression2)

Semantics: The goal is satisfied if the value of **Expression1** is smaller than the value of **Expression2**.

>

Syntax: Expression1 > Expression2; >(Expression1,Expression2)

Semantics — The goal is satisfied if the value of **Expression1** is greater than the value of **Expression2**.

=<

Syntax — Expression1 =< Expression2;
=<(Expression1,Expression2)

Semantics — The comparison is successful if the value of **Expression1** is smaller than or equal to the value of **Expression2**

>=

Syntax — Expression1 >= Expression2;
>=(Expression1,Expression2)

Semantics — The comparison is successful if the value of **Expression1** is greater than or equal to the value of **Expression2**

=

Syntax — Expression1 = Expression2;
=(Expression1,Expression2)

Semantics — The comparison is successful if the value of **Expression1** is equal to the value of **Expression2**

\=

Syntax — Expression1 \= Expression2;
\=(Expression1,Expression2)

Semantics — The comparison is successful if the value of **Expression1** is not equal to the value of **Expression2**

7.4 Knowledge Base Predicates

A Prolog program is realised within the system's knowledge base or database. Prolog offers some built-in predicates in order to create and manipulate this knowledge base. The user can upload self-defined clauses to the existing knowledge base with **consult(Filename)**. **reconsult(Filename)** allows the clauses to be re-read, during which process any changes to the corresponding clauses are made by means of the **assert** predicate: **asserta** places the clauses at the beginning and **assert** at the end of the database. The user can also remove clauses from the knowledge base; this takes place with the help of the **retract(Functor)** predicate. With this the first clause which matches the corresponding functor is removed. If several clauses exist under this functor name then they can be removed from the knowledge base by means of **abolish(Functor, Arity)**.

With **consult** the clauses are generally placed at the end of the knowledge base. The control over adding clauses is, however, much better in a Prolog session. Thus it might be that a clause needs to be placed before all other clauses with the same functor. This means that it is found ahead of all other clauses with the same functor when searching through the knowledge base. Because of **asserta** clauses appear in the knowledge base in the reverse order from that in which they were typed in: this corresponds to a stack (a so-called cellar store). In many Prolog implementations **assert** and **asserta** are identical.

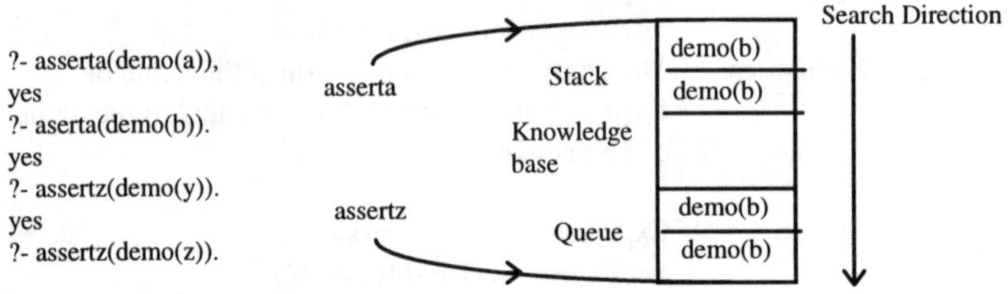

Fig. 2.9: Working principles of **asserta** and **assertz**

In other applications it may be necessary for a clause to be inserted after all clauses with the same functor and the same arity. This corresponds to the so-called queue. This is achieved by means of the **assertz** predicate. The clauses are then added to the end of the knowledge base.

asserta

Syntax	asserta(Head,Body)
Semantics	**asserta** constructs a clause **Head:- body** from **Head** and **Body** and adds this to the start of the database.
Examples	`?- asserta(demo(start)).` `yes`
Remarks	On backtracking over **asserta** the clause remains in the database

assertz

Syntax	assertz(Head,Body)
Semantics	**assertz** constructs a clause **Head:- Body** from **Head** and **Body** and inserts this at the end of the database. Head must be an atom or a structure in order for the functor of the clause to be clear.
Examples	`?- assertz(demo(end)).` `yes`

abolish

Syntax	abolish(Procedurename,Arity)
Semantics	**abolish** deletes a procedure from the database. The parameters **Procedurename** and **Arity** exactly specify the procedure and clauses of this name are removed from the database.

Examples	`?- abolish(aub,a).`
	`no`
	`?- abolish(demo,1).`
	`yes`

retract

Syntax	retract(Head,Body)
Semantics	**retract** deletes the first clause from the database for which unify with both arguments **Head** and **Body**. If no suitable clause is found in the database then retract ends with fail. After a successful retract the **Head** and the **Body** are instantiated to the corresponding parts of the deleted clause so that the values concerned may be further processed. The **Body** of a fact is true.
Examples	`?- retract(demo).` `yes`
Remarks	A deleted clause is never reinstated in the database if a failure leads back to **retract**. Instead and in contrast, the next matching clause is deleted. In this way all matching clauses can be removed from the database recursively.

The user can also display the knowledge base. This is carried out by the **listing(Functor)** predicate, in which the inclusion of a functor produces a display of all these functors regardless of their arity. Omitting a functor displays the whole knowledge base.

listing

Syntax	listing; listing(Functor)
Semantics	If no argument is given then **listing** writes all the user-defined clauses of the database to the current output stream. When present, an argument indicates the functor of the clauses to be listed (regardless of their arity). **listing** can not only be used for debugging but also in order to confirm the present state of the knowledge base.
Examples	`?- listing.` `..... (listing of the Prolog database)`
Remarks	**listing** does not show built-in predicates.

Example: Test Session

```
?- asserta(demo(a)).
?- asserta(demo(b)).
?- asserta(demo(c)).
?-listing(demo).
/* demo/1 */
demo(c)
demo(b)
demo(a)
?- retract(demo(X)).
?- listing(demo)
/* demo/1 */
demo(b)
demo(a)
?- abolish(demo,1).
?- listing(demo).
yes
```

```
?- asserta(demo(a)).
?- asserta(demo(b)).
?- asserta(demo(c)).
?-listing(demo).
/* demo/1 */
demo(a)
demo(b)
demo(c)
?- retract(demo(X)).
?- listing(demo)
/* demo/1 */
demo(b)
demo(c)
?- abolish(demo,1).
?- listing(demo).
yes
```

Example: Implementing the Predicate "Abolish"

```
new_abolish(Name,Arity):-
      functor(Predicate,Name,Arity),
      deleteclause(Predicate).
deleteclause(P):- retract(P), fail.
deleteclause(P):- retract((P:- Tail)), fail.
deleteclause(P).
```

Example: Input of Clauses

```
new_clauses:-
      loop,
      read(Text),
      test_and_assertz(Text).
test_and_assertz(end).
test_and_assertz(Text):- assertz(Text),!,fail.

loop.
loop:- loop.
```

Remarks Concerning the assert and retract Operators

These operators enable the Prolog database to be manipulated, i.e., insertion, **assert,** or deletion, **retract,** of clauses. It is however necessary to be aware of the side effects of these operators.

- The literal **assert(x)** always succeeds. As a side effect of this "success" clause x is added to the program.
- The literal **retract(x)** eliminates a clause from the program which it can unify with, otherwise it fails.
- The side effects of the operators are not influenced by backtracking.

Here is an example of the use of **assert** operators - a meta-interpreter which provides an interactive "shell": it asks the user for information which it needs to prove queries. The predicate **askable** specifies in advance the goals which can not be made by the user to the interpreter (notice the order in which the **solve** clauses are used!). Answers to the questions are stored. If the answer to a question about `A` was positive (`yes`) then `A` was confirmed otherwise (`no`) `untrue(A).` This information is used by the predicate *known* in order to avoid repeated questions about the same goal:

```
solve(true).
solve([A,B]):-      solve(A), solve(B).
solve([A,B]):-      clause([A,B]),
                    solve(B). /* Are A,B clauses? */
solve(A):-
            askable(A),
            not(known(A)),
            ask(A,Answer),respond(Answer,A).
ask(A,Answer):- display_query(A),read(Answer).
respond(yes,A):- assert(A).
respond(no,A):- assert(untrue(A)),fail.
known(A):- A.
known(A):- untrue(A).
display_query(A):- write(A),write(" ? ").
```

It would be easy to extend this "shell" so that it also produces explanations for such questions that the user responds to with the question "why?" (for this the rules used would also need to be memorised and presented on request).

The existence of these operators is motivated as follows:

1. With **assert** and **retract** database manipulation operators can be implemented.
2. They permit the formulation of mechanisms to ensure consistency.
3. They compensate in some way for Prolog systems which do not have garbage collection.

With **assert** and **retract**, variables of whatever sort can also be simulated. The Prolog program itself - the set of clauses, in our case the extension of the known predicate - is used to represent a state. The operators **assert** and **retract** are also operators for the transformation of logic programs.

The proof search for a query and a given Prolog program can refer to itself (and therefore the corresponding logical theory) when using **assert** and **retract**. The real purpose of logic programming: creating programs whose characteristics can be read off directly, is endangered. The semantics of general queries is at odds with the semantics of Prolog queries:

- the order and premises of clauses are an important aspects of the program - they need to be harmonised with the order of the intentional side effects.
- the side effects of **assert** and **retract** are not reversed in backtracking.

This is not least due to the fact that the operators are, in a procedural sense, *program transformations*, whilst, in a declarative sense, they should be seen as *serving to guarantee* truth values.

When using the interactive "shell", described above, the situation of a material inconsistency[2] can arise in that during the interaction a fact stored as untrue can, on further program transformations, become provable and therefore also directly guaranteed. If the dubious guarantees are in the Prolog database in the following order:

```
A.
:
:
untrue(A).
```

then `untrue(A)` counts as a *prior* (and therefore notably alogical) guarantee for the truth value of `A`.

[2] Not however a formal inconsistency as the system is not aware that the user regards the predicate untrue as a form of negation!

7.5 Structure Predicates

Structure predicates serve to determine the datatype of a term.

atom(*X*)

Semantics: atom checks to see if the argument *X* is instantiated with a non-numeric atom.

Examples:
```
?- atom(ollie).
yes
?- atom(15).
no
?- atom(A).
no
```

atomic(*X*)

Semantics: Checks if the argument *X* is instantiated to an atom or number.

Examples:
```
?- atomic(15).
yes
?- atomic(A).
no
?- A is 3+4, atomic(A).
A=7
yes
```

integer(*X*)

Semantics: Checks if the argument *X* is instantiated to a whole number.

Examples:
```
?- integer(50).
yes
?- integer(X).
no
```

nonvar(*X*)

Semantics: Checks if the argument *X* is instantiated to a non-variable term.

Examples:
```
?- nonvar(X).
no
?- nonvar(a,(X,Y)).
X=_G12
Y=_G13
yes
```

var(*X*)

Semantics	Checks if the argument *X* is an unbound variable.

Examples	`?- var(X).`
	`yes`
	`?- var(23).`
	`no`
	`?- X=X,var(X).`
	`X=_G13`
	`yes`

struct(*X*)

Semantics	Checks if the argument *X* is a structure.

Examples	`?- struct(b).`
	`no`
	`?- struct([a,b,c]).`
	`yes`

7.6 Comparison Predicates

Prolog offers an array of predicates for comparing terms, these will be presented briefly in this section.

=

Syntax	Term1=Term2
Semantics	The comparison is successful if **Term1** and **Term2** unify. The value of the resulting variable substitution is made available for further processing.

Examples	`?- germany=D.`
	`D=germany`
	`yes`
	`?- germany=D,EC.`
	`no`

Remarks	The comparison includes the trivial identity test.

==

Syntax	Term1==Term2
Semantics	The comparison is successful if **Term1** and **Term2** are equal. Terms with different variables are not equal.

Examples	`?- p(a,b)==p(b,a).`
	`no`
	`?- p(a,b)==p(a,b).`
	`yes`

\=

Syntax	Term1 \= Term2
Semantics	The comparison is successful if the terms do not unify. The values of the variables are not available later.

Examples	`?- f(X) \= f(X).`
	`no`
	`?- p(a,X) \= p(b,Y).`
	`yes`

\==

Syntax	Term1 \== Term2
Semantics	The comparison is successful if the terms are unequal. Terms which differ only with respect to variables are unequal.
Examples	`?- X \== X.` `no`

compare

Syntax	compare(Op,Term1,Term2)
Semantics	**compare** carries out a comparison between **Term1** and **Term2** according to an internal sorting order (Variables-Numbers-Atoms-Terms). **op** is instantiated with <, = or >, according to the result of the comparison. If it is instantiated when called then **compare** is a test. **op(=A,B)** is equivalent to **A==B**.

Examples	`?- compare(Op,'abc',[97,98,99]).`
	`op==`
	`yes`
	`?- compare(=,[a],T).`
	`no`

Example: FOR-NEXT Loop and the ASCII Table

```
for(Loopvariable,Loopvariable,End).
for(Loopvariable,Start,End):-
      Start < End,
      Next is Start + 1,
      for(Loopvar,Next,End).
ascii_code(From,To):-
      for(X,1,80),
      write('*'),
      X=80,
      for(Y,From,To),
      write(' '),
      put(Y),
      write(' '),
      Y >= To,nl,
      for(Z,1,80),
      write('*'),
      Z=80,nl.
next(_):- fail.
next:- fail.
```

Exercises for the Topic

1. Work out the possibilities of a permutation by the *n*-over-*k* calculation. Write a program to calculate Fibonacci numbers.

Correct thinking is based on cause and effect and leads to logical, constructive planning; wrong thinking frequently leads to inner tension and nervous breakdown.
- Dale Carnegie -

3 LOGIC

FOUNDATIONS

Topic 8

In this section the most important terminology of logic is explained. Some terms will be treated that are dealt with more fully later on.

Syntax

The expression "syntax" is a central term in logic. The syntax determines how logical propositions appear. Here parallels can be drawn with human language. In human language there are also certain syntactic constraints which are adhered to and to which everyone who uses the language must adhere in order to be able to be understood. It is similar for logic. The syntax is, so to speak, the grammar of the logic.

The syntax determines on the one hand how the logical expressions appear and on the other how conclusions may be drawn from these logical expressions. This could be compared to the basic mathematical operations. The basic mathematical operations have symbols for multiplication, division, addition and subtraction which are indicated by the symbols $\times$, $\div$, $+$, $-$. There are precise regulations for these basic mathematical operators. It is the same in logic. Basic mathematical operators could be seen to be AND and OR which are represented by $\wedge$, $\vee$. For both of these "basic mathematical operators" of logic there are precise rules, as in mathematics.

Along with these "computational symbols" of logic, which are called conjunctions, syntax also contains the alphabet of the language. The alphabet is examined more closely, below.

The symbols used in syntax do not give any indication of their meaning. Semantics are necessary for this. For this reason all symbols used in syntax are, with the exception of the conjunctions, considered to be equal.

Semantics

Semantics is the science of semantic expressions. Semantic expressions constitute the relationship between the linguistic and non-linguistic elements. Semantics permits the interpretation and interpretation of the symbols used in syntax.

The meaning of the symbols used in the syntax can be derived from the semantics. Here is a small example:

The letter "F" itself, when it is used syntactically, has no meaning: more precisely, no meaning can be derived from it. Only with the help of the corresponding contextual semantics can meaning be recognised. Thus the letter "F" could, e.g., be the symbol for the position of a fire extinguisher or the first letter on number plate referring to the town of Frankfurt.

Alphabet

The alphabet contains the symbols used in the syntax. It is a finite set of all the symbols allowed by syntax. In the syntax, or alternatively, the semantics only those symbols may be used which are formed from letters of the alphabet. This includes the empty word, too.

Calculus

A calculus is a procedure which generates new "permissible" strings of symbols from those which are permitted. A calculus consists of a number of rules, for each of which their applicability and results are exactly defined. The order in which the rules are used is not defined. If a prescription as to the order in which the rules are to be used is added then this is known as an *algorithm*.

For example: Chaining rule

$A \to B$	if A then B
$B \to C$	if B then C
$A \to C$	if A then C

Logical Formulae

A logical formula is a formula composed of syntactic symbols which should express some meaning. In order to say "Every German is a European" then the logical formula could be represented as:

$$\forall x(Gx \to Ex)$$

In which "$\forall x$" means "for all x it is true that", and "$\to$" means implies, i.e., if the first condition is true then the second is also true: G stands for German and E stands for European.

Relationship between Syntax and Semantics

The following clarifies the relationship between syntax and semantics. The whole semantics which are represented in this figure by *W** represents the knowledge base. W is that part of the knowledge base which is required for the solution of a given problem.

Example: Search Procedures

- Syntactic expressions: state tree, problem, situation
- Semantic expressions: state space, reduction space, game space
- Calculus: Search procedure, breadth-first search, depth-first search, ...

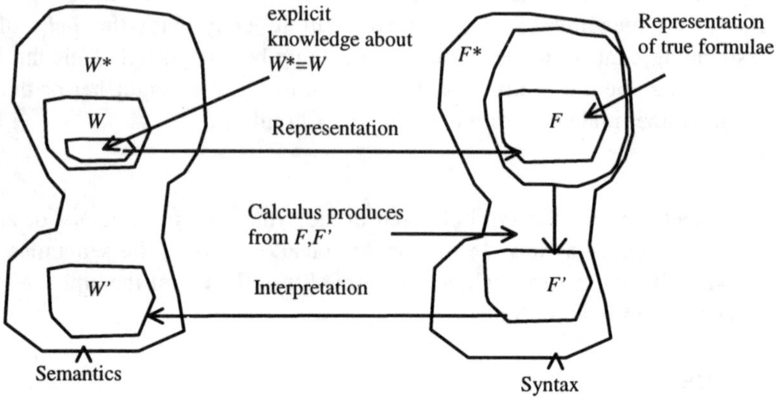

Fig. 3.1: Relationship between syntax and semantics

Correct ⇔ solution path in the search tree; solution path in the search space
Completeness ⇔ if the solution path is valid for the search space then the procedure finds a solution path in the search tree (each winning position can be calculated)

Proof Procedure

In logic there are two important procedures in proof determination, namely semantic and syntactic proof.

Semantic methods (model theory)
The relationship between logical sentences is investigated with respect to their truth value by comparison with an external domain. Semantic proof is performed with the help of a truth table. Truth tables are presented under the theme of propositional logic.

The vocabulary used here is:
true, false, interpretation, satisfiable, model implication, semantic consequence.

Syntactic methods (proof theory)
Logical sentences are investigated with respect to the other sentences by using inference rules. The most important inference rules are: Modus Ponens, resolution calculus and Herbrand's calculus.

The vocabulary employed here is:
axiom, inference, theorem, proof, consistency, syntactic consequence.

Figure 3.2 clarifies the relationship between both proof procedures.

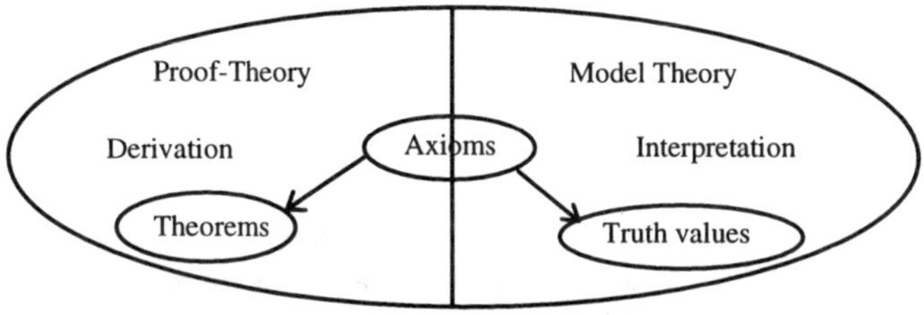

Fig. 3.2: Relationship between proof procedures

8.1 Axiom Systems

What does "to axiomatise" mean?

This expression means finding formulae which describe a situation and its characteristics by means of a chosen language. From this further formulae can be derived. Therefore an axiom system can be thought of as a set of formulae from which all other formulae, which are valid for the situation, follow.

An axiom system consists of the following three components

- a language
- axioms
- inference rules

By choice of language the language elements with which the axiom system is furnished are determined. Syntax and semantics of the language are defined thus. Typical logics are propositional logic or predicate logic. It is, of course possible to select natural language as a language of the axiom system in which the syntax and semantic must be precisely defined. In the following we shall look at the language of predicate logic.

Axioms are the mathematical propositions (sentences) which are fundamentally accepted yet can not be proved. For example it is not possible to prove that "exactly one straight line passes through two points" even if this seems entirely obvious. On the other hand, the opposite of this sentence is mathematically plausible even if it seems to contradict our common sense. Therefore today the meaning of axioms is seen to be the "basic facts of reality" and they are held to be the *unprovable basis of a theory*.

To what extent this theory is suited to describing reality is considered out of bounds. A theory of course, contains more than axioms as it needs symbols, i.e., a language and rules of derivation with whose help formulae can be developed. Propositions, which can be obtained from axioms and must prove them, are known in mathematics as propositions or theorems.

Inference rules are prescriptions which describe pure, formal operations with logical symbols. Their general form is as below:

$$\frac{S_1, \dots S_n}{S} \quad \text{with } S_1, \dots, S_n\ S \text{ as sets of formulae}$$

This form of representation means that S follows from S_1, ... S_n. The formulae above the line, i.e., S_1, ... S_n are the premises and that under the line is the conclusion, S. The inference rules must be correct, i.e., the conclusion must logically follow from the premise. If these rules are drawn up correctly then additional formulae can be derived. Typical examples for inference rules are introduction, elimination and Modus Ponens. An example for Modus Ponens:

P	if P is true
$P \rightarrow Q$	from P, Q follows
Q	then Q is true

It should also be pointed out that the selection of axioms and inference rules is not based on any regulated basis. The choice is essentially left open. However, certain criteria apply to axiom systems. These are:

- *Freedom from contradiction*
  This means that a proposition and its opposite (negation) can not be produced at the same time. The appearance of such contradictions always indicates an unusable axiom system.
- *Completeness*
  An additionally produced axiom system must be complete. All propositions of the theory must be derivable from it. If any single one is not derivable then the system must be extended.
- *Independence*
  No axiom should be included which can be derived from another. It might as well be crossed out. This constraint is not that strong. It is sometimes practical to use such superfluous axioms, e.g., it obviates numerous proofs for the proposition about the internal angles of a triangle if it is used as an axiom.
- *Decidability*
  It must be possible to determine the truth or falsity of the formally derived expressions.

Example: The axiom system represents the assessment regulations of a university. The language is that of natural language. The following axioms are given:

A_1: Everyone who has passed a Prolog exam has passed the Prolog module.
A_2: Everyone who has passed the Prolog module is entitled to sit the diploma exam.

A_3: Hilary has passed the Prolog exam.

As an inference rule, Modus Ponens (MP), is selected. The derivation is as follows:

1:	Hilary has passed the Prolog module.	A_1,A_3,MP
2:	Hilary is admitted to the exam.	1,A_2,MP

This example just illustrates a possible fragment of the assessment regulations. Further axioms are required in order to draw new conclusions.

Belief is love of the invisible, trust in the impossible.
- Johann Wolfgang von Goethe -

4 PROPOSITIONAL LOGIC

Propositional logic is a subarea of mathematical logic which was founded by Aristotle and then became part of philosophy. Starting with the works of De Morgan, Boole and Frege in the middle of the last century, mathematical logic was formalised and can be regarded as a mathematical theory. Propositional logic is a two-valued logic because each proposition can only take two values, namely true or false.

Propositions can be connected to each other and conclusions may be drawn and laws derived from these connections. A proposition in propositional logic is seen to be a construct which can not be taken apart any further and is characterised only by its truth. The inner structure of the proposition is investigated: this is the task of predicate logic which follows propositional logic in the hierarchy of logics. This notion is comparable to chemistry, which works primarily with atoms (propositions), which combine to form molecules (connected propositions) and behave according to certain laws. The components of the atom, that is the relationship between nucleus and shell, is considered next. It is only considered when it is required (predicate logic).

Before an axiom system for propositional logic is constructed, below, the fundamental expressions and possible connections in propositional logic are looked at in more detail.

PROPOSITIONS

A proposition is a statement about which it is sensible to ask whether or not it is "true" or "false". True propositions are, e.g.:

- Man is mortal
- A square has four sides
- $3 \times 2 = 6$

False propositions are, e.g.:

- Socrates was German
- The moon is square
- $16 \div 4 = 5$

Such propositions can readily be transformed into Prolog:

- is_mortal("Man").

is_foursided("Square").   etc.

There are linguistic constructs to which no meaningful truth value can be assigned. Here are some utterances which are not propositions:

- Command: Come to me!
- Names: Multiplication
- Questions: Are you well?

PROPOSITIONAL FORM

In this "propositional variables" (atoms) are also used and are indicated with lower case letters *a, b, c, ...* . These are symbols which do not signify a particular proposition but are, rather, place holders for propositions and are only substituted for by meaningful propositions. A propositional form is a language construct which contains at least one variable and, after the replacement of the variables, is turned into a true or false proposition, e.g.:

- X is a prime number
- Y is a European town

There are satisfiable and non-satisfiable propositional forms. Propositional forms which result in a true proposition for at least one substitution are called satisfiable and the others, non-satisfiable propositional forms. Satisfiable propositions can:

- be generally valid if they turn into true propositions for all substitutions;
- partially valid if they hold true for one but not, however, for all substitutions.

PROPOSITIONAL CONNECTIONS

With the help of so-called *conjunctions*:
AND (∧, &, conjunction), OR (∨, ;, disjunction), if ...then (→, implication), if-and-only-if (iff, ↔, equivalence), negation (not, ¬)
many atomic propositions can be connected with each other to form complex combined propositions which are also called formulae (well-formed formulae). for example:

- it is warm ∨ it is cold
  reads: It is warm or it is cold.
- it is warm → ¬ it is cold
  reads: If it is warm then it follows that it is not cold.

it is warm ∧ ¬ it rains → it is a nice day
  reads: If it is warm and it is not raining then it follows that it is a nice day.

Simplified:

- $P \vee Q$
- $P \rightarrow Q$
- $[P \wedge \neg R] \rightarrow S$

The truth of the newly combined propositions depends only on the truth values of the part propositions (atomic propositions) which appear in it. In propositional logic this is called the *Extensionality Principle*.

The main task of propositional logic is to investigate which propositions are true, based on their logical form, and what relationship the propositions have to one another.

Topic 9
Axiom Systems in Propositional Logic

As already defined an axiom system consists of:

- the syntax of the language
- the semantics of the language
- logical axioms
- inference rules

In this section an axiom system for propositional logic is constructed.

9.1 Syntax of Propositional Logic

The syntax of the axiom system contains both the symbolic system as well as the grammar, according to which the propositions can be constructed. The formalised elements of this system are called formulae. Syntax is, therefore, purely concerned with the structural composition of formulae and possible transformations. In the following text these symbols are defined.

Propositional Variables

An atom is a unary predicate. It corresponds to an elementary logical proposition, i.e., without connection.

Literal

When differentiated by means of positive or negative propositional variables then a literal is produced. A literal can, for example, just as easily be the variable P as its negation $\neg P$.

Clauses

A clause is a disjunction of atoms or, put differently, a finite, possibly empty set of literals. For example in set notation:
$\{\{P\},\{P,Q\},\{Q,R\},\{R\}\}$

Horn Clauses

These are implications which are made up of just one atomic formula as a conclusion and several atomic formulae linked by "AND" as premises. The formulae can not contain any "OR", "negation" or "equivalence". This subset of propositional logic is called Horn logic. It is made up of clauses with at most one positive literal, so-called Horn clauses

There are four permissible types of Horn clause:

1. General Horn Clauses

   $$P \leftarrow Q_1 \wedge Q_2 \wedge \ldots \wedge Q_n \qquad n \geq 1$$

   These constitute Prolog's rules.

2. Horn clauses without Tail (no premises)

   $P \leftarrow$

   This constitutes Prolog facts.
3. Horn clauses without head (no conclusion)

   $\leftarrow Q_1 \wedge Q_2 \wedge ... \wedge Q_n \qquad n \geq 1$

   This constitutes Prolog querying.
4. Empty Horn clauses

   $\leftarrow$

   These clauses are always false and correspond to the Prolog "fail" construct.

Conjunctive Connection

A propositional logic formula is in conjunctive normal form (CNF) when it is in the form of a conjunction $P_1 \wedge P_2 \wedge P_3 \wedge ... \wedge P_n$ in which the individual elements (P_1-P_n) are disjunctions of the form $P_{11} \vee P_{12} \vee P_{13} \vee ... \vee P_{1m}$. The elements of disjunctions must be propositional variables or negations of propositional variables, i.e., a conjunction of disjunctions of literals. For example:

$$(P \vee Q) \wedge (\neg P \vee Q \vee R) \wedge (P \vee \neg R)$$

Disjunctive Connection

A propositional logic formula is in disjunctive normal form (DNF) when it is in the form of a disjunction $P_1 \vee P_2 \vee P_3 ... P_n$ in which the individual elements (P_1-P_n) are disjunctions of the form $P_{11} \wedge P_{12} \wedge P_{13} \wedge ... \wedge P_{1m}$. The elements of disjunctions must be propositional variables or negations of propositional variables, i.e., a disjunction of conjunctions of literals. For example:

$$(P \wedge Q) \vee (\neg P \wedge Q \wedge R) \vee (P \wedge \neg R)$$

Transformation of a formula into CNF or DNF

A formula can be turned into conjunctive or disjunctive normal form by means of the following procedure.

1. Elimination of all implications and equivalences in the formula, with the help of the following two equivalence rules:

   $P \rightarrow Q \equiv (\neg P \vee Q)$

   $P \leftrightarrow Q \equiv ((\neg P \vee Q) \wedge (\neg Q \vee P))$
2. Removal of all sub-formulae still in the formula of the form $\neg(P \wedge Q)$ or $\neg(P \vee Q)$, with the aid of De Morgan's equivalence rules:

   $\neg(P \wedge Q) \equiv \neg(\neg P \vee \neg Q)$

   $\neg(P \vee Q) \equiv (\neg P \wedge \neg Q)$
3. Reducing all double negatives in the formula, with the aid of the equivalence rule for double negatives:

   $\neg\neg P \equiv P$
4. Removal of all sub-formulae in the formula of the form $P \wedge (Q \vee R)$ or $P \vee (Q \wedge R)$, with the distribution equivalence rule:

   $(P \wedge (Q \vee R)) \equiv ((P \wedge Q) \vee (P \wedge R))$

   $(P \vee (Q \wedge R)) \equiv ((P \vee Q) \wedge (P \vee R))$

After carrying out these four steps the formula will be in conjunctive or disjunctive normal form.

Example for transformation into CNF

$(P \rightarrow Q) \rightarrow (\neg R \rightarrow (S \wedge T))$

1. $\neg(P \rightarrow Q) \vee (\neg R \rightarrow (S \wedge T))$
   $\neg(\neg P \vee Q) \vee (\neg\neg R \vee (S \wedge T))$
2. $[\neg\neg P \wedge \neg Q] \vee [\neg\neg R \vee [S \wedge T]]$
3. $[P \wedge \neg Q] \vee [R \vee [S \wedge T]]$
4. $[P \wedge \neg Q] \vee [R \vee S] \wedge [R \vee T]]$
   $\{P \vee [(R \vee S) \wedge (R \vee T)]\} \wedge \{\neg Q \vee [(R \vee S) \wedge (R \vee T)]\}$
   $\{[P \vee (R \vee S)] \wedge [P \vee (R \vee T)]\} \wedge \{[\neg Q \vee (R \vee S)] \wedge [\neg Q \vee (R \wedge T)]\}$

Matrix Method

The matrix method, also called "connections method", avoids the creation of new formulae. Instead of this the refutation of the formula being investigated is derived directly from its internal structure. In order to cover the basic ideas we shall restrict ourselves to propositional logic in conjunctive normal form.

The formulae are represented as two dimensional matrices, which are not really anything other than a different notation for formulae in negation normal form (NNF), in which conjunctions are written vertically and disjunctions horizontally, and thus the connectives similarly - the brackets are omitted, by convention. In the matrix method, the formula-matrix is established once, at the beginning, and then all that is noted are the paths through the matrix which are complementary. The derivation process is, therefore, concerned with generating new paths, instead of new sets of formulae, as components of the search space.

The matrix of a formula G, in negation normal form, is defined inductively as follows:

- if G is a literal then $[G]$ is the matrix for G.
- if G is a disjunction $(k_1 \vee ... \vee k_n)$ with $n \geq 2$, in which all k_i are conjunctions or literals then $[M_1 ... M_2]$ is the matrix for G if M_i in each case represents the matrix for k_i.
- If G is a conjunction $(D_1 \wedge ... D_n)$ with $n \geq 2$ in which all D_i are disjunctions or literals then $\begin{bmatrix} M_1 \\ : \\ : \\ M_n \end{bmatrix}$ is the matrix for G if in each case M_i represents the matrix for D_i.

If X is a finite set of formulae in NNF then the matrix for X is defined by the matrix of the conjunctions of all the formulae from X.

For example:
a) The matrix for the formula
$P \wedge (Q \vee S) \wedge (\neg P \vee (\neg Q \wedge R)) \wedge (Q \vee \neg S)$
appears as below:

$$\begin{bmatrix} & P & \\ Q & & S \\ & & \neg Q \\ \neg P & & \\ & & R \\ Q & & \neg S \end{bmatrix}$$

A matrix represents a formula *positively* in DNF:
$(\neg P \wedge Q \wedge R) \vee (\neg Q \wedge \neg R) \vee (P \wedge Q)$
in matrix form:

$$\begin{bmatrix} \neg P & \neg Q & P \\ Q & \neg R & Q \\ R & & \end{bmatrix}$$

The *negative* matrix represents the negation of the clauses:
$\neg((\neg P \wedge Q \wedge R) \vee (\neg Q \wedge \neg R) \vee (P \wedge Q))$
$(P \vee \neg Q \vee \neg R) \wedge (Q \vee R) \wedge (\neg P \vee \neg Q)$
The negative matrix is obtained by turning the positive matrix 90° anticlockwise and a toggling of the signs of the elements, i.e., negating the elements with ¬.

The Horn Matrix

A Horn matrix represents the transformation of Horn clauses into a matrix. They can be recognised in that they have only one positive literal in the positive representation and only one negative literal in the negative representation (positive representation: columns in DNF, lines in CNF; opposite in the negative representation). Examples:

b) CNF: $P \wedge (\neg P \vee Q) \wedge (\neg Q \vee R) \wedge (\neg R)$

CNF positive $\begin{bmatrix} P & \\ \neg P & Q \\ \neg Q & R \\ \neg R & \end{bmatrix}$ CNF negative $\begin{bmatrix} R & Q & P & \neg P \\ & \neg R & \neg Q & \end{bmatrix}$

c) DNF $P \vee (\neg P \wedge Q) \vee (\neg Q \wedge R) \vee (\neg R)$

DNF positive $\begin{bmatrix} P & \neg P & \neg Q & \neg R \\ & Q & R & \end{bmatrix}$ DNF negative $\begin{bmatrix} R & \\ Q & \neg R \\ P & \neg Q \\ \neg P & \end{bmatrix}$

Prolog form: $\begin{bmatrix} R \\ Q\text{:- } R \\ P\text{:- } Q \\ \text{:- } P \end{bmatrix}$

Path through a matrix

If M is a matrix then a (complete) path through M is a list of literals which is produced when a sub-matrix is selected from each line of the matrix and is treated as follows:

- if this sub-matrix contains just one literal then add it to the existing list.
- if there is then a matrix, M', with a conjunction or disjunction then select a complete path through M' and add all the literals on this path to the existing lists.

In example a) $(P, Q, \neg P, Q)$ and $(P, Q, \neg Q, R, \neg S)$ are paths through this matrix but $(P, Q, \neg Q, \neg S)$ is not. *A* path is complementary if it holds a complementary literal pair. *A* matrix is complementary if all its complete paths are complementary.

9.2 Semantics of Propositional Logic

The semantics of the axiom system embodies the meaning of the sentences or alternatively the determination of which determines the assignment of truth values to propositions. The truth value of a proposition depends, basically, on the truth values of the atomic propositions. The complete proposition is either true or false. In this it is unimportant if the elementary propositions are factually true or false; what is important is that they are logically true or false. For example:

factually true: 4+5=9
logically true: 4+5=9 or 2+5 $\neq$ 9
factually false: 4+5=8
logically false: 4+5=8 and 2+5=9

In the following the semantics of propositional logic is further investigated.

Interpretation

The assignment of truth to an elementary proposition is known as "assigning variables" or interpretation.

Henry is a man := true
Henry is a woman := false
Henry is a man & ¬(Henry is a woman) := true.

Definition of Conjunctions by Truth Tables

In contrast to propositions, for which the meaning of the proposition (true/false) is dependent on the context (e.g., the utterance "It is raining" depends on the truth value of the place and situation of the utterance), the meaning of conjunctions is based on the truth values of the individual propositions alone and not their content. For this reason conjunctions can be defined with the help of truth tables which are based exclusively on truth values and are independent of the context of the propositions.

Q	P	$\neg Q$	$Q \wedge P$	$P \vee Q$	$Q \rightarrow P$	$Q \leftrightarrow P$
t	f	f	f	t	f	f
t	t	f	t	t	t	t
f	t	t	f	t	t	f
f	f	t	f	f	t	t

Fig. 4.1: Truth table

Remarks:

- The negation of the sentence "The bird is white" does not mean that "The bird is black" but, rather, "It could also be black, brown, yellow and ...".
- The sentence "She is not only clever but hard working" can be formulated as "She is clever and she is hard working".
- It is worth noting about implication that if the first proposition (premise) is false then the whole proposition is true since the conclusion is not subject to any conditions.
  A= The moon is square.
  B= The cheese is green.
  $A \rightarrow B$ is a true proposition due to the false first proposition (premise) *A* the validity of *B* is not proved.
  $A \rightarrow B = (\neg A) \vee B$
  $= \neg A \vee \neg(\neg B)$
  $\neg B \rightarrow \neg A$
  For example:
  "If it rains then the harvest will grow" is equivalent to:
  "If the harvest does not grow then it has not rained".
  It is not correct to say:
  "If the harvest grows then it has rained".
- The proposition "If and only if the switch is closed then the current will flow" means: "If the switch is closed the current flows and if the current flows the switch is closed".

Model of a Formula

Using the truth table for conjunctions, a single truth value (true or false) can be assigned for every possible interpretation. An interpretation in which a formula is true is known as a model.

Example: $(A \vee B) \wedge (A \vee \neg B)$

There are two different propositional variables, so there are $2^2=4$ possible interpretations:
$\alpha=\{f,f\}$; $\beta=\{f,t\}$; $\gamma=\{t,f\}$; $\delta=\{t,t\}$

In formulae with few propositional variables this is a sensible approach with which to determine the truth value of the entire formula. This approach is called the "Truth Table Method". In this the whole formula is subdivided into part-formulae and then their truth values are determined. Then, by the connections of the sub-formulae, the truth value for the whole formula can be determined.

A	B	$A \vee B$	$A \vee \neg B$	$(A \vee B) \wedge (A \vee \neg B)$
t	t	t	t	t
t	f	t	t	t
f	t	t	f	f
f	f	f	t	f

Under both interpretations $\gamma=\{A=\text{true}, B=\text{false}\}$ and $\delta=\{A=\text{true}, B=\text{false}\}$ the whole formula is true therefore these two interpretations are models of the formula.

Satisfiability of a Formula

A formula is satisfiable if it has at least one model of the formula. For example:

a) Harry is a husband & (Harry is a wife) := false
α {Harry is a husband} := true
{Harry is a wife} := false

b) Harry is a man $\rightarrow \neg$(Harry is a wife) := true
α satisfies b) but not a).

If there are no such models then the formula is unsatisfiable.

Consistency of the Formula

Given a set of formulae S with the set of variables $V=\{P_1, P_2, \ldots P_n\}$ an interpretation α is *consistent* if all formulae in the interpretation α are true.

Example: $S=\{P \vee Q, \neg P \vee \neg Q\}$; $V=\{P,Q\}$

P	Q	$P \vee Q$	$\neg P \vee \neg Q$
f	f	f	t
f	t	t	t
t	f	t	t
t	t	t	f

The interpretations $\alpha=\{f,t\}$ and $\beta=\{t,f\}$ are consistent with *S*, since all formulae of *S* (here $P,Q,P\vee Q$ and $\neg P\vee\neg Q$) are true in both interpretations.

A set *S* of formulae is consistent if at least one consistent interpretation exists. In this example *S* would be consistent.

Logical Consequence

A formula *F* is a logical consequence of a set of formulae *S* if *F* is satisfied in all models of *S*. A logical consequence constitutes a semantic proof of a theory. An attempt is made, with the aid of inference rules and previously derived theorems, to prove the validity of a theory. The notation for logical consequence is:

$$S \models F$$

e.g., $\{Q\vee P, \neg Q) \models P$

Proof:

Q	P	$Q\vee P$	$\neg Q$	P	
t	t	t	f	t	
t	f	t	f	f	
f	t	t	t	t	← ✓
f	f	f	t	f	

✓ identifies the interpretation that makes $Q \vee P, \neg Q$ and P true.

Theory

If A_1, A_2, ..., A_n are logical formulae then the totality of formulae which can be derived from A_1, A_2, ... A_n are known as propositional theories with respect to the axiom system A_1, A_2, ... A_n. All formulae which can be derived from this are called sentences or *theorems* of the theory.

Given the two axioms A_1: $P\rightarrow Q$ and A_2: P then Q is a theorem with respect to the axiom since $P \rightarrow Q$ constitutes Modus Ponens.

Every interpretation of the propositional variables P_1, P_2, ... P_n of a theory in which all the axioms take on a truth value is known as the *model of a theory*. A theory is called *consistent* if it has at least one model. A theory is known a inconsistent if it does not have a model, or, put differently, if for every formula *F* it is true that: $Th \models F$ and $Th \models \neg F$.

Tautology

A propositional logic formula is called a tautology or logically valid if all possible interpretations are models of the formula, i.e., the formula is true under all interpretations. The notation of a tautology is:

$$1 \| \models F$$

Examples:
a. The formula F=Henry is a man $\vee$ $\neg$(Henry is a man) is a tautology since all possible interpretations α={W} and β={f} make the formula true.

b. The formula $F=(A \vee B, \neg A) \models B$ is a tautology for all possible interpretations of B.

Some tautologies:
a. $\models A \wedge (A \rightarrow B) \rightarrow B$
b. $\models \neg B \wedge (A \rightarrow B) \rightarrow \neg A$
c. $\models (A \rightarrow B) \rightarrow ((A \vee C) \rightarrow (B \vee C))$

Proof of tautologies:
There are three different procedures to determine whether or not a formula is a tautology.
1. Truth tables
2. Boolean algebra
3. Normal forms

The three different procedures will be explained by means of an example:

$$\models ((P \rightarrow Q) \wedge P) \rightarrow Q$$

As can be seen from the truth table, if the formula is true under all interpretations then we are dealing with a tautology.

1. Truth table

P	Q	$P \rightarrow Q$	$(P \rightarrow Q) \wedge P$	$((P \rightarrow Q) \wedge P \rightarrow Q$
f	f	t	f	t
f	t	t	f	t
t	f	f	f	t
t	t	t	t	t

2. Use of boolean algebra

$(P \wedge (P \rightarrow Q)) \rightarrow Q$
$\neg(P \wedge (\neg P \vee Q)) \vee Q$
$(\neg P \vee (P \wedge \neg Q)) \vee Q$
$((\neg P \vee P) \wedge (\neg P \vee \neg Q)) \vee Q$
$(\text{true} \wedge (\neg P \vee Q)) \vee Q$
$\neg P \vee \neg Q \vee Q$
$\neg P \vee \text{true}$
true

3. Normal form

A propositional formula in CNF is a tautology only if in every conjunct at least one propositional variable appears negated once and one further time unnegated.

$((\neg P \vee Q) \wedge P) \leftarrow Q$
$\neg((\neg P \vee Q) \wedge P \vee Q)$
$\neg(\neg P \vee Q \vee \neg P \vee Q)$
$(\neg\neg P \wedge \neg Q) \vee \neg P \vee Q$
$(P \wedge \neg Q) \vee \neg P \vee Q$
$((P \wedge \neg Q) \vee \neg P) \vee Q$
$((\neg P \vee P) \wedge (\neg P \vee \neg Q) \vee Q)$
$(Q \vee \neg P \vee P) \wedge (Q \vee \neg P \vee \neg Q)$

Since a propositional variable appears in each conjunct, negated in one case and not negated in the other, the formula is a tautology.

Equivalence

A further important expression is propositional equivalence. Two propositions P and Q are exactly equivalent if the formula $P \leftrightarrow Q$ is a tautology, i.e., $\models P \leftrightarrow Q$. That is: in order to prove that the two propositions P and Q are equivalent, it has to be shown that the combined formula $P \leftrightarrow Q$ is a tautology.

Some equivalences:
a. $\models (A \rightarrow B) \leftrightarrow (\neg B \rightarrow \neg A)$
b. $\models (A \vee B) \leftrightarrow (B \vee A)$
c. $\models A \wedge (A \vee B) \leftrightarrow A$

Substitutions

If two propositions $(P \leftrightarrow Q)$ are equivalent then the proposition P in the formula can be replaced by Q without changing the truth value. For example:

$P \leftrightarrow Q$ is true.

From $(P \wedge R) \vee S$ it is possible to deduce $(Q \wedge R) \vee S$.

This almost amounts to a new rule of inference, since it is possible to derive valid new propositions by means of equivalence.

9.3 Logical Axioms of Propositional Logic

The axioms of propositional logic are the foundations which are held to be completely true and require no further proof. They are non-derived propositions from which all others are deduced. The derivation proceeds with the help of logical inference rules.

As_1: $[\neg P \rightarrow P] \rightarrow P$
As_2 $P \rightarrow [\neg P \rightarrow Q]$
As_3: $[P \rightarrow Q] \rightarrow [[Q \rightarrow R] \rightarrow [P \rightarrow R]]$

Equivalence Rules

Identity	$P \rightarrow P$
Idempotence	$P \vee P \equiv P$
	$P \wedge P \equiv P$
Commutativity	$P \vee Q \equiv Q \vee P$
	$P \wedge Q \equiv Q \wedge P$
	$P \leftrightarrow Q \equiv Q \leftrightarrow P$
Associativity	$[P \vee Q] \vee R \equiv P \vee [Q \vee R]$
	$[P \wedge Q] \wedge R \equiv P \wedge [Q \wedge R]$
Absorption	$P \vee [P \wedge Q] \equiv P$
	$P \wedge [P \vee Q] \equiv P$
Distribution	$P \wedge [Q \vee R] \equiv [P \wedge Q] \vee [P \wedge R]$
	$P \vee [Q \wedge R] \equiv [P \vee Q] \wedge [P \vee R]$
Double negation	$\neg\neg P \equiv P$
De Morgan	$\neg[P \vee Q] \equiv \neg P \wedge \neg Q$
	$\neg[P \wedge Q] \equiv \neg P \vee \neg Q$
Tautology	$P \vee Q \equiv P$ if P is a tautology
	$P \wedge Q \equiv Q$ if P is a tautology
Unsatisfiability	$P \vee Q \equiv Q$ if P is unsatisfiable
	$P \wedge Q \equiv P$ if P is unsatisfiable
Conditional elimination	$P \rightarrow Q \equiv \neg P \vee Q$

9.4 Inference Rules in Propositional Logic

Inference rules are derivation rules which are used to derive a new proposition from a set of propositions.

The set of true propositions is called a "premise" and the deduced proposition a "conclusion".

If the premise is true and consistent then it is not possible to simultaneously derive a proposition and its negation.

The following are the most important inference rules:

Modus Ponens (separation rule)

P	if P is true
$P \rightarrow Q$	Q follows from P
Q	then Q is true

Modus Tollens (refutation rule)

$$\frac{P \to Q \quad \neg Q}{\neg P}$$

Modus Barbara (chaining rule)

$$\frac{P \to Q \quad Q \to R}{P \to R}$$

Resolution

A generalisation of Modus Ponens which is simpler for computers.

$$\frac{A \quad \neg A \vee B}{B}$$ resolvent

$$\frac{\neg P \vee A_1 \vee A_2 \vee \ldots \vee A_n \quad P \vee B_1 \vee B_2 \vee \ldots \vee B_n}{A_1 \vee A_2 \vee \ldots \vee A_n \vee B_1 \vee B_2 . \vee \ldots \vee B_m}$$

Metasymbol

|= means the semantic deduction (it is in general true that).

Th |= F indicates that the formula F in the Theory is true with the help of the truth table (semantic proof).

|- means the syntactic deduction (it is true that).

Th |- F indicates that the formula F was derived from the theory by means of an inference rule (syntactic proof).

With the help of these expressions we can set the following criteria for inference rules.

Soundness

An inference rule is sound if and only every theorem, which can be derived from a set of axioms by the inference rule, is a logical consequence of the axioms. If the axioms are valid and the inference rule sound then the logical proof is sound.

From T |- A_F follows T |= F,

i.e., all axioms from the theorems to be proved are also logical consequences of the axioms.

Completeness

We say that the inference rule is complete if and only if every theorem, which is a logical consequence of a set of axioms, can be derived from the axioms with the help of the inference rules. The converse of the proposition that logical proofs are complete, i.e., that every logical consequence can be proven:

From Th |= follows Th |-

was first proved for an axiom system in 1930 by Gödel.

In summary, if a proof method is sound and complete then the following must hold:

T |= F iff T |- F

Exercises on the Topic

1. Transform the following formula into CNF:
   $[P\rightarrow Q]\rightarrow[\neg R\rightarrow[S\wedge T]]$
   $[\neg P\rightarrow R]\vee[P\wedge\neg Q\leftrightarrow R]$

2. Given the formula
   F: $P\rightarrow[Q\wedge[[P\vee Q]\rightarrow[R\Leftrightarrow P]]]$
   and the interpretation $\alpha=\{P:=\mathrm{w},Q:=\mathrm{f},R:=\mathrm{w}\}$ is the formula true?

3. Find an interpretation for the formula $\neg(A\Leftrightarrow(B\vee\neg C))$ which makes the formula true and an interpretation which makes the formula false.

4. Prove the following deductive rule with the help of Boolean algebra:
   $\neg(A\rightarrow B)\wedge\neg(C\rightarrow\neg B)\rightarrow(A\rightarrow\neg C)$

5. Given these theories
   Pa1: $P\vee Q$
   Pa2: $P\rightarrow Q$
   Pa3: $\neg P$
   Prove that Q is a logical consequence of the theory.

Topic 10
Proof Procedures in Propositional Logic

There are two ways in which the truth of a proposition can be proved: the direct method of "experimentation" by which one seeks to verify if the content of the proposition exists in reality and the indirect method by which one derives the proposition to be proved from logical derivations of propositions previously known or taken to be true.

- G. Asser, 1974 -

This topic gives an overview of various proof procedures of propositional logic. The following procedures have been selected from a broad spectrum:

1. syntactic methods
2. semantic methods
3. proof by contradiction
4. resolution

10.1 Syntactic Methods

Syntactic methods examine logical sentences with respect to their derivability from other sentences by means of inference rules or transformations.

Given the theory Th with the formulae:
Pa1: $P \vee Q$
Pa2: $P \rightarrow \neg Q$
Pa3: $\neg P$

Prove that Q is a theorem of the theory if Q can by derived from the formulae.

Procedure:

1. Transform Pa1 by the following criteria:
   $P \vee Q \equiv \neg P \rightarrow Q$
   From which we get
   Pa1': $\neg P \rightarrow Q$
2. Use the Modus Ponens inference rule with the formula Pa3 and Pa1' so that we obtain:
   Pa3: $\neg P$
   Pa1': $\neg P \rightarrow Q$
   ———————
   Q

Therefore the logical conclusion is that Q is a theorem of the theory Th.

10.2 Semantic Methods

In semantic methods the procedure makes use of truth tables. A truth value is entered into the table for every formula. This means that if an interpretation of a formula is true then this interpretation is a model of the formula and, therefore, the formula is a theorem of the theory.

a) Given the theory Th
$\neg P$
$P \vee Q$
Prove that Q is a theorem of the theory Th.

Procedure:
We draw up a truth table and search for a model.

P	Q	$P \vee Q$	$\neg P$	Q
t	t	t	f	t
t	f	t	f	f
f	t	t	t	t
f	f	f	t	f

In line 3 we see that all interpretations of the theory are true and have this found a model of the theory. We conclude from this that Q is a logical consequence of the theory.

b) Given the following theory:
$\neg P$
$P \wedge Q$
Search for a model.

P	Q	$P \wedge Q$	$\neg P$	Model?
t	t	t	f	no
t	f	f	f	no
f	t	f	t	no
f	f	f	t	no

We see that we have not found a model and that the theory is not satisfiable.

10.3 Proof by Contradiction

In proof by contradiction, or indirect proof, the negation of the assertion is added to the preconditions. Instead of always proving B from A ($A \vdash B$) we now attempt to prove a contradiction (indirect proof) from A and $\neg B$ ("hypothesis") ("if the hypothesis is to be overturned then we have then proved B from A").

An explanation by implicature:

$Th \cup \neg F$ |= [] iff Th |= ($false \leftarrow \neg F$)
that is:
$Th \cup \neg F$ |= iff Th |= F
With the assumption that the inference system is complete and sound:
$Th \cup \neg f$ |- iff Th |- F

Example: given the theory:
$Th=\{P \vee Q, P \rightarrow \neg Q, Q\}$
prove that $\neg P$ is a theorem of the theory, i.e., Th |- P.

Procedure:

1. We add the negation of the assertion to our theory.
   $Th'=\{P \vee Q, P \rightarrow \neg Q, Q, P\}$
2. Use the inference rule Modus Ponens:
   $P \rightarrow \neg Q$
   P
   ___
   $\neg Q$
3. We add the recent true conclusion to Th' and get:
   $Th''=\{P \vee Q, P \rightarrow \neg Q), Q, P, \neg Q\}$
   By Q and $\neg Q$ we achieve contradiction.

Disadvantages of Modus Ponens:

- it does not aim at the answer
- it derives what can be derived

This leads to the existence of irrelevant atoms.

Modus Tollens

Modus tollens shows that if $\neg A$ is given and B follows from A then the conclusion $\neg B$ is correct.

$\neg A$	Cars do not stop.
$B \rightarrow A$	If a serious accident occurs then cars stop.
$\neg B$	No serious accident has occurred.

Another way of writing modus tollens: $\{\neg A, (B \rightarrow A)\}$ |- $\neg B$
If B is true, from $(B \rightarrow A) \leftrightarrow (w \rightarrow A)$ follows: $\{A, A\}$ |- []
For example: given the theory Th:$\{Q, P \rightarrow Q, \neg P\}$, prove that P is a theorem of the theory. Th |- P

1. We add the negation of the assertion to the theory and get: $Th'=\{Q, Q \rightarrow P, \neg P, \neg P\}$
2. We use the modus tollens inference rule: $\{\neg P, Q \rightarrow P\}$ |- $\neg Q$
   We add the conclusion $\neg Q$ to the theory Th and get contradiction:
   $\{Q, \neg Q\}$ |- []

10.4 Resolution

Ground resolution is a restricted form of Robinson's method, with whose help a finite set of ground clauses can be tested for their unsatisfiability:

Definition: If *C*1 and *C*2 are ground clauses. A ground clause *C* is a (ground-) resolvent of *C*1 and *C*2 if there is an atom of the form:

1. *C*1 contains ¬*Q*;
2. *C*2 contains *Q* and
3. *C* is the disjunction of literals of *C*1, without *Q*, and the literal of *C*2, without *Q*. If C1=¬Q and *C*2=*Q* then the empty clause is a (ground) resolvent of *C*1 and *C*2.

*C*1*:* {*P*,¬*Q*}
*C*2*:* {*Q*,*S*}
C: {*P*,*S*}

The resolution inference rule generally implies that the resolvent is a logical consequence of *C*1 and *C*2,

In general:
C={*C*1-{*Q*}} ∪ {*C*2-{¬*Q*}}

Proof:

P	*Q*	*S*	*C*1:{*P*,¬*Q*}	*C*2:{*Q*,*S*}	*C*:{*P*,*S*}	Model
t	f	t	t	t	t	yes
t	f	f	t	f	t	
t	t	t	t	t	t	yes
t	t	f	t	t	t	yes
f	f	t	t	t	t	yes
f	f	f	t	f	f	
f	t	t	f	t	t	
f	t	f	f	t	f	

As we have found models, we can conclude that {*P*,*S*} is a theorem of the theory.

Examples for Resolution

*C*1	*C*2	*C*:Resolvent
{*P*,*Q*,*R*}	{*S*,*T*,¬*P*}	{*Q*,*R*,*S*,*T*}
{*P*,*Q*}	{¬*Q*,*S*}	{*P*,*S*}
{*T*}	{¬*T*}	[]
{*P*,*Q*,*R*,*S*}	{*P*,*Q*,¬*R*,*S*}	{*P*,*Q*,*S}*

Theorem Proof by Resolution

Given the theory:
Pa1*:* *P*∨ *Q*

Pa2: $P \rightarrow \neg Q$
Pa3: $\neg P$

Prove that Q is a logical consequence of the theory.

1. Add $\neg Q$ to the theory and transform into clausal form:
   $S=\{\{P,Q\},\{\neg P,\neg Q\},\{\neg P\},\{\neg Q\}\}$
2. $\{P\}$ is a resolvent of $\{P,Q\}$ and $\{\neg Q\}$.
   Add it to S so that we get:
   $S'=\{\{P,Q\},\{\neg P,\neg Q\},\{\neg P\},\{\neg Q\},\{P\}\}$
3. The resolvent of $\{\neg P\}$ and $\{P\}$ is an empty clause.
   Add the empty clause to S:
   $S''=S' \cup []$
4. S'' now contains the empty clause;
   S'' is unsatisfiable and must therefore be a theorem of the theory.

Exercises for the Topic

1. For the log function
   log(ab)=log a + log b
   is true. Prove, using Modus Ponens, that log 1 = 0.

2. The following theory is given:
   Pa1: it rains ∨ it snows ∨ it is dry
   Pa2: it is warm
   Pa3: it is not raining
   Pa4: it is not snowing
   Pa5: it is nice → it is good for walking
   Pa6: [it is dry ∧ it is warm] → it is nice
   Prove that "it is dry" is a logical consequence of the theory.

3. Show whether or not the following theory is consistent with the help of Modus Ponens.
   $B \rightarrow \neg A$
   $C \rightarrow B$
   $C \rightarrow A$
   $D \rightarrow C$
   D

4. Prove the associativity law with the help of truth tables.
   $P \vee (Q \wedge R) \equiv (P \vee Q) \wedge (P \vee R)$

5. Given the following theory Th:
   Pa1: $\neg P \rightarrow Q$
   Pa2: P
   Prove whether or not $\neg Q$ is a theorem of the theory with the help of truth tables.

6. Given the theory Th:
   Pa1: $P \rightarrow \neg Q$
   Pa2: $\neg R \rightarrow P$
   Pa3: Q
   Prove if R is a theorem of the theory Th with the help of truth tables.

7. With the condition *log(a/b)=log a-log b* the fact that *log 1=0* should be proved. Use the modus tollens proof procedure.

8. The following theories are given:
   Pa1: $P \rightarrow Q$
   Pa2: $\neg Q$
   Prove whether or not $\neg P$ is a theorem of the theory.

9. Show that the resolvent of any two Horn clauses is always a Horn clause.

10. Carry out resolution on the following two clauses:
    a. male(*X*):- father(*X*).
    b. father(*X*):- parents(*X*), not mother(*X*).

11. Carry out theorem proving by means of resolution on the following theory:
    Pa1: $P \leftrightarrow Q$
    Pa2: Q
    Prove that P is a logical consequence of the theory.

12. Negate the following propositional logic clauses and use the resolution principle to show that the resultant set of clauses is not satisfiable.
    a. $(P \vee Q) \rightarrow (Q \vee P)$
    b. $(P \rightarrow Q) \rightarrow ((R \vee P) \rightarrow (R \vee Q))$
    c. $(\neg P \rightarrow P) \rightarrow P$
    d. $(\neg Q \rightarrow \neg P) \rightarrow ((\neg Q \rightarrow P) \rightarrow Q)$
    e. $((P \rightarrow Q) \rightarrow P) \rightarrow Q$

The winner is always he who can love,
tolerate and forgive, not he who knows
better and judges.
- Hermann Hesse -

5 PREDICATE LOGIC

In propositional logic it is possible to establish whether or not a proposition is true or false. When a true or false value is found for a proposition then there is no further possible use for propositional logic. Predicate logic is therefore an extension of propositional logic which means that all laws which are valid in propositional logic are also valid in predicate logic.

In predicate logic, a distinction is made in the representation between the objects (individuals) and the characteristics (predicates) which are expressed about them. This means that predicates do not just embody the characteristics of individuals but can also indicate the relationships between several individuals.

Let us look at the following fragment of the real world:

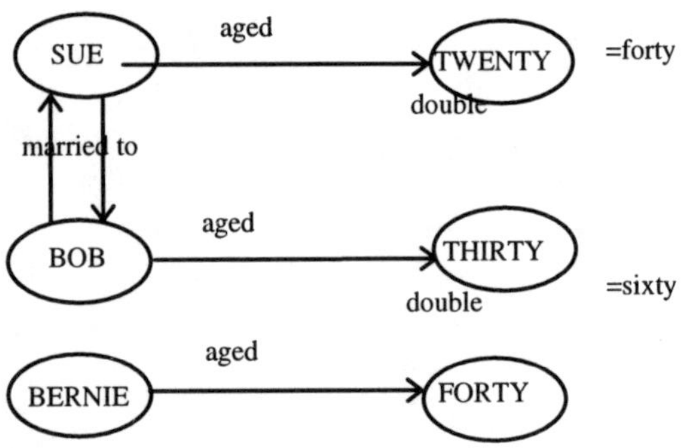

In this "relational structure" objects are identified by constants.
{Susie, Bob, Bernie ... }

The relations are defined with predicate symbols:
married_to(Susie,Bob);

and the construction of an object by means of others we shall call function symbols:
double_of(Twenty,Forty).

Predicate logic also establishes symbolic expressions for the general validity of propositions. These expressions are known as variables: they can be placed at positions at which constants would otherwise stand. A further form of the general validity of propositions are universal quantifiers. These express that the proposition is true for any symbol. The opposite of the universal quantifier is the so-called existential quantifier, which expresses the notion "there is ...".

The following example is intended to indicate the power of predicate logic:

The following characteristics are fundamental to the natural numbers:
1. For every number there is one and only one successor.
2. There is no number which is immediately followed by one.
3. For every number other than 1 there is one - and only one - immediate predecessor.

The domain of individuals over which the quantifiers range is that of the natural numbers: x, y, z are variables. In addition two binary predicates are required: follows(x,y) and equal(x,y). The first predicate means "y immediately follows x", the second predicate "x is equal to y". The sentences then have the following predicate logic form.

1. $\forall x \exists y(\text{follows}(x,y) \wedge \forall z(\text{follows}(x,z) \rightarrow \text{equal}(y,z)))$
2. $\neg(\exists x\ \text{follows}(x,1))$
3. $\forall x(\neg\text{equal}(x,1) \rightarrow \exists y(\text{follows}(y,x) \wedge (\forall z(\text{follows}(z,x))) \rightarrow \text{equal}(y,z))))$

Predicate logic consists of two hierarchical forms:
- First Order Predicate Logic: in this quantification is over constants and variables. For example: "All people are mortal."
- Higher order predicate logic: in this the predicate variables are quantified. For example: "Two people are exactly identical if they have the same features."

Topic 11

Axiom System of Predicate Logic

In predicate logic, too, the axiom system consists of:

- language (syntax, semantics)
- logical axioms
- inference rules.

In this section the axioms of predicate logic are given.

11.1 Syntax of Predicate Logic

In addition to the syntax of propositional logic the following symbols are defined:

Alphabet

The alphabet of predicate logic is the set of its symbols. These symbols are:

- the set of constants: *a, b, c*
- the set of variables: *x, y, z*
- the set of predicates: *P, Q, R*
- the set of function symbols: *f, g, h*
- additional symbols: $\vee, \wedge, \rightarrow, \neg, \leftrightarrow, \forall, \exists$

Term

- Terms are constants, variables or function symbols *a,x,f(b,y,z),f(g(x),y,z)*
- For every function symbol *f* and for *n* terms $t_1, t_2, \dots t_n$ the following is also a term: $f(t_1, t_2, \dots t_n)$.

Ground Term

A ground term is a term with a specified variable.
f(g(a),b,c)

Arity

Arity indicates the number of terms.

$f(a,b)$	function of binary arity
$P(f(a,b),x,y)$	predicate of arity three
f^0	constant
add(x,y)	add x to y (function)
smaller(x,y)	test if $x < y$ (predicate)

Atom

An atom is an expression which can not be logically subdivided. Atoms are sequences of characters. They indicate predicates and operators. They begin with a small letter and can consist of letters, number and special characters.

married(Susie,Bob)	Susie is married to Bob
aged(Bob,double(20))	Bob is aged two times twenty

Literal
A literal is an atom or negated atom. Non-negated propositions are called positive literals and negative propositions are negative literals.

loves(max, margaret)	Max loves Margaret.
¬loves(max,mary)	Max does not love Mary.

Well-Formed Formulae
A formula is the symbolic representation of a spoken utterance. It is a syntactic construct and serves to express facts and relations by means of language. A formula is produced when the objects, relations and functions of an utterance are replaced by the corresponding predicates, constants, variables, symbols etc. A predicate can be seen to be a formula. Formula are linked propositions, e.g., if F and G are formulae then the following are also formulae:
$\neg F, F \wedge G, F \vee G, F \leftarrow G, \exists x F, \forall x F$

Quantifiers
The two quantifiers are:

- The existential quantifier (particular quantifier) $\exists x$F — Means that that a constant a exists for which F is true.
  $\exists x$ aged$(x,40)$ — "There exists an x aged 40."
- The universal quantifier (generalising quantifier) $\forall x$F — Means that for all constants F is true.
  $\forall x(\text{nat}(X) \rightarrow x > \text{predec}(x))$ — For all x if x is a natural number then it is true that x is greater than the predecessor of x

Variables which are bound to quantifiers are known as bound (quantified) variables. Unbound variables are known as free variables.

$\forall x \forall y[\text{married}(x,y) \rightarrow \text{married}(y,x)]$

The existential quantifier can be represented as a negation of the universal quantifier.
$\exists x\text{A} \equiv \neg \forall x \neg \text{A}$

Clauses
A clause is a formula of the form:

$\forall x_1, \forall x_2, \ldots, \forall x_n(L_1 \vee L_2, \ldots, L_n)$

Further types of clause are:

- non-Horn-clauses: $P_1, \wedge P_2, \ldots P_n \rightarrow Q_1 \vee Q_2, \ldots, Q_m$
- Horn clauses: $P_1, \wedge P_2, \ldots, P_n \rightarrow Q$
- query clauses: $P_1, \wedge P_2, \ldots, P_n \rightarrow$
- fact: $\rightarrow P$
- empty clause: $\rightarrow$

Program

A program consists of a finite set of clauses.

11.2 Semantics of Predicate Logic

The semantics of predicate logic states that: the meaning of logical formulae, produced by means of syntactic rules, is only valid in the abstract world which we have created. The truth values are, therefore, only defined there. They can only apply in their domains (be true) or not (be false).

In order to define the meaning of logical formulae a relationship between the formal language and the environment must be created. The propositions involved refer to individuals and include relations and functions.

Interpretation of a Formula

In interpretation the relationship between the alphabet of the language and its environment is created. For this every constant must be contained in the alphabet and an element (object) of the environment (domain) must be assigned to it. A relationship is assigned to every predicate symbol which is described in the domain. Furthermore, every function symbol must be assigned to a function which is defined in the domain.

Formally: an interpretation I in a language L is a non-empty set of objects D, which is known as the domain of the interpretation and an association.

- To every constant exactly one element of the domain is assigned. $c \in L$ with $c \in D$.
- To every n-place predicate symbol a relation is assigned which map the respective n-values of the domain into a single value, namely "true" or "false".
  $p \in L$ with $p \subseteq D^n$ $(=D \times \ldots \times D)$
- To every *n*-place function symbol a function is assigned which map from the respective *n*-values of the domain into a single value, namely "true" or "false".
  $f \in L$ with $f: D^n \rightarrow D$

The following example clarifies the meaning of the domain in the interpretation of a formula:

$$F=\forall x\, p(f(x,a),x)$$

- the natural numbers are declared to be in the domain, D={1,2,3, ...}

- we assign the number 1 to the constants *a*
- function *f* is defined as multiplication
- as for predicate symbols we determine that *p* stands for "=".

This means that for the formula: $F = x \times 1 = x$
The interpretation is now:

For all natural numbers *x* it is true that: $x \times 1 = x$

In this way, the formula is given a concrete meaning by means of an interpretation.

This formula applies to the domain of natural numbers. In another environment, e.g., the inheritance of physical characteristics by a son from his father, it is not necessarily true since a son is not necessarily taller than his father.

In order to extend the formula and then to draw the correct conclusions, the new terms must be made aware of the domain at the outset. We add a unary predicate symbol to the domain and declare:

q=is_primenumber

We also add a function *g* which is defined as addition:

$g=y+z$

We give the variables *y* and *z* the values: $y=2$; $z=3$.

These formulae are now joined by the connective ($\wedge$) to produce the new formula:

$F=\forall x\, p(f(x,a),x) \wedge q(g(y,z))$.

This formula also applies in the domain of natural numbers, since the multiplication of all natural numbers by 1 is a natural number and the addition of 2 and 3 results in a prime number.

Variable Instantiation

If a formula exists in which there are variables to be interpreted then all variables in the formula must be assigned an element of the universe.

$\{x_1/e_1, x_2/e_2, .. x_n/e_n\}$

In this *x* is the variable and *e* the assigned element.

The formula $x+y$ evaluates to 2 given the interpretation $\{x/1, y/1\}$; with the interpretation $\{x/3, y/5\}$ it evaluates to 8.

Model

If a formula in an interpretation is true then this interpretation is the model of this formula. A model exists if there is an interpretation of a formula such that the truth value of this formula is true. A formula can have several models.

For example: for the formula *p(f(x,a),x)* with the interpretation:

- the domain is the set of natural numbers
- *f* stands for addition
- *p* stands for ">" "greater than .."
- the formula *p(f(x,a),x)* stands for $x+a > x$.

No model exists for this formula: $x+0 > x$ is a false proposition.

Satisfiable

A formula is known as satisfiable if a model exists for this formula. For example: is the formula *p(f(x,a),x)* satisfiable?

If

1. the number 1 is assigned to the constant *a*,
2. *f* stands for multiplication,
3. *p* stands for "=",
4. the value 7 is assigned to varible *x*, i.e., $\{x/7\}$.

then the formula *p(f(x,a),x)* is produced for $7 \times 1 = 7$. This formula is satisfiable.

Generally Valid

A formula is generally valid if it is true for all interpretations. Generally valid formulae are known as tautologies. For example: is the formula *p(f(x,a),x)* generally valid?

If

1. the domain is the set of natural numbers,
2. the number 1 is assigned to the constants *a*,
3. *f* stands for the set of multiplications,
4. *p* stands for "=",

then the formula *p(f(x,a),x)* is produced for $x \times 1 = x$, that is for the proposition:

For all natural numbers *x* the following is true: $x \times 1 = x$

This proposition is true and it follows from this that this formula is generally valid.

Logical Consequence

S is a set of formulae and *F* a formula. If, for every interpretation and instantiation, the models of *S* are also models of *F* then we say that *F* is a logical consequence of the set of formulae *S*, i.e.:

$$S \models F$$

S is called a set of premises or set of assumptions and *F* the conclusion of the consequence. The formula *F* follows logically from the set of formulae and means that it is produced by dint of the all the premises being fulfilled, independently of assignment and interpretation , i.e., all the formulae of *F* result from the satisfaction of *F*.

The logical consequence symbol $\models$ and the connective $\rightarrow$ are often confused. The difference lies in the fact that the $\rightarrow$ connective is set between the formulae of the object language to produce a formula of the object language; the insertion of the logical consequence symbol $\models$ results in a proposition of the meta-language. If the formula $F \rightarrow G$ is satisfied for an interpretation and instantiation then it does not mean that *G* logically follows from *F* $(F \models G)$. This is only the case if the formula $F \rightarrow G$ is generally valid.

Below is a list of some elementary rules for logical consequences in which *F* and *G* are formula and *x* variables.

F	$\models F \vee G$	
F	$\models G \rightarrow F$	
$F \wedge G$	$\models F$	
$F \wedge G$	$\models G \rightarrow F$	
$F \wedge G$	$\models F \leftrightarrow G$	
$(F \rightarrow G) \wedge (G \rightarrow H)$	$\models F \rightarrow H$	Transitivity w.r.t. the implication
$G \wedge (G \rightarrow F)$	$\models F$	Modus ponens
$\neg F \wedge (G \rightarrow F)$	$\models \neg G$	Modus tollens
$\forall x F$	$\models \exists x F$	For a non-empty domain
$\forall x F \vee \forall x G$	$\models \forall x (F \vee G)$	
$\exists x (F \wedge G)$	$\models \exists x F \wedge \exists x F$	

Fig. 5.1: Rules for Logical Consequence

These rules can be includes as inference rules in an axiom system (cf. Modus Ponens, Modus tollens).

For example: given

1. $\forall x(\forall y((\text{mother}(x) \wedge \text{child\_of}(y,x)) \rightarrow \text{loves}(x,y)))$
2. mother(suzanne)$\wedge$child_of(andrea,suzanne)
3. loves(suzanne,andrea)

We shall show that 3 is a logical consequence of 1 and 2. Given an interpretation which is a model for 1 and 2 then it is true that;

a. $\models \forall x(\forall y((\text{mother}(x) \wedge \text{child\_of}(y,x)) \rightarrow \text{loves}(x,y)))$

b. $\models$ mother(suzanne) $\wedge$ child_of(andrea,suzanne)

In order for "a" to be true it is necessary to instantiate variables. The constants "suzanne" and "andrea" are used for this and the following situation arises:

c. $\models$ (mother(suzanne) $\wedge$ child_of(andrea,suzanne) $\rightarrow$ loves(suzanne,andrea)

This proves that 3 is a logical consequence of 1 and 2, since "loves(suzanne,andrea)" is true for the interpretation and is therefore a model.

Truth Value of Formulae

When is a formula true?

In order to determine the truth validity of formulae, an interpretation and an instantiation of variables is required for these formulae.

- The formula $P(T_1,T_2,...,T_n)$ is true if and only if the predicate assigned by the interpretation of *P* is true.
- If *F* and *G* are formulae then the truth value of the formulae $\neg F$, $F \& G$, $F \rightarrow G$ can be obtained from the truth table.
- If *F* is a formula then $\exists xF$ is true if a constant exists which makes *F* true.
- If *F* is a formula then $\forall xF$ is true for all values of *x*.

Given the theory *Th*:

1. $\forall x(r(x) \rightarrow p(x) \vee q(x))$
2. $r(a) \wedge r(b)$

and the interpretations:

α={ *a*:= Adam, *b*:= Eve
p "is a woman"
q "is a man"
r "is a person"}

Is *p*(*a*) a logical consequence of *Th*?

Formula 1 means:
For all *x* if *x* is a person then *x* is either a man or a woman.

If the value "Adam" substitutes for *x* then the formula in α is true since "Adam" is a person and a man. If "Eve" is substituted then the formula is true since Eve is a person and a woman.

This formula is satisfiable as a model exists for every case which makes the formula true.

This formula is generally valid since it is true for all possible interpretations.

Formula 2 means: *a* is a person and *b* is a person.

If the constants *a* and *b* are replaced by their interpretations Adam and Eve then the formula means: Adam is a person and Eve is a person.

This proposition is true.

Eve is substituted for constant *b*; *q(Eve)* is not a logical consequence of the theory as Eve is not a man.

11.3 The Logical Axioms

As mentioned already, the axioms of predicate logic are unprovable formulae. the basic formulae of the domain are established as required according to the chosen domain which the axiom system should describe.

Logical Equivalence

The "≡" symbol is used for logically equivalent. After the definition $F \equiv G$ is written to indicate that the formulae F and G are logically equivalent.

Logical equivalence is used in order to derive certain formulae. Here are some important rules which can be used, if needed. F, G, H are formulae; x,y are variables.

$F \equiv F \wedge F$	Idempotence wrt. the conjunction
$F \equiv F \vee F$	Idempotence wrt. the disjunction
$\neg\neg F \equiv F$	Double negation
$F \rightarrow G = \neg F \vee G$	
$F \rightarrow G \equiv \neg G \rightarrow \neg F$	Contraposition law
$F \leftrightarrow G \equiv (F \rightarrow G) \wedge (G \rightarrow F)$	
$\neg(F \vee G) = (F \rightarrow G) \wedge (G \rightarrow F)$	
$\neg(F \vee G) \equiv \neg F \wedge \neg G$	De Morgan's law
$\neg(F \wedge G) \equiv \neg F \vee \neg G$	De Morgan's law
$\neg \forall x F \equiv \exists x \neg F$	
$\neg \exists x F \equiv \forall x \neg F$	
$\forall x \forall y F \equiv \forall y \forall x F$	
$\exists x \exists y F \equiv \exists y \exists x F$	
$\forall x (F \wedge G) \equiv \forall x F \wedge \forall x G$	Distributivity of ∀
$\exists x (F \wedge G) \equiv \exists x F \wedge \exists x G$	Distributivity of ∃

For the following laws the variable x is free for formula F but bound for formula G.

$\forall x F \equiv F$

$\exists x F \equiv F$

$\forall x (F \wedge G) \equiv F \wedge \forall x G$

$\forall x (F \vee G) \equiv F \vee \forall x G$

$\exists x (F \wedge G) \equiv F \wedge \exists x G$

$\exists x (F \vee G) \equiv F \vee \exists x G$

11.4 Inference Rules

In the area of predicate logic various valid inference rules can be made available to an axiom system. We shall only look at some well-known rules. It is not absolutely necessary for all the rules mentioned here to be established in an axiom system. Only those rules which are absolutely necessary for the derivation of new formulae should be selected. This means that it is possible for there to be only one rule defined in an axiom system. It is important to point out that the rules used should be sound. Only then can the derivability of new formulae be guaranteed. The soundness of the inference rules can be directly proven from the definition of the semantics of the predicate logic language.

Modus Ponens

Modus Ponens, also known as the implication elimination rule, means that for every formula of the form F and $(F \rightarrow G)$ the formula G follows. F and $(F \rightarrow G)$ constitute the premises, G the conclusion. The rule is written as below:

$$\frac{F \qquad F \rightarrow G}{G}$$

Modus Tollens

Modus Tollens can almost be seen to be the opposite of Modus Ponens. The formula $\neg G$ follows from the premises $\neg F$ and $(G \rightarrow F)$. Here is the formulation:

$$\frac{\neg F \qquad G \rightarrow F}{\neg G}$$

Replacement Rule

If, in formula F, the part formula F' is replaced by the formula G' then the resulting formula G is a formula and from $F' \leftrightarrow G'$ then $F \leftrightarrow G$ logically follows.

This rule can be understood as: F consists of F' and F''. F' is replaced by G' which produces a formula G is produced consisting of G' and F''. The equivalence of F and G is a logical consequence of that of F' and G'.

$$\frac{F' \leftrightarrow G'}{F \leftrightarrow G}$$

Conclusion: if F, F', G, G' are formulae then according to this rule F' and G' are logically equivalent just as are F and G. The rules of logical equivalence are also used in this inference.

Universal Quantifier Introduction Rules

The universal quantifier can be introduced if a formula F follows from a set of formulae and the variable x is not free in this set of formulae. The introduction rule can be represented as below:

$$\frac{F(x)}{\forall x F(x)}$$

Existential Quantifier Introduction Rule

The existential quantifier introduction rule states: if a formula F exists which consists of a term t for which x in $F(x)$ is free then the formula $\exists x F(x)$ is true.

$$\frac{F(t)}{\exists x F(x)} \qquad \text{The term } t \text{ is free for } x \text{ in } F(x).$$

Universal Quantifier Elimination Rule

This rule states that for every formula of the form $\forall xF$, in which x is a free variable in F, a new formula follows $F\{x/t\}$, i.e., the variable x is replaced by a term t which is free for x. The representation is as follows:

$$\frac{\forall xF}{F\{x/t\}} \qquad \text{The term } t \text{ is free for } x \text{ in } F(x)$$

Existential Quantifier Elimination Rule

If a constant c is not contained in the formula $F(x)$ then the variable x which is bound to the existential quantifier is replaced by c. The existential quantifier is thereby removed.

$$\begin{array}{ll} \exists x F(x) & \\ F(c) & \qquad \text{The constant } c \text{ does not appear in } F(x). \end{array}$$

Example:

1. $\forall x(\forall y(\text{mother}(x) \wedge \text{child\_of}(y,x) \rightarrow \text{loves}(x,y)))$
2. mother(martha) $\wedge$ child_of(tom,martha)

Elimination of universal quantifiers in 1:

1a. $\forall y(\text{mother(martha)} \wedge \text{child\_of}(y,\text{martha}) \rightarrow \text{loves}(\text{martha},y))$

Elimination of universal quantifiers in 1a:

1b. mother(martha)$\wedge$child_of(tom,martha)$\rightarrow$loves(martha,tom)

Modus Ponens applied to 2 and 1b:

loves(mary,tom)

11.5 Consistency, Soundness, Completeness of an Axiom System

Certain requirements are placed on an axiom system. Along with requirements for independence and freedom from contradiction, the question of consistency, soundness and completeness is examined.

Definition: an axiom system AS is inconsistent with respect to a set of formula S if it is true that:

$$S \vdash_{As} F \wedge S \vdash_{AS} \neg F$$

Accordingly every axiom system should be **consistent**, i.e., it should be not possible to derive the negation of an already derived formula.

One of the most important requirements of an axiom system is soundness. For a set of formulae *S* and a formula derivable from *F* the following definition applies:

Definition: an axiom system AS is sound if for every set of formulae *S*, every formula which is derivable from *S* is a logical consequence, i.e.,:

$$S \vdash_{AS} F, \text{ then } S \models F.$$

Completeness is a further requirement of an axiom system. The intuitions behind it can be explained as follows:

It is expected of an axiom system that the notion of derivable formulae is covered by that of generally valid formulae. This is expressed in the definition as follows:

Definition: An axiom system AS is complete if for every set of formulae *S* every formula which follows from *S* is derivable, i.e.,

$$S \models F, \text{ then } S \vdash_{AS} F.$$

Example:
Here we give the reader an example of a small axiom system in the area of predicate logic. Firstly, we describe just the axioms and the inference rules.

Variables:	x	
Predicates:	schoolchild	is a school child
	student	is a student
	alevels	has "A" level qualifications
	entrance	has met entrance requirements
	uni	goes to university

Axioms:	
A_1	$\forall x(\text{student}(x) \rightarrow \text{entrance}(x))$
A_2	$\exists x(\text{schoolchild}(x) \wedge \text{alevels}(x))$
A_3	$\exists x(\text{entrance}(x) \rightarrow \text{uni}(x))$
A_4	$\exists x(\text{schoolchild}(x) \wedge \text{alevels}(x) \rightarrow \text{entrance}(x))$

Inference rules:	
I_1	Elimination of universal quantifiers
I_2	Transitivity with respect to implication

11.6 Axiomatic Theories

We must now make sure that we are clear about the meaning of the expression "Theory". A theory consists of a language by means of which sentences can be expressed independently of a domain. Axioms are the basic sentences of a theory. With the set of axioms, new, indeed very complex, sentences can be developed. These sentences, also called theorems, are the logical consequence of the axioms. For a theory, a sound and complete axiom system should be available.

Predicate calculus can, for example, be seen as a concept of the theory. It consists of a formal language and formal rules. In addition, there is a sound and complete axiom system in which the true sentences can be derived by means of a small number of axioms and inference rules. This theory is generally not used. This is because one is generally interested in a particular domain in which only given predicates and function constants are admissible.

Of course work is carried out purely on theories in the area of predicate logic. Certain theories relate back to other more expressive logical systems which need not concern us here. Here we just wish to look at the theory of the first order, i.e., the particular version of predicate logic for a given domain.

In summary we maintain that the goal of a theory is to derive all the true sentences of the domain under consideration on the basis of the axioms.

Theorems are, therefore, valid sentences which are derived from the axiom system. A derivation of a theorem is the ordered list of axioms, inference rules and previous theorems, which produced this theorem.

11.7 Inconsistency, Decidability, Completeness of a Theory

The expressions consistency and inconsistency will now be explained. A theory can either be consistent or inconsistent. Here is the definition of inconsistency.

Definition: a theory T is inconsistent if for some formula F the following holds:

$$T \vdash F \text{ and } T \vdash \neg F.$$

A further important notion is the decidability of a theory. This, essentially, follows from consistency or inconsistency. The following definition introduces the theme of decidability.

Definition: a theory T is decidable if neither a formula F nor its negation can be derived from the theory T.

Definition: a theory is complete if every formula of the language is a theorem or a negation of a theorem.

Remark on the completeness of a theory:
An incomplete theory can become complete by introducing new axioms which are valid in the theory.

If a theory is complete then the corresponding axiom system is complete.

11.8 Relationship between Axiom System and Theory

Having explained all the necessary expressions, we can demonstrate the relationship between an axiom system and a theory.

In the definitions of section 11.5 a set of formulae was mentioned repeatedly. As a theory is nothing more than a set of formulae the expression "set of formulae" can be used interchangeably with "theory". This results in the following definitions:

Definition: an axiom system is **sound** if every formula *F* which is derived from theory *T* is a logical consequence of *T*, i.e.:
$T \vdash_{AS} F$, then $T \models F$.

Definition: An axiom system AS is **complete** if for every theory *T* every formula *F* which logically follow from the theory *T* can be derived, i.e.:
$T \models F$, then $T \vdash_{AS} F$.

The basis of a theory is, therefore, the axiom system. If such a basis exists then a theory is axiomatisable.

The question of decidability of the axiom system can now be explained. If a theory is decidable then this is also true of the axiom system since the axiom system constitutes the basis of a theory.

An axiom is **decidable** if it is possible to determine whether or not a theory *T* in AS is consistent.

An axiom system is **semi-decidable** if it is always possible to determine the inconsistency and sometimes also possible to determine the consistency.

An axiom system is **undecidable** if neither the formula nor its negation can be derived from a theory T.

Remarks:
- Propositional logic is decidable.
- Predicate logic is undecidable.
- Full predicate logic is semi-decidable.

Example: Example 11.5 is repeated in order to complete it.

The theorem "There are students who go to university" shall be derived with the existing axioms and inference rules. Here is the derivation:

Theorem: $\exists x(\text{student}(x) \rightarrow \text{uni}(x))$
1. $\forall x(\text{student}(x) \rightarrow \text{entrance}(x))$ (A1)

2. student(t) $\rightarrow$ entrance(t) 1,(I1)
3. $\exists x$(entrance(x) $\rightarrow$ uni(x)) (A3)
4. $\exists x$(student(x) $\rightarrow$ uni(x) 2,3,(I2)

11.9 Exercises for the Topic

1. Express the following sentences in predicate logic:
   a. Either it is raining or it is not raining.
   b. Every student who studies computing must take an option apart from sport.
   c. Every natural number which is not equal to 0 has another number which succeeds it.
   d. If x is a father or x is a mother then x is a parent of someone.
   e. If x is a parent and feminine then x is the mother of someone.
   f. Everyone who is a parent has a child.

2. Express the following sentences in predicate logic. Use the emboldened word as predicates.
   a. Not everything that **gleams** is **gold**.
   b. **All** is **well** that **ends well**.
   c. The **end justifies** the **means**.
   d. Harry **likes** himself and no one else. (use the predicate =)
   e. For all **natural** numbers there is none which is **smaller** than all the others.

3. Re-write the following formulae in the form $H \leftarrow B_1, B_2, \ldots, B_n$.
   a. $\forall X(p(X) \vee \neg q(X))$
   b. $\forall X(p(X) \vee \neg \exists Y(q(X,Y) \wedge r(X)))$
   c. $\forall X(\neg p(X) \vee (q(X) \rightarrow r(X)))$
   d. $\forall X(r(X) \rightarrow (q(X) \rightarrow p(X)))$

4. Derive the following formula using the list of logical consequences and logical equivalences.
   a. $\forall x(F(x) \rightarrow G) \equiv \exists x f(x) \rightarrow G$
   b. $\exists x(F(x) \rightarrow G(x)) \equiv \forall y F(y) \rightarrow \forall y F(y) \rightarrow \exists x G(x)$
   c. $(F \vee G) \wedge (\neg F \vee H) \models G \vee H$
   d. $F \rightarrow (G \leftrightarrow H) \models (F \wedge G) \rightarrow H$

5. Construct the derivation in an axiom system for the following schema.
   $\forall x(a \wedge b) \rightarrow \forall x(a) \wedge \forall x(b)$

Topic 12
Converting a Formula into Clausal Form

If we wish to formalise a problem and goal using a logic program then the sentences are generally written directly in clausal form. Sometimes it is more natural to write the sentences in first order predicate logic and then to convert them to clausal form.

There are simple algorithms for converting any first order predicate logic sentence into a set of clauses. The transformation follows several systematic steps, in which use is made of the commutativity and associativity characteristic of "∧" and "∨", as well as the removal of superfluous brackets. We also ensure that, by suitably renaming variables, the two quantifiers refer to the same variables as in the original sentence.

Before we describe the process let us have a look at skolemisation.

12.1 Skolemisation

Skolemisation is just a process for giving an existing thing a name. If the thing which exists is dependent on certain variables then the name of this should be reflected by marking these variables as parameters - otherwise it is possible for the information content to be lost. This is the idea behind skolemisation.

The following cases are possible:

- $\forall x \exists y\, p(x,y)$
  means: for every x there is a y such that the predicate is true, i.e., there is a functional dependency between x and y which is given by:
  $y=f(x)$ such that:
  $\forall x \exists p(x,y) \Rightarrow \forall x \forall y p(x,y)$ is true.
- $\exists x \forall y \neg p(x,y) \Rightarrow \neg \forall x \forall y p(x,y)$
  x is not dependent on a variable. Therefore, the existential quantifier can be replaced by the universal quantifier.
- $\exists x p(x)$
  x is independent. We introduce a constant and call it a "skolem constant".
  $\exists x p(x) \Rightarrow p(a)$
  Once the existential quantifiers have been replaced the remaining universal quantifiers can be removed.
- $\forall xz \exists p(x,z,y)$
  In this case the y is dependent on two variables so:
  $\forall xz p(x,x,f(x,z))$

The Transformation

The conversion follows several steps, as below:

1. Removal of implication (→) and equivalence (↔):
   - $A \rightarrow B \equiv \neg A \vee B$
   - $A \leftrightarrow B \equiv [B \vee \neg A] \wedge [A \vee \neg B]$

2. Bring negation as far as possible into the formula:
   - $\neg\neg A \equiv A$
   - $\neg(B \vee A) \equiv (\neg B \wedge \neg A)$ De Morgan
   - $\neg(B \wedge A) \equiv (\neg B \vee \neg A)$
   - $\neg\forall x p(x) \equiv \exists x \neg p(x)$
   - $\neg\exists x p(x) \equiv \forall x \neg p(x)$
3. Conjunction and disjunction are replaced as far as possible, by:
   - $A \vee (B \wedge C) = (A \vee B) \wedge (A \vee C)$
   - $A \vee \forall x B = \forall x(A \vee B)$
   - $A \vee \exists \mathrm{x} B = \exists \mathrm{x}(A \vee B)$
   - $\forall x(A \wedge B) = \forall x A \wedge \forall x B$
4. Renaming of variables:
   - so that the two quantifiers have the same variables.
5. Removal of existential quantifiers:
   - skolemisation as described
6. Removal of universal quantifiers:
   - since all variables are universally quantified.
7. Conversion into CNF using De Morgan:
   - $\neg(A \wedge B) = \neg A \vee \neg B$
   - $A \vee (B \wedge C) = (A \vee B) \wedge (A \vee C)$
8. Removal of operators by writing as sets:
   - $P \wedge (Q \vee R) = \{\{P\},\{Q,R\}\}$
9. Renaming of variables so that:
   - no variable appears in more than one clause.

Example: Given the following formula:

$\forall x\{\{\forall y p(x,y)\} \rightarrow \neg\{\forall y q(x,y) \rightarrow r(x,y)\}\}$

Step 1: $\forall x\{\neg\{\forall y p(x,y)\} \vee \neg\{\forall y \neg q(x,y) \vee r(x,y)\}\}$

Step 2: $\forall x\{\exists y \neg p(x,y)\} \vee \{\exists y q(x,y) \wedge \neg r(x,y)\}\}$

Step 3: $\forall x\{\exists y \neg p(x,y) \vee (\exists y q(x,y) \wedge \neg r(x,y))\}$

Step 4: $\forall x\{\exists y \neg p(x,y) \vee (\exists z q(x,z) \wedge \neg r(x,z))\}$

Step 5: $\forall x\{\neg p(x,f_1(x)) \vee (q(x,f_2(x)) \wedge \neg r(x,f_2(x)))\}$

Step 6: $\neg p(x,f_1(x)) \vee (q(x,f_2(x)) \wedge \neg r(x,f_2(x)))$

Step 7: $(\neg p(x,f_1(x)) \vee q(x,f_2(x))) \wedge (\neg p(x,f_1(x)) \vee \neg r(x,f_2(x)))$

Step 8: $\{\{\neg p(x,f_1(x_1)),q(x,f_2(x))\}\{\neg p(x,f_1(x)),\neg r(x,f_2(x))\}\}$

Step 9: $\{\{\neg p(x_1,f_1(x_1)),\mathrm{q}(x_1,f_2(x_1))\}\{\neg p(x_2,f_1(x_2)),\neg \mathrm{r}(\mathrm{x}_2,f_2(x_2))\}\}$

Binding Rules

$\neg$	binds stronger than	$\wedge,\vee$
$\wedge,\vee$	bind stronger than	$\rightarrow$
$\rightarrow$	binds stronger than	$\leftrightarrow$

Example:

$\neg A \wedge B$	transformation	$(\neg A) \wedge B$
$A \vee B \rightarrow C \wedge D$	transformation	$(A \vee B) \rightarrow (C \wedge D)$
$A \leftrightarrow B \rightarrow B$	transformation	$A \leftrightarrow (B \rightarrow B)$

Some Useful Conversions

$F \leftarrow (G \vee H)$	$\Rightarrow$	$F \leftarrow G$
$F \leftarrow (G \leftarrow H)$	$\Rightarrow$	$F \leftarrow H$
		$F \leftarrow \neg H$
$F \leftarrow (G \leftrightarrow H)$	$\Rightarrow$	$F \leftarrow G \wedge H$
		$F \leftarrow \neg G \wedge \neg H$
$(F \vee G) \leftarrow H$	$\Rightarrow$	$F \leftarrow \neg G \wedge H$
$(F \wedge G) \leftarrow H$	$\Rightarrow$	$F \leftarrow H$
		$G \leftarrow H$
$(F \leftarrow G) \leftarrow H$	$\Rightarrow$	$F \leftarrow G \wedge H$
$F \leftarrow \exists y G(y)$	$\Rightarrow$	$\forall y (F \leftarrow G(y))$
		y can not appear in F

Note that the symbols: ←,→,if,:- are identical (in Prolog).

12.2 Exercises for the Topic

1. Read the following expressions in natural language and skolemise them. Give the skolem function a suitable name.
   a. $\exists x \neg \text{secretary}(x)$
   b. $\forall x \exists y[\text{person}(x) \rightarrow \text{has\_father}(x,y)]$
   c. $\forall x \exists y[\text{teacher}(x) \rightarrow [\text{teaches}(x,y) \wedge \text{student}(y)]]$

2. Express the following sentence in clausal form using just the predicate "likes".
   a. Hugh likes everyone.
   b. Hugh like someone.
   c. Everyone likes everyone.
   d. Everyone likes someone.
   e. Someone likes everybody.
   f. Someone likes somebody.
   g. No one likes Hugh.
   h. No one likes nobody.
   i. No one likes somebody.
   j. No one likes everyone.

3. Transform the following formulae into clausal form.
   a. $\forall x[p(x) \rightarrow [\forall y p(y) \rightarrow p(f(x,y)) \wedge \neg \forall y[q(x,y) \rightarrow p(y)]]]$
   b. $\forall x \forall y[q(x,y) \leftrightarrow \forall u(p(g,u) \vee p(x,u))]$
   c. $p(x,y) \leftrightarrow q((y) \leftarrow q(x))$
   d. $\neg \forall x p(x) \rightarrow \exists x \neg p(x)$
   e. $\forall x \exists y\{[p(x,y) \rightarrow q(y,x)] \wedge [q(y,x) \rightarrow r(x,y)]\} \rightarrow \exists x \forall y[p(x,y) \rightarrow r(x,y)]$
   f. $\neg\{(\forall x\{p(x) \rightarrow \{p(f(x,y)) \wedge \neg \forall y\{q(x,y) \rightarrow p(y)\}\}\}$
   g. $\neg \exists p(x) \rightarrow \forall x \forall y(p(x,y) \rightarrow \neg r(y))$

The worth of man arises from the
limitations of his spirit.
- Blaise Pascal -

6 HERBRAND PROOF PROCEDURE

In order to work with logic programs, a procedure is required with whose help sentences can be derived, i.e. propositions from a set of basic sentences - so-called axioms. The totality of the axioms is also called a logic program; that is if, with the help of a machine, the conclusions (or theorems), which are drawn from the basic component resources, are taken into account. This makes it possible to realise applications such as automated deduction systems and expert systems for knowledge representation. Thus, when the realm of mathematics and logic had gained structure and stability in the "enlightenment"; as ever more complex proofs could be carried out according to fixed procedures and programmable machines were finally available, these important tasks could be given over to computers. An algorithm, which described the steps for the derivation of predicate logic theorems, was, however, required. One of these procedures was the Herbrand proof procedure.

It was necessary to guarantee that that which a human could derive from the axioms, could also be derived using this procedure in finite time. This requirement was fulfilled by the development of this method. Nevertheless, this procedure could not overcome the inherent problem of predicate logic: so-called undecidability. This problem can not be solved in simple predicate logic either by other procedures or by humans. This meant that the procedure achieved what is necessary to cover most applications of knowledge-based computing in simple predicate logic.

On the other hand people wanted to stay with predicate logic since what had suddenly been achieved, i.e., the advantages of mechanised proof, should not just be thrown away. Hence the inherent undecidability was accepted.

In return, people felt that they had something about which there had been much speculation: objectivity. A seemingly context-independent authority which could provide answers by means of scientific querying independent of the human sphere of experience. The competence of this authority were however, restricted to responding to highly constrained questions. The aim is thus apparent: the computer has to find the situation, as long as there is one. "What?" is not queried but rather "How and Why?". Interesting, related results of this proof are not considered.

If one could, for example, combine three axioms in order to prove something of amazing brilliance then a mechanical proof device would not be able to do it - let alone notice it. The human user has to formulate this as a concrete query -

the mechanical brainwave which gets near to this discovery by accident is not possible. Polya's requirement that "One has to be able to guess a mathematical sentence before it can be proven" (see Lakatos, "Proof and Contradictions") remains the only way, the pseudo-chance discovery as a by product, as "manna", must be denied.

The Herbrand proof procedure is of no relevance to practical applications today - since SLD-resolution[3] became popular as a logically equivalent procedure. The latter is more powerful, i.e. faster, because it necessitates many fewer steps.

[3] The topic of SLD-resolution follows, later.

Topic 13

Herbrand Domains

13.1 Explanation of Technical terms

Interpretation, Assignment, Universe

A formula is just a pile of characters and symbols without a concrete meaning. It must, therefore, be interpreted in order to receive a meaning; i.e., in order to be able to be determined "true" or "false". For this, it is necessary to explain a universe which specifies the objects which can be used in place of variables or constants. Each constant is assigned exactly one element. Furthermore, each *n*-place functor must be assigned a function which maps every value of the universe to a value within it. And, finally, every predicate must be assigned a function which maps every value of the universe to "true" or "false" (see remark in the next chapter).

An assignment of variables relates every variable of the formula to an element of the universe. It is, thus, possible to use the functor-functions and to perform truth value evaluation by means of the predicate-functions, as each argument now corresponds to an object of the universe. The whole formula can now be assigned a truth value with the logical connections by the definition of the operators and quantifiers. As an interpretation usually permits more than one assignment several different truth values can be determined for an interpretation - at least, that is, if open formulae are being used.

Example of an interpretation:
As formula we shall consider: $\forall x\colon p(f(x,a),x)$

- the universe is the set of natural numbers
- the constant α is assigned the number 1
- the two-place functor *f* stands for the multiplication of two natural numbers
- the two-place predicate *p* is true if and only if both its arguments are arithmetically identical - otherwise it is false.

We therefore interpret the formula as:

$$\forall x\colon equal(times(x,1),x)$$

or, in Queen's English: for all natural numbers which can be used in place of *x* the following is true:

$$x \times 1 = x$$

For the example of assignment $x=5$ results in $5\times1=5$ - therefore a true proposition. As this comparison is true for all natural numbers the whole formula is true.

Truth Value of a Formula, Model

If the formula is exclusively, and always, true under an interpretation, and under all conceivably possible variable assignments, then the interpretation concerned is known as a model for the formula. This emphasis is redundant with respect to logic programming as it is already concerned with universally quantified formulae.

The above example is, therefore, a model as the truth value of the whole formula is "true" independent of whatever value is initially given to x.

I would like to make a further remark with respect to the function which assigns a "truth value" to a predicate in an interpretation and, thus, indirectly assigns the "truth value" to the formula: it is totally clear that a meaning belongs to a symbol or a sentence of symbols. "No object without a subject and no subject without an object", Schopenhauer is supposed to have said. That means that the semantics of a predicate lies in the domain of the truth, correctness or soundness of a proposition - or otherwise. This is not achieved by a special function which gives an absolute meaning to an absolute symbol. It is always so - therefore not only is a special function required here but, and more problematically, a simple mathematical function can not do this.

An element of the set of predicate designators is not mapped along with an object, to another from the set of magically produced symbolic meanings ({t,f} or also {0,1} or some other "semantic set"), in order to give a predicate meaning. It already has it, albeit potentially. Instead of this, an object which can potentially mean true or false, is projected onto a word or a symbol for "true" or "false".

Logical Consequence

A formula F is a logical consequence of a set of formulae S if every model for S is also one for F. This is then true: $F_1 \,\&\, F_2 \,\&\, ... \,\&\, F_n \Rightarrow F$
since in all cases in which the interpretation is not a model for S, the constraint is false and, therefore, the proposition true, independently of whether or not it is also a model for F. The definition also requires the presence of logical consequence, so that its validity is similarly unaffected. If it is a model for S and not for F then in the case of F it is still an instance of logical consequence hence the sentence would be false. And, finally, if an interpretation is both a model for S as well as for F, then F is logically consistent and the above proposition would be true.

If this conclusion is reformulated, somewhat, then the following results:
$F_1 \,\&\, F_2 ... F_n \neg F \Rightarrow 0$
Although we know that at the meta-level at which Modus Ponens seems to operate this formula must result, since it is based on nothing more than the principle of indirect proof, we do not appear to be in the position to carry out this reformulation according to well-defined laws. Similar laws may apply to the meta level, we just lack the syntax, the laws themselves and a meta calculus. Intuitively, we would formulate the following:

$F_1 \,\&\, F_2 \,\&\, ... \,\&\, F_n \Rightarrow F$
$iff\, \neg(F_1 \,\&\, F_2 \,\&\, ...\&) \vee F$
$iff\, \neg F_1 \vee \neg F_2 \vee ... \vee \neg F_n \vee F \vee 0$

iff $\neg(F_1 \& F_2 \& ... \& F_n \& \neg F) \vee 0$
iff $F_1 \& F_2 \& ... \& F_n \& \neg F \Rightarrow 0$

in which "iff" means "if and only if" and is intended, here, to stand for equivalence.

13.2 Herbrand Interpretation, Universe and Basis

Definition: Herbrand Universe

The Herbrand universe is defined as the set of all ground terms (terms without variables) which can be constructed from the constants and functors which appear in the given set of formulae *P*. This means that not only are all the constants occurring contained in the Herbrand universe (*HU*) but also those *n*-place tuples $f(\text{Constant}_1, ... \text{Constant}_n)$ can be produced with the functors. This expands the *HU* since this *n*-place tuple is now an element of the *HU*. Additional ones are, once again, produced as the elements, produced by means of the functors, become arguments to which new *n*-place tuples $f(\text{Term}_1, ... Term_2)$, and therefore, new elements can be assigned. If there are no constants in *P* then a "dummy constant" is assumed with which all elements can be constructed by means of the function rule. The *HU* is, in the case of existing functors, the result (which is never attained but clearly defined) of an endless recursion. For example:

- *P:*
  $p(x)$: $q(f(x),g(x))$
  $r(g)$:-
  $\mathbf{L}=\{p,q,r,f,g\}$
  $HU=(P)_L=\{h,f(h),g(h),f(f(h)), g(f(h)),g(g(h)), ...\}$
- Δ: a set of formulae
  $\Delta=\{\{p(a,b)\},\{q(b),r(c)\}\}$
  $HU(\Delta)=\{a,b,c\}$
- $\Delta=\{\{p(b)\},\{q(f(x),g(y))\}\}$
  $HU(\Delta)=\{b,f(b),g(b),f(f(b)),f(g(b)),g(g(b)), ...\}$
- $\Delta=\{\{p(x)\},\{\neg p(y)\}\}$
  $HU(\Delta)=\{h\}$

Definition: Herbrand Basis

The Herbrand basis of a program is the set of all "ground clauses" which can be formed if variables are substituted for elements of the *HU*. For example:

- *P:*
  $p(x)$:- $q(f(x),g(x))$
  $r(g)$:-
  $\mathbf{L}=\{p,q,r,f,g\}$
  $HU=\{a,f(a),g(a),f(f(a)),g(f(a)),g(g(a)), ...\}$
  $HB=\{p(a),q(a,a),r(a),p(f(a)),p(g(a)),q(a,f(a)),q(f(\text{a}),a), ...\}$

- $\Delta=\{\{p(a,b)\},\{q(b),r(c)\}\}$
  $HU=\{a,b,c\}$
  $HB=\{\{p(a,b)\},\{q(b),r(c)\}\}$
- $\Delta=\{\{p(b)\},\{q(f(x)),g(y)\}\}$
  $HU=\{b(f(b),g(b), \dots\}$
  $HB=\{\{p(b)\},\{q(f(b)),g(b)\},\{q(f(g(b)),g(g(b))\}, \dots$
- $\Delta=\{\{p(x)\},\{\neg p(y)\}\}$
  $HU=\{a\}$
  $HB=\{\{p(a)\},\{\neg p(a)\}\}$
- owns(owner(cat),cat).
  happy(*x*):- owns(*X*,cat).
  HU={cat,owner(cat),owner(owner(cat,cat)), ...}
  HB={owns(*X*,*Y*)|*X*,*Y*∈ *HU*} ∪ {happy(*X*)| *X* ∈ *HU*}

Remarks

- if Δ contains constants and functions then *HU* is infinite.
- if Δ contains only constants then *HU* is finite.
- if Δ contains no constants then the constant *h* is added.
- If *HU* is infinite then *HB* is infinite.

Definition: Herbrand Interpretation

A Herbrand interpretation consists of the Herbrand universe, a given function assignment for functors and some truth value evaluation for *n*-place predicates. In addition, every constant symbol is assigned an identically-named constant from the Herbrand universe.

An interpretation *I* for a set of formulae Δ is called *HI* if the following is true:

- the universe of the interpretation is *HU*.
- every constant is assigned the same constant of *HU*.
- every n-place function symbol *f* is assigned a function which has, respectively, n ground terms $t_1, \dots t_n$ from *HU* constructed on the basis of the element $f(t_1, \dots t_n)$ from *HU*.
- every ground atom is assigned either the value true or false.

The assignment of predicates is left open, this means that various Herbrand interpretations can then only be differentiated by the assignment of predicates. For example:

$P: \neg p(a)$
$\qquad \exists x p(x)$
$HU(P)=\{a\}$
$HB(P)=\{p(a)\}$
$III_1=I_1=\{\},HI_2=\{p(a)\}$
HI_1 is not a model of $\exists x p(x)$;
HI_2 is a model of $\exists x p(x)$, but not of $\neg p(a)$

Assuming that the universe is the totality of natural numbers; we assign "0" to α and "uneven" relation(<1>,<3>,<5>, ...) to *P*; there is a model as "0" is not uneven" and "an uneven number exists, e.g., 1".

Definition: Herbrand Model

The Herbrand interpretations, which are models for a set of formulae Δ, are Herbrand Models. In order to prove unsatisfiability it is sufficient to consider just the Herbrand interpretations.

- if Δ has a model then it has *HM* and it is satisfiable
- Δ is therefore unsatisfiable if it has no *HM*.
- if Δ has no *HM* then it does not mean that Δ is unsatisfiable; Δ can have other models.

For example:
$\Delta=\{p(a),\exists x\neg p(x)\}=\{p(a),\neg p(x)\}$
$HU=\{a\}$
$HB=\{p(a),\neg p(a)\}$
0 is assigned to constant α; the predicate *p* maps 0 to "true".
{p(0):= true,
¬p(0):= false}
Δ has a model but no *HM*! The Herbrand interpretations for Δ are:
$HI=\{\{\},\{p(a)\}\}$
None of these interpretations is a model for Δ.

Definition: Ground Program

A ground program is understood to be the set of all clausal expressions which result from the permitted instantiations of elements from *HU*. Predicates are also elements of *HB* in this. For example:

*P*1: likes(tom,*X*):- likes(*X*,logic).
likes(henry,logic).
HU(*P*1): {tom,henry,logic}
GP(*P*1): likes(tom,tom):- likes(tom,logic).
likes(tom,henry):- likes(henry,logic).
likes(tom,logic):- likes(logic,logic).
likes(henry,logic).

Example: *P*2 is:
likes(chris,*X*):- likes(*X*,logic).
likes(bob,logic):-
HU={chris,bob,logic}

G(*P*2):
likes(chris,chris):- likes(chris,logic).
likes(chris.bob):- likes(bob,logic).

likes(chris,logic):- likes(logic,logic).
likes(bob,logic).

HB=
{likes(chris,chris),likes(chris,logic),likes(chris,bob),likes(logic,chris),likes(logic, logic),likes(logic,bob),likes(bob,chris),likes(bob,logic),likes(bob,bob)}

HM: *false:=false*
true:= true
false:=false
true

With these interpretations, all clauses *G(P)* are true. This interpretation is an HM for *P*.

Definition: Herbrand Theorem

If a set of clauses is unsatisfiable then its Herbrand basis is also unsatisfiable.

Given: theory *Th*, formula *F* and ground program *GP*, $Th \cup \{\neg F\}$ is unsatisfiable if and only if $GP\{Th \cup \neg F\}$ is unsatisfiable.

13.3 Semantic Trees

A semantic tree is a graphical representation of all Herbrand interpretations of a set of formulae *P*. The nodes of this tree are the truth values of the predicates of *P*, or more accurately, of the corresponding *HB*. The two daughter nodes of each node correspond to the two truth values of a predicate: the left represents the case in which the predicate is true and the right that in which it is false. Both nodes again link this state to that of a further predicate of the *HB*. Because there are also two truth values for this then the daughter node also has two subnodes which represent the truth values of the new predicate. The same applies to the new subnodes until no more predicates of the *HB* are unused.

As an example we shall use the following set of formulae:
p(a).
q(b).
q(X):- p(X).

$HU=\{a,b\}$
$HB=\{p(a),p(b),q(a),q(b)\}$
$GP=\{p(a),q(b),\neg p(a)\vee q(a),\neg p(b)\vee q(b)\}$

Each terminal node of every leaf, along with every path leading to it, defines the logical states of all of the predicates occurring in the *HB* which belong to *P*. In the potentially infinite tree all the possible permutations of states are represented such that the semantic tree shows all possible Herbrand interpretations of a set of formulae *P*.

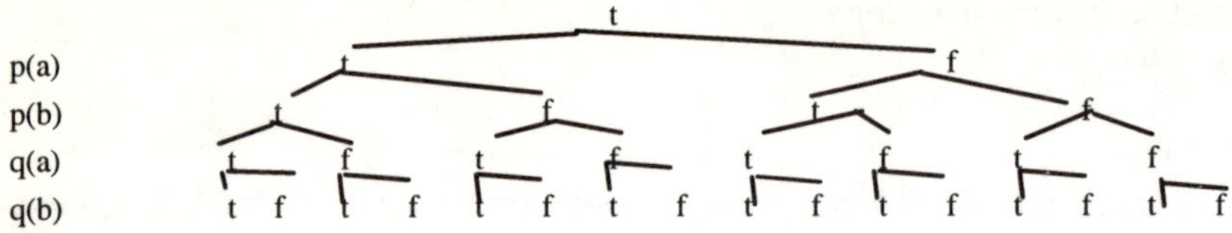

p(a)	t	t	t	t	t	t	t	t	f	f	f	f	f	f	f	f
¬p(a)∨q(a)	t	t	f	f	t	t	f	f	t	t	t	t	t	t	t	t
¬p(b)∨q(b)	t	f	t	f	t	t	t	t	t	f	t	f	t	t	t	t
P in total	t	f	f	f	t	f	f	f	f	f	f	f	f	f	f	f

Fig. 6.1: A Semantic tree

The now instantiated predicates of a leaf or path can be used to perform logical connections by means of operators and quantifiers. The predicates defined in this way can be used to evaluate clauses, particularly those of the *GP* and also those of the *P*. In the case of there being variables then all the possible connections implied by the quantifiers can be carried out by instantiating to elements of *HU*. This makes it possible to evaluate the quantified clauses themselves.

That is, all the clausal expressions contained in *GP* can be evaluated with "true" or "false" and all the universally-quantified clauses are, themselves, given a truth value. If all the evaluated clauses of *P* or, similarly, all expressions which are contained in *GP* are produced then the truth value of *P* itself, or that of the logic program, is given under the interpretation for the path to a leaf. If it is "true" then it relates to the Herbrand model - if it is false then the logic program is not satisfied. If there is no Herbrand model then the evaluation of the logic program at all leaves, and therefore under all possible interpretations, is "false", making *P* unsatisfiable.

A leaf at which formula *P* is falsified is a *failure node*. An inference node is a node whose successor nodes are failure nodes or inference nodes. An inference node, along with all its failure nodes, is called a failure tree.

Definition

- If a semantic tree is satisfiable then its failure tree is unsatisfiable.
- If all terminal nodes of the failure tree are failure nodes then the tree is unsatisfiable.
- A semantic tree is unsatisfiable if its root node is an inference node.

Example:

$\Delta=\{p(x)\vee q(x),\neg p(a),\neg q(b)\}$
$HU=\{a,b\}$
$HB=\{p(a),q(a),p(b),q(b)\}$
$HM1=HI=\{p(a),\neg q(a),\neg p(b),q(b)\}$

$HM2 = HI = \{\neg p(a), \neg q(a), \neg p(b), q(b)\}$
$HM1$ does not satisfy $\neg p(a)$ or $\neg q(b)$
$HM2$ does not satisfy $p(x) \vee q(x)$

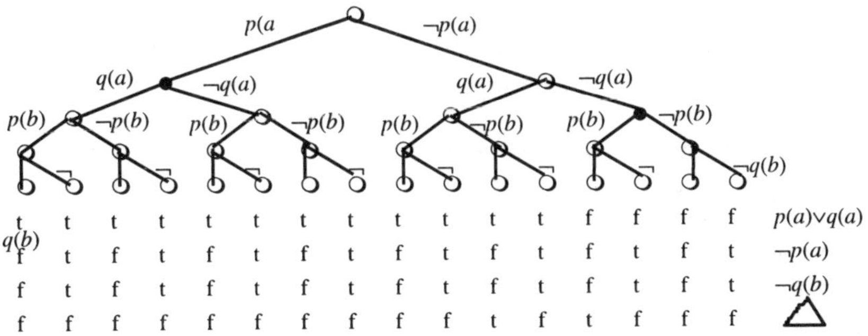

Fig. 6.2: A Semantic Tree with Failure Nodes

Example:

$\Delta = \{\neg p(x) \vee q(x), p(f(y)), \neg q(f(y))\}$
$HU(\Delta) = \{a, f(a), f(f(a)), f(f(f(a))), \ldots\}$
$HB(\Delta) = \{p(a), q(a), p(f(a)), q(f(a)), p(f(f(a))), \ldots\}$

If a node in a tree is not a failure node but both successor nodes are failure nodes then this node is an inference node.

The inference node is indicated in fig. 6.2 by a 3.

- below marker 1 all interpretations do not satisfy the clause $\neg p(x) \vee q(x)$.
- All interpretations beneath marker 2 do not satisfy the clause $\neg q(f(y))$

We conclude from this:
$\{\neg p(x) \vee q(x), \neg q(f(y))\}$ the new clause $\neg p(f(y))$.

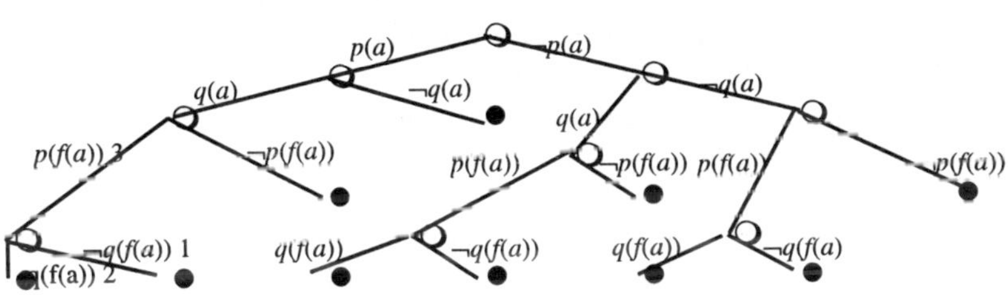

Fig. 6.3: A Semantic Tree with Inference Nodes

13.4 Proof Procedure

The last comment means that the proof procedure can not produce a solution for the logic program in conjunction with a query. The falsehood of the set of formulae under investigation must therefore be shown at every terminal node; in this case there is no Herbrand interpretation for them.

This is particularly meaningful if, firstly, a logic program exists which is known to be satisfiable and, secondly, it is sought to determine if the negation can be derived from the program. This is, of course, always the case if the logic program is itself unsatisfiable since "from falsehood anything follows". How is that so in inferencing?: if the condition is false then it is already true ....

This means that this will show up in the Herbrand proof procedure since, with respect to a query, the resultant set of formulae would still be unsatisfiable. In practice what is sought is whether or not the query is derived because of this trivial case or because of a real "derivation" from the logic program: for this reason, care should be taken to determine the satisfiability of a program when writing it. If it is unsatisfiable then its contradictory nature must be removed before anything can be achieved with theorems - although or, indeed, because of, the fact that any theorem can be derived from it. The Herbrand proof procedure is recommended for such a satisfiability test. If the *HB* terminates then satisfiability can be determined, if not then it nevertheless represents a small plus, in not succeeding to prove unsatisfiability. If such a test is successfully completed then it is possible to draw further conclusions, as long as there is no intention to use SLD resolution immediately, by means of the Herbrand procedure.

Of course, sometimes we do not just want to know if the negation of a query is a logical consequence of a set of formulae. A query has the form:
$\forall x_1 \forall x_2 \ldots \forall x_k \neg(A_1 \& A_2 \& \ldots \& A_n)$
or in clausal form: $A_1, A_2, \ldots A_n \Rightarrow$
Negation would look as below:
$\exists x_1 \exists x_2 \ldots \exists x_k A_1 \& A_2 \ldots A_n$

If it can be considered to be a logical consequence, i.e., if the set of formulae is unsatisfiable in connection with the query then it does not mean anything more than "there are values for the variables such that all partial expressions A_1, A_2 ... & A_n together (i.e., $A_1 \& A_2 \& \ldots \& A_n$) follow from the set of formulae". As we have said this does not suffice: we would like to know what the values are. SLD resolution is available for this.

With a somewhat fiddly "trick", the Herbrand procedure can be used for this. To do this, all we need to do is to use all combinations of elements of *HU* instead of using the variables, and carry out the procedure so that the query reads: $A_1 \& A_2 \& \ldots \& A_n \Rightarrow$ whose negation as a possible theorem is represented as: $A_1 \& A_2 \& \ldots \& A_n$.

By omitting quantifiers, it can immediately be seen whether or not these combinations are valid. As this is an automated procedure this process is, in principle, possible, however for large or infinite *HU* (due to functors), or for combinations of many variables, this technique would be ruled out, in that there would be no solution to this problem.

In this sense, the definition of a correct answer is still very interesting. A correct answer is an instantiation of some of the variables of the query for which the chain of expressions is a logical consequence. If variables remain in the chain of expressions then this formula must be a logical consequence of the set of formulae for all respectively remaining values of variables; in the case of instantiation of the other variables it would be a correct answer. Formally, a query $A_1 \& A_2 \& \ldots \& A_n \Rightarrow$ looks as follows:

$$\forall x_1 \forall x_2 \ldots \forall x_k \neg(A_1 \& A_2 \& A_n)$$

In which $\cup(A_1 \& A_2 \& A_n)$ represents the formula which results if the variables of the query, which are to be instantiated by the instantiation of $\cup$, are instantiated accordingly and $x_1, x_2, \ldots, x_n$ are the remaining variables.

The Consistency Proof for a formula whose HB *is infinite*

The last open question really means: How does the procedure operate in the case of an infinite *HB*? Since, as already mentioned, in connection with semantic trees, the whole tree is, eventually, searched, i.e., all permutations evaluated to "true" or "false" and, in accordance with the rule in *P* or the ground program, they are linked to each other and evaluated. That is, if there is a case in which the whole set of formulae or logic program is evaluated to "true" then it is satisfiable, otherwise it is not.

This can, moreover, take a very long time as there are $2^{(\text{cardinality}(HB))}$ possible evaluations which can, for larger HB, be associated with a long computing time (although the algorithm can, if circumstances permit, terminate after the evaluation of the first *HB* - if the concern is just the satisfiability of the query; this said, time is (in principle) limited. Here is the algorithm again:

1. Presume: $\Delta = \{\}$
2. Produce a subset Δ' of *HB*(*F*), such that $\Delta \subseteq \Delta'$.
3. Prove if Δ' is satisfiable by exploring all permutations assigning formulae in Δ' as true.
4. If unsatisfiability is discovered then stop; *HB*(*F*) is unsatisfiable else go to 2.

- If *F* is unsatisfiable then we shall find a subset of *HB*(*F*) which is satisfiable in finite time.
- If *F* is satisfiable then we *continue for ever and are never able to prove satisfiability*.

Example for an infinite HB:
$F = \forall x \exists y\ \text{has\_father}(x,y) \wedge \exists x \forall y \neg \text{has\_father}(y,x)$

1. Renaming of variables
   $\forall x \exists y$has_father(x,y)) $\wedge$ $\exists w \forall z \neg$has_father(z,w)
2. Elimination of $\exists$
   $\forall x$ has_father(x,f(x)) $\wedge \forall z \neg$has_father(z,a)
   in which f=skolem-function, a=skolem constant
3. Skolem Normal Form
   has_father(x,f(z)) $\wedge$ $\neg$has_father(z,a)
4. HU={a,f(a),f(f(a)),f(f(f(a))), ... etc}
5. HB={has_father(a,f(a)) $\wedge$ $\neg$has_father(a,a),
   has_father(f(a),f(f(a)) $\wedge$ $\neg$has_father(a,a),
   has_father(a,f(a)) $\wedge$ $\neg${has_father(f(a),a), ...}}

As long as unsatisfiability remains undiscovered there is no conclusion about the satisfiability of F!

The Consistency Proof of a Formula whose HB *is Infinite*

Another heuristic procedure is, however, required with infinite HB. The semantic tree is, in practice, searched level by level. Several levels can be explored at once.

Firstly, one or more elements of the HB are taken. If there is already a subtree with branches which are not failure nodes and do not belong to failure trees then they are linked, by the presently existing leaves and the paths to them, to logical states given to them which they return anew. For the new elements of the HB, we take both possible values and carry out the linking to every leaf for all sub-permutations of the new values.

If there is still no subtree, the procedure is in the initial stages, this predicate is the only one that can be investigated and no other links are possible.

The linking either takes place according to the clauses involved in P, in which the new predicates of HB occur or according to the instantiated clauses of GP. If failure nodes are produced in this way then these are noted and need not be investigated in the next iteration.

If there are no more which are not failure nodes and which do not belong to any failure trees[4] then it is possible to stop. If not then this sequence must be repeated.

Example for a finite HB

F=$\forall x$(employed_by(x,ibm))$\rightarrow$has_tie_colour(blue)

- Skolem Normal Form
  employed_by(x,ibm)$\rightarrow$has_tie_colour(blue)

---

[4] This is really just for completeness as they are no longer produced as they are already blocked at the failure nodes themselves and noted as such.

- *HU*={ibm,blue}
- *GP*(*F*)={ employed_by(ibm,ibm)→has_tie_colour(ibm,blue),
  employed_by(blue,ibm)→has_tie_colour(blue,blue)}

A satisfiable true assignment of HB is:
{ employed_by(ibm,ibm):= false,
employed_by(blue,ibm):= false,
has_tie_colour(ibm,blue):= false,
has_tie_colour(blue,blue):= false}

Therefore F is satisfiable!

13.5 Exercises for the Topic

1. Define the Herbrand universe for a given set of formulae *S* if *S* contains the following:
   a. two constants **a**, **b** and two unary function symbols **f**,**g**,
   b. a constant **a** and a binary function symbol **f,**
   c. no constants but a unary function symbol **f.**
2. Find the Herbrand basis for the following formula:
   $F=\forall x \exists y$ has_father$(x,y) \wedge \exists x \forall y \neg$*has*_father$(y,x)$
3. Give the Herbrand Universe and the Herbrand basis for the following programs.
   a.
   ```
   likes(chris,Anyone):- buys(Anyone,this-book).
   buys(Anyone,this-book):- sensible(Anyone).
   sensible(you).
   ```
   b.
   ```
   p(f(X)):- q(X,g(X)).
   q(a,g(b)).
   q(b,g(b)).
   ```
   c.
   ```
   p(s(X),Y,s(Z)):- p(X,Y,Z).
   p(0,X,X).
   ```
4. For Herbrand universe *HU*={*a*,*b*,*c*,*d*} and the Herbrand interpretation *HI*={*p*(*a*),*p*(*b*),*q*(*a*),*q*(*b*),*q*(*c*),*q*(*d*)} which of the following formulae are true in the interpretation?
   a. $\forall \mathrm{X} p(\mathrm{X})$
   b. $\forall \mathrm{X} q(\mathrm{X})$
   c. $\exists \mathrm{X}(q(\mathrm{X}) \wedge p(\mathrm{X}))$
   d. $\forall \mathrm{X}(q(\mathrm{X}) \rightarrow p(\mathrm{X}))$
   e. $\forall \mathrm{X}(p(\mathrm{X}) \rightarrow q(\mathrm{X}))$
5. Given the program *P*:
   ```
   link(a,b).
   link(b,c).
   path(X,Z):- link(X,Z).
   path(X,Z):- link(X,Y),path(Y,Z).
   ```
   With the clause: C: path(a,c)
   a Write the ground program *GP*(*P*∪¬*C*) assuming *HU*={*a*,*b*,*c*}
   b. With the help of the Herbrand procedure show that *GP*(*P*∪¬*C*) is unsatisfiable.

A world without deduction would be a world
without science, technology, social.
- Convention and Culture

7 RESOLUTION METHODS

There are numerous procedures for searching for the proof of a given predicate logic sentence. The most obvious is to start with a set of axioms and systematically derive all possible sentences from it, in the hope of producing the sentence in question. Such a procedure is known as *generate and test.* This procedure is constructive but blind.

A completely different approach is *reductio ad absurdum* which is used by the so-called *resolution* method:

- the negation $\neg F$ of the formula F to be proved is assumed.
- it is proved that the conjunction of the axioms Ax and $\neg F$ is unsatisfiable, i.e.: $Ax \cup \{\neg F\} \models []$
- by assuming the axioms are valid the falsehood of $\neg$F and, therefore, the truth of F is determined.

This procedure is known as proof by refutation. Its acceptance rests or falls however with the acceptance of *tertium non datur*, as it is simply proven that as the negation of the given formula is a contradiction the formula itself can, therefore, not be false. Church's and Turing's theorems fixed, once and for all, the non-existence of decision procedures for the validity of predicate logic formulae. The resolution method - as for any other proof method - is only a semi-decidable procedure. We shall come back, later, to questions of the soundness and completeness of the resolution method.

RESOLUTION IN PROPOSITIONAL LOGIC

Resolution in propositional logic is called ground resolution. It is a limited form of Robinson's method which can be used to test the unsatisfiability of a finite set of ground clauses.

Definition: C_1 and C_2 are ground clauses. A ground clause C is the (ground) resolvent of C_1 and C_2 if there is an atom A of the form:

1. C_1 contains $\neg A$
2. C_2 contains A
3. C is the disjunction of the literals of C_1 without $\neg A$ and the literals of C_2 without A.

If $C_1 = \neg A$ and $C_2 = A$ then the empty clause [] is a (ground) resolvent of C_1 and C_2. For example:

$C1$:{employee(X),¬manager(X)}
$C2$: {manager(w),¬seniormanager(w)}
$C2$: {employee(x),¬seniormanager(x)}

C is the "resolvent".

Definition: *Th* is a set of ground clauses and C a ground clause. C is then derivable from *Th* by means of Ground resolution:

$$Th \vdash_g C$$

if there is a sequence $C_1 \ldots C_n = C$ such that:

- C_i is a ground clause ($i \in \{1, \ldots, n\}$)
- for each C_i with $i \in \{1, \ldots, n\}$ then either

$$C_i \in Th$$

or $k,l \in \{1, \ldots i - 1\}$ is true such that the (ground) resolvent of C_k and C_l is C_i.

It is obviously true that: if C is a (ground) resolvent of two ground clauses C_1 and C_2 then any desired Herbrand interpretation I is valid:

$$\text{if } I \models C_1 \text{ and } I \models C_2 \text{ then } I \models C.$$

Derivations made by resolution have the related important characteristic that they are truth preserving - called *sound*. As the following resolution shows ground resolution is also complete with respect to the totality of satisfiable, finite sets of clauses.

A finite set *Th* of ground clauses is unsatisfiable if and only if it is a derivation of the empty clause [] from *Th* by means of ground resolution:

$$\not\models Th \text{ iff } Th \vdash_g []$$

The question of "which" ground instances of a formula in skolem normal form to prove by contradiction "when" the proof is to be brought forward is still open. Only resolution with unification provides the answer to this.

RESOLUTION IN PREDICATE LOGIC

In the case of ground resolution there is both a positive and a negative literal (for the same relation symbol), of two ground clauses, to explore for their suitability at every resolution step. The corresponding clauses are produced (more or less on demand) by a generator. Robinson's key idea - avoiding the instantiation of ground instances of a hypothesis ¬F, which are irrelevant to the proof, basically lies in relating this suitability test to the support of the selection of more interesting ground instances.

In crudely simple terms, the generalisation of ground resolution from general resolution lies in:

- resolving any desired clauses which may contain variables based on the starting hypothesis F and
- employing the process of matching complementary literals (called unification) to reduce the set of ground instance candidates of ¬F

In this way the individual steps of resolution become too costly but, as there are fewer resolution steps overall, the overall derivation becomes decidedly faster - ultimately a whole class of ground instances are tested for their unsatisfiability in one step. In contrast to the *generate and test* form of resolution this is a kind of *"specialise to resolve"* form.

As all forms of resolution can only work with unquantified formulae, these formulae are transformed into skolem normal form before being processed - using a specific procedure - as is shown in the next section. In the topic of that section we introduce the expressions required for describing the resolution method.

Topic 14

Substitution

A substitution θ is a representation which assigns a finite set of variables v_1, v_2, ..., v_n (which may contain variables) to terms t_1, t_2 ... t_n. We describe this as:

$$\theta=\{v_1/t_1, v_2/t_2, ..., v_n/t_n\}$$

The application of a substitution θ to a formula F is written in postfix: $F\theta$. For example:

$F=p(x,y,v); \theta=\{x/A,y/f(B),z/w\}; F\theta=p(A,A,f(B),v)$

If t_1, ... $t_n \in HU$ then θ is a *ground substitution*:
F=likes(x,y); $\theta=\{x/$chris, $y/$logic$\}$, $F\theta$=likes(chris,logic)
We lengthen the idempotent substitution: $F\theta=(F\theta)\theta$; i.e., for each substitution $\{v_1/t_1, v_2/t_2, ..., v_n/t_n\}$ no variable v_i may occur in t_i. For example:
F=likes(x,y);$\theta=\{x/y,y/$logic$\}$
$F\theta$=likes(y,logic)
$(F\theta)\theta$=likes(logic,logic) is not allowed!

A non-idempotent substitution can be transformed to an idempotent substitution by using the substitution on itself.
$\theta^1=\{x/f(a,\mathbf{y}),y/f(b,\mathbf{z}),z/c\}$ is not idempotent
$\theta^2=\{x/f(a,f(b,\mathbf{z})),y/f(b,c),z/c\}$ is not idempotent[5]
$\theta^3=\{x/f(a,f(b,c)),y/f(b,c),z/c\}$is idempotent

The variables in bold are not permitted and must be replaced. We proceed, in steps, to transform the clause into the idempotent clause θ^3. It is not possible to make it idempotent for every possible substitution.

Composition

The composition of two substitutions θ and λ, written as $\theta o \lambda$, is that substitution which is produced by applying λ to the term θ and adding the binding of λ to that of θ.

Given:
$\theta=\{x_1/t_1, ...x_n/t_n\}$
$\lambda=\{y_1/u_1, ... y_m/u_m\}$
$\theta o \lambda=\{x_1/t_1\lambda, ..., x_n/t_n\lambda, y_1/u_1, ... y_m/u_m\}$

λ is applied to every term t_i of θ and then the substitution of λ added to the list. Finally, all substitutions x_i/t_i for $x_i/t_i\lambda$, for which $x_i=t_i\lambda$ is true and those replacements y_i/u_i for which y_i is contained in $\{x_1, x_2, ... x_n\}$, are removed. For example:

- $\theta=\{x/f(y),y/z\}$
  $\lambda=\{xz/john,y/Bill,z/y\}$

---

[5] $\theta^2=\theta o \theta$

$\theta o\lambda=\{x/f(Bill),y/y,x/John,y/Bill,z,y\}$
$=\{x/f(Bill),z/y\}$

- $\theta=\{w/G(x,y)\}$
  $\lambda=\{x/A,y/B,z/C\}$
  $\theta o\lambda\{w/G(A,B),x/a,y/B,z/C\}$

The order in which the two substitutions are composed is clearly important.

The composition has the following characteristics:

- $\theta o\lambda$ is functional
- $F(\theta o\lambda) = (F\theta)o\lambda$
  $(\theta o\lambda)o\sigma=\theta o(\lambda o\sigma)$

Composition is generally not commutative. For example:
$F=p(x,g(y),z)$
$\theta=\{x/f(y)\};\lambda=\{y/a,z/b,x/c\}$
$F\theta=p(f(y),g(y),z)$
$F\theta\lambda=p(f(a),g(a),b)$
$F\lambda=p(c,g(a),b)$
$F\lambda\theta=p(c,g(a),b)$

14.1 Exercises for the Topic

1. Apply the following substitutions to the formulae:
   a. θ={*x*/mum(*y*),*y*/chris}; *F*=likes(*x*,dad(*y*))
   b. θ={*x*/mum(chris),*y*/chris}; *F*=likes(*x*,dad(*y*))
   c. θ={*x*/elizabeth};*F*=∃*x* wife(*x*,*y*)←husband(*x*,*y*)&married(*y*,*x*)

2. Are the following substitutions allowed?
   a. {*x*/mum(*y*),*y*/chris}
   b. {*x*/x}
   c. { }
   d. {*x*/2,*x*/3}
   e. {*x*/2,*x*/2}
   f. {*x*/*y*,*y*/*x*}
   g. {*x*/2,*y*/2,*y*/*x*}
   h. {*f*(*x*)/*f*(y)}

3. Compute the composition $\sigma^*=\sigma_1 o\sigma_2$ in which:
   a. $\sigma_1=\{w/f(x,y)\},\sigma_2=\{x/a,y/b,z/c\}$
   b. $\sigma_1=\{x/f(y),y/z\}$, $\sigma_2=\{x/a,y/b,z/y\}$
   c. $\sigma_1=\{x/f(a,y),w/f(u,z)\},\sigma_2=\{x/f(a,a),y/b,v/c\}$
      Prove that $F\sigma^*=(F\sigma^1)\sigma^2$ in which $F=p(v,x,y,w)$

4. Which of the following sentences are correct?
   a. $\sigma\theta=\delta\theta$ implies $\sigma=\delta$

b. $\theta\sigma=\theta\delta$ implies $\sigma=\delta$

c. $\sigma=\delta$ implies $\sigma\theta=\delta\theta$

Topic 15

Unification

For each step of resolution it is necessary that both a positive literal *P* and a negative literal $\neg P$ (of the same relation symbol) be semantically equal.

$p(x,\text{barry}),p(\text{andy},y)$
$\theta=\{x/\text{andy}, y/\text{barry}\}$
$\text{p}\theta=p(\text{andy},\text{barry})$

In general, given two terms the question is: are they unifiable? What is the unifier?

Definition: Unifier
A substitution γ is a unifier for a finite set of simple expressions:
$\Phi:=\{\phi_1, \phi_2, \ldots \phi_k\}$ if it is true that:

$$\phi_1\gamma=\phi_2\gamma= \ldots = \phi_k\gamma$$

The set Φ is *unifiable* if and only if there is a unifer for it.
$\phi_1=p(a,y,z)$; $\phi_1=p(x,b,c)$
$\gamma=\{x/a,y/b,z/c\}$
$\phi\gamma=p(a,b,c)$.

If, for example, $\phi_1\equiv p(t_1, \ldots. t_n)$, $\phi_2\equiv p(\text{u}_1, \ldots, u_n)$
then a unifier is a solution of the equality mechanism:
$t_1=u_1, t_2=u_2, \ldots, t_n=u_n$

Problems of Unification

It is not always possible to find a unifier for two expressions. This can have the following consequences:

- arguments can not be unified if a variable is not available: $\phi=\{p(f(x),a),p(y,f(w))\}$;
  is not unifiable as the second argument can not be unified.
- The variables may be nested hence unification takes place in two stages:
  - $\phi=\{p(f(x),z),p(y,b)\}$
    $\sigma=\{y/f(a),x/a,z/b\}$
  - $\phi=\{\text{human}(x),\text{human}(\text{uncle}(y))\}$
    $\sigma=\{x/\text{uncle}(w),\text{w}/\text{harry},y/\text{harry}\}$
  - a variable can only be instantiated to a constant. The variable *x* can not be unified
    $\phi=\{p(x,x),p(\text{andy},\text{barry})\}$

Example for Unification

- $\phi=\{f(x,y),f(g(a),b)\}$
  $\sigma=\{x/g(a),y/b\}$

- $\phi=\{f(x,a),f(a,y)\}$
  $\sigma=\{x/a,y/a\}$
- $\phi=\{f(g(a),b),f(h(a),b)\}$
  not unifiable
- $\phi=\{f(b,g(a,y)),f(x,z)\}$
  $\sigma=\{x/b,z/g(a,c),y/c\}$

Definition: *Variants*
Two expressions ϕ_1 and ϕ_2 are variants of one another if there is a substitution θ and σ with:

$$\phi_1=\phi_2\theta \textit{ and } \phi_2=\phi_1\sigma.$$

If the two expressions are variants of each other then there is always a corresponding substitution θ' and σ' which can simply be seen to be variable renamings.

Definition: most general unifier (mgu)
A most general unifier for θ of a set $\phi:=\{\phi_1, ..., \phi_n\}$ is a unifier of which every other unifier $\{\phi_1, ..., \phi_n\}$ is a variant. That is, every unifier can be derived from θ by specialisation. For example:

- $\phi=\{\phi_1, \phi_2\}=\{p(A,y,z),p(x,y,z)\}$
  $\theta=\{x/A\}$ most general unifier
  $\lambda=\{y/B,z/C\}$
  $\gamma=\theta o\lambda=\{x/A,y/B,z/C\}$ specialisation of θ
- $\phi=\{\phi_1, \phi_2\}=\{p(f(x),z),p(y,a)\}$
  $\theta=\{y/f(x),z/a\}$
  $\gamma=\theta o\lambda=\theta\{x/a\}$

The following example clarifies this term with reference to the Herbrand Universe:
likes(chris,y);likes(x,mum) and
HU={chris,mum,dad}
possible substitution=$HU\times HU$

A most general unifier θ can be readily determined (provided that it is unifiable). The procedure for this can easily be explained with the help of a few expressions.

Definition: *complementary pair*
Two literals are complementary if they have the same predicate symbol and one is positive and the other negative.

elephant(w) and $\neg$elephant(w)

Definition: A *divergent pair*
A pair of non-identical terms in the same position in the predicate. For example:

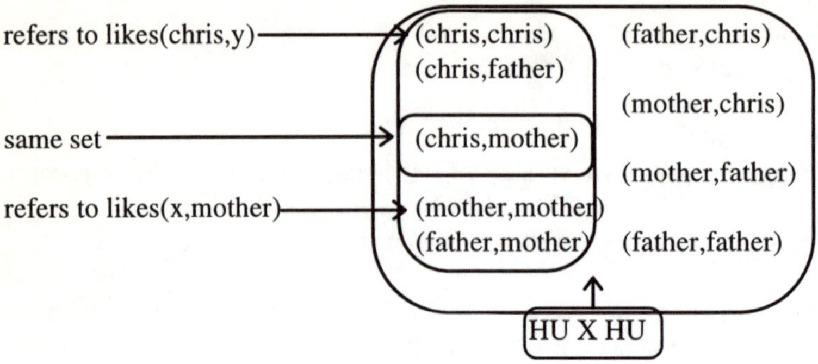

Fig. 7.1: Most General Unifier of the Herbrand Universe

$p(x,y,z)$
$p(u,v,f(w))$
Divergent pairs:= $<x,u>;<y,v>;<z,f(w)>$
Expressions are matched from left to right and the divergent pair placed in a list:

$$Dis(\phi):=\{x,u;y,v;z,f(w)\}$$

Unification Procedure

Let's imagine two stacks S and θ. At the start stack S contains the pairs of terms for which a unifier is sought. Stack θ is empty.

```
Begin: Loop
       if stack S empty
       then: stop; θ is a most general unifier
       else: Begin: comparison;
             Each time the top pair of terms is
             removed from the stack S and a pair
             <e1,e2>=<S1θ,S2θ> is constructed.
       if e1 and e2 are equal
       then: no substitution is required
       e.g., <e1,e2>=<x,x> and this is called
       an identity substitution
       goto Begin
       else: if e1 and e2 are different constants
       then: Error; the terms are not unifiable.
             e.g., <e1,e2>=<a,b>
       else: if either e1 or e2 is a function term
             and the other a constant
       then: error; the terms are not unifiable.
             e.g., <e1,e2>=<g(x),a>
       else: if e1 and e2 are function terms with
```

```
                different function symbols
        then: error: the terms are not unifiable.
                e.g., <e1,e2>=<g(x),f(x)>
        else: do the function terms have the same
                function symbol
        then: the pair of arguments are written back
                to the stack and the function symbols are
                removed.
                e.g., <e1,e2>=<g(x),g(y)>
        else: if e1 and e2 are variables
        then: add the binding e1/e2 to the stack θ
                the order <e1,e2> must be preserved.
                e.g., <e1,e2>=<x,y>
        else: if e1 or e2 is a variable which appears
                within the other terms (occurs check)
        then: error; the terms are not unifiable.
                e.g., <e1,e2>=<x,f(x)>
        else: if e1 is a variable
        then:       add the binding e1/e2 to the stack θ
                e.g., <e1,e2>=<x,a>
        else: if e2 is a variable
        then: add the binding e2/e1 to the stack θ
                e.g., <e1,e2>=<x,a>
        else go to Begin.
        End: comparison
End: loop
```

The algorithm is clarified by means of an example:
p(a,w,x,f(f(x))
p(z,g(y),g(z),f(y)

At the start the stack *S* contains the pair of terms: <e1,e2>:
a. <*a,z*>
b. <*w,g(y)*>
c. <*x,g(z)*>
d. <*f(f(x)),f(y)*>
and stack θ is empty. The terms are fetched from stack *S* and compared.

Pair of terms a.: Constant *a* and variable *z*; this pair is stored on stack θ in the form *z/a.*

Pair of terms b.: Variable *w* and function *g(y)*; this pair is stored on the stack in the form *w/g(y).*

Pair of terms c.: Variable *x* and function *g(z)*; θ is applied $<e_1\theta,e_2\theta>=<x,g(x)>$; *x/g(a)* is stored in stack θ.

Pair of terms d.: Both terms are functions with the same function symbol; θ is applied $<e_1\theta,e_2\theta>=<f(f(g(a))),f(y)>$. The pair of terms $<f(g(a)),y)$ is added to the stack *S*. On the next iteration only the function *f(g(a))* and the variable *y* remains. They are stored in stack θ in the form $y/f(g(a))$.

On termination stack *S* is empty and stack θ represents the most general unifier:

$$\theta=\{z/a,w/g(y),x/g(a),y/f(g(a))\}$$

The algorithm does not guarantee an idempotent substitution. *y* is not substituted in the example. By applying θ once again to itself we produce the idempotent form of the unifier:

$$\theta^2=\{z/a,w/g(f(g(a))),x/g(a),y/f(g(a))\}$$

15.1 The Occurs Check

The test if a variable *v* occurs in *t* is usually known as occurs check. If, it is not performed, for reasons of efficiency then that alone could lead to the above algorithm showing a worst-case exponential behaviour. This means that the soundness of the resolution method in use can no longer be guaranteed. This prevents even the lowliest of Prolog interpreter manufacturers from omitting it. For example:

$S=\{p(x,x),p(y,f(y))\}$

1. $\theta_0=\{\}$
2. $D_0=<e_1,e_2>=<x,y>$
   $\theta_1=\{x/y\};S\theta=\{p(y,y),p(y,f(y))\}$
   $D_1=<e_1,e_2>=<y,f(y)>$
   $\theta=<y,f(y)$

y occurs in *f(y)*; therefore, *S* is not unifiable.

Problems of Omitting Occurs Check

Omitting occurs check destroys the correctness of resolution:

a.
```
test:- p(x,x).
p(x,f(x)).
:- test.
```
Answer: yes; the answer is false!

b.
```
test:- p(x,x).
p(x,f(x)):- p(x,x).
:- test.
```
Answer: Prolog loops endlessly.

c.
```
test:- concat(u-u,v-v,a-(w-w)).
concat(x-y,y-z,x-z).
:- test.
```
Answer: yes, i.e., the result of appending two empty lists is {a}!

15.1 Exercises for the Topic

1. Determine whether or not the following atoms are unifiable. If yes then give both (idempotent form) of their mgu. If possible give the least general unifier, lgu.
   a. $p(\mathrm{a},x)$ and $p(y,b)$
   b. $p(x,x)$ and $p(y,z)$
   c. $p(x,y)$ and $p(y,x)$
   d. $p(t(x,t(x,b)))$ and $p(t(a,z))$
   e. $p(t(x,t(x,b)))$ and $p(t(a,t(a,z)))$
   f. $p(x,f(y))$ and $p(f(y),x)$
   g. $p(x,f(x))$ and $p(f(z),f(z))$
   h. $p(f(a),x)$ and $p(x,a)$

Find the most general unifier for the following sentences, if one exists.
a. $S=\{p(f(y),w,g(z)),p(u,u,v)\}$
b. $S=\{p(f(y))),w,g(z)),p(u,v,v)\}$
c. $S=\{p(a,x,f(g,y))),p(z,h(z,w),f(w))\}$
d. $S=\{p(a,x,f(g(y))),p(z,f(z),f(a))\}$
e. $S=\{p(john(x,f(g(y))),p(z,f(z),f(w))\}$
f. $S=\{p(f(a),g(x)),p(y,y)\}$
g. $S=\{p(a,x,h(g(z))),p(z,h(y),h(y))\}$

Topic 16

Consistency Checking with Resolution

We now have at our disposal the full set of tools for the description of the general method of resolution:

Robinson Theorem: a set of clauses *S* is unsatisfiable if and only if the empty clause [] is derivable from *S*:

$$|\neq S \textit{ iff } |\text{-} []$$

Given a set of formulae *F*:

1. transform *F* into a set of clauses *S*.
2. find a new resolvent of the pair of clauses in *S* and add them to *S*.
3. if [] is produced then stop; *F* is unsatisfiable.
4. if no further resolvent can be produced then stop; *F* is satisfiable; else goto 2.

Unsatisfiability can be reached in finite time.

Satisfiability can be reached if there is a finite set of resolvents in S.

The Proof of a Theorem with Resolution

Prove that *F* is a theorem of the theory *Th*.

1. transform *Th* into the set of clauses *S*.
2. transform $\neg F$ into the set of clauses *C*.
3. Produce $R=S\cup C$.
4. Find the resolvent in *R*.
   a. [] is produced; it follows from this that: *Th* |- *F*
   b. no further resolvent is found; it follows from this that: *Th* |-/ *F*
   c. further resolvents are found; it follows from this that: *Th* |-/ *F*

Observation: Although the proof of Th |- F is semi-decidable in predicate logic, it is decidable for a finite number of resolvents.

16.1 Query by Resolution

We shall demonstrate a query by resolution with the aid of an example.

Example: A Family Database
$M(x)$ means x is a man
$G(x,y)$ means x and y are brothers and or sisters
$B(x,y)$ means x is the brother of y
$F(x,y)$ means x is the father of y

$\forall xyF(x,y)\rightarrow M(x)$
$(\forall xyw)F(x,y)\wedge F(x,w)\rightarrow G(y,w)$
$(\forall xy)G(x,y)\wedge M(x)\rightarrow B(x,y)$
F(george, henry)
F(george,sean)

$F(\text{sean},\text{liz})$

Query: Who is the brother of henry?
$\exists xB(z,\text{henry})$?
Conversion of the axioms to normal form:

1. $\neg F(x,y) \lor M(x)$
2. $\neg F(x,y) \lor \neg F(x,w) \lor G(y,w)$
3. $\neg G(x,y) \lor \neg M(x) \lor B(x,y)$
4. $F(\text{george},\text{henry})$
5. $F(\text{george},\text{sean})$
6. $F(\text{sean},\text{liz})$
7. $\neg B(z,\text{henry})$

In order to carry out resolution we need to carry out substitution. We replace x by george and y by sean in 2.

$\neg F(\text{george},\text{sean}) \lor \neg F(\text{george},w) \lor G(\text{sean},w)$

Resolution with 5 produces:

8. $\neg F(\text{george},w) \lor G(\text{sean},w)$	by 5 & 2 {x/george/,y/sean}
9. $G(\text{sean},\text{henry})$	by 4 & 8 {w/henry}
10. $M(\text{sean})$	by 6 & 2 {x/sean, y/liz}
11. $\neg G(\text{sean},y) \lor B(\text{sean},y)$	by 10 & 3 {x/sean}
12. $B(\text{sean},\text{henry})$	by 9 & 11 {y/henry}
13. []	by 12 & 7

It can be seen from 12 that Sean is the brother of Henry.

Example: given the formula:
$Th = \neg p(a) \land \forall x(p(x) \lor q(f(x)))$
$F = \exists z q(z)$

Prove: Th |- F
We negate F: $\forall z \neg q(z)$ add it to the theory Th and derive the empty set.

1.	$\neg p(a)$	
2.	$p(x) \lor q(f(x))$	
3.	$\neg q(z)$	
4.	$q(f(a))$	Resolvent 1 and 2, substitution x/a
5.	[]	Resolvent 3 and 4, substitution $z/f(a)$

16.1 Exercises for the Topic

1. Negate the following predicate logic clauses and use the resolution principle in order to show contradiction.
   a. $\forall x(p(x) \rightarrow p(x))$

b. $(\neg(\forall x p(x))) \rightarrow \exists x \neg p(x)$
c. $(\forall x(p(x) \wedge q(x)) \rightarrow \forall x p(x) \wedge \forall y q(y))$
d. $\exists x \forall y p(x,y) \rightarrow \forall y \exists x p(x,y)$

2. Given the following set of axioms *Ax* and theorems $t(z)$, show that $Ax \vdash t(z)$. Carry out the proof by means of resolution and determine the value of z.
   a. $p(x) \& q(x,y) \rightarrow t(x)$
   b. $r(y) \& q(y,x) \rightarrow t(x)$
   c. $p(a)$
   d. $q(b,c)$
   e. $t(a)$
   f. $r(b)$

Given the theory:
a. $p(x,y) \leftrightarrow (q(y) \leftarrow q(x))$
b. $q(c) \leftarrow q(b)$
c. $q(b) \leftarrow q(a)$

Prove if $p(a,c)$ is a logical consequence of the theory by means of Resolution.

It is not the size of the task which is decisive but how we approach the understanding of the most small.
- Theodore Fontane -

8 RESOLUTION STRATEGIES

DISADVANTAGES OF THE RESOLUTION PRINCIPLE

- A clause can be produced more than once.
- Clauses which are logically weaker than the existing ones can be derived.
- Clauses can be produced which are not usable later and thus lead to an increase in the number of clauses
- Several clauses can be produced at the same time because the program tries several possibilities at the same time.

Many scientists are trying to find solutions to these problems but as yet without luck! There are numerous simplifications of the resolution principle. The art of building resolution-based theorem provers probably lies foremost in finding a suitable strategy for selecting clauses to resolve with each other. These strategies do not generally, however, achieve the completeness of the general resolution rule.

Below, the most important resolution strategies,[6] for limiting the search space for combinable clauses, are be sketched out in broad brush strokes. We shall study one resolution strategy, namely *SLD resolution,* which is especially suited for application in the Horn clause subset of clausal logic, in more detail.

ELIMINATION OF TAUTOLOGIES

Each clause which contains a literal as well as its negation is eliminated. Such clauses would cause the performing of irrelevant resolutions - they are ultimately universally valid and can not, therefore, contribute to the invalidity of clauses.

"SET-OF-SUPPORT" RESOLUTION

If resolution is controlled by the "set-of-support" rule then the totality of clauses is, firstly, divided into two disjunct sets *T* and *S - T*, such that *S - T* is a satisfiable set of clauses (usually the theory *Th* itself). *T* is then called the set-of-support. Two clauses may only be resolved with each other if at least one of the two clauses is supported by *T* - that is if it is contained in *T* or has a parent clause which is contained in *T*.

---

[6] This list is obviously incomplete.

This strategy preserves completeness (provided that the theory *Th* is really satisfiable). It is also worth noting because it behaves well, preventing anything ensuing on the basis that P and $\neg P$ belong to a contradictory theory (something which can arise unintentionally).

P_1 AND N_1 RESOLUTION

In P_1 resolution, we are concerned with restriction of general resolution such that two clauses can only be resolved with each other if one of them is a positive clause. It is regarded as an extension of the set-of-support form of resolution (a set of all positive clauses is taken as the set-of-support - set-of-support resolution can be used not only on an initial set of clauses but also if at least one clause is positive) and is therefore complete.

Similarly, for N_I Resolution two clauses can only be resolved with each other if one of them is negative. The same comments as for P_1 resolution apply.

P_1 and N_1 Resolution get their own meaning by their relationship to Hyper-resolution.

HYPER-RESOLUTION

The procedure for hyper-resolution is outlined below:

1. Either a single mixed or negative clause, the so-called *Nucleus*, and as many positive clauses, so-called *electrons*, are selected as there are negative literals in the nucleus.
2. These clauses are melded into a single positive clause in one step (hence the name hyper-resolution) in which every negative literal of the nucleus is resolved with one of the literals in one of the electrons.
3. The hyper-resolvents consist thus of the positive literals of the nucleus along with one of the literals of the electrons about which nothing can be resolved.

Hyper-resolution is, really, just an efficient variant of P_1 resolution (the same is true of so-called negative Hyper-resolution which is similarly related to N_1 resolution). Hyper-resolution is, therefore, a similarly complete procedure.

INPUT RESOLUTION

In input resolution the restriction which applies is that at least one of the clauses to be resolved must be a non-derived (so-called *input clause*) clause.

As the following example shows, input resolution is incomplete:

$$\{P \vee Q, P \vee \neg Q, \neg P \vee Q, \neg P \vee \neg Q\}$$

It is not possible to use input resolution to decide (just P and $\neg P$ or Q and $\neg Q$ are derivable, but not both as none of them are input clauses). Input resolution is, however, complete for sets of Horn clauses.

Input resolution is compatible with the set of support rule, i.e., a combination of set of support and input resolution does not produce any strengthening of incompleteness.

Under ordered input resolution a further restriction is imposed, namely, that disjunctions are presented in a given order (from left to right) for resolution.

LINEAR RESOLUTION

Linear resolution is an extension of input resolution in which two clauses can only be resolved with each other if at least one of them is an input clause or has already been presented for resolution.

Linear resolution is complete and compatible with the set-of-support rule (even if additional ordering criteria are imposed).

ENTITY RESOLUTION

In entity Resolution, two clauses can only be resolved with each other if at least one is an entity clause (a resolvent always has fewer literals than the longest of its parent clauses - each step of resolution therefore appears to get nearer to the goal of the derivation).

This constraint clearly entails the loss of completeness, but it is worth noting that it is complete for sets of Horn clauses.

A weakening of entity resolution is possible by not carrying out entity resolution in exclusivity but in preference.

SUBSUMPTION RESOLUTION

Each of the clauses C_1 subsumed by C_2 is taken from the set of clauses to be considered for resolution. The following definition is hence true:

Definition: a clause C_1 subsumes a clause C_2 if there is a substitution θ such that:

$$C_1\theta \subseteq C_2$$

If the empty clause can be derived with the help of C_2 then it can also be done - in no more than a similar amount of time - for C_1.

Two forms of subsumption are usually distinguished:

- *forwards subsumption*: in this form newly derived clauses which are subsumed by an existing clause (i.e., an input or derived clause) are eliminated.
- *backwards-subsumption*: in this form all existing clauses which are subsumed by a newly derived clause are eliminated.

In order to avoid the repeated elimination of the same clause a newly derived clause is checked to establish if, by forwards subsumption, it can be eliminated before any other clauses are eliminated by backwards subsumption.

Topic 17

SLD Resolution

SLD Derivation

In introducing SLD derivation[7] we must, once again, extend our descriptive apparatus.

Definition: *Calculation rule BR*
A calculation rule determines which literal of a query is selected.

G_i is a goal clause: $\leftarrow A_l, A_m, \ldots, A_k$ and C_{i+1} a Horn clause: $A \leftarrow B_i, \ldots B_n$ and *BR* is, in addition, a calculation rule. The goal G_{i+1} is derived from G_i and C_{i+1} by the unifier $\theta_{i=1}$ if it is true that:

1. A subgoal A_m was selected by *BR* from G_i.
2. If A_m and A are equal (match) a more general unifier θ_{i+1} results for A_m and A.
3. G_{i+1} is the new goal:
   $\leftarrow (A_l, \ldots A_{m-1}, B_1, \ldots, B_n, A_{m+1}, \ldots, A_k)\theta_{i+1}$

The following is obviously true for such a triple (G_{i+1}, G_i, C_{i+1}):

G_{i+1} is a resolvent of G_i and C_{i+1}.

Definition: *SLD derivation*
P is a program, *G* a goal and *BR* a calculation rule. An SLD derivation of $P \cup G$ with respect to BR consists of a (finite or infinite) series:
$<G_0;C_0>, <G_1;C_1>, \ldots, <G_{n-1};C_{n-1}>, <G_n;C_n>$

in which G_{i+1} is a resolvent of G_i and a clause C_{i+1} from *P* with θ_{i+1} via BR.

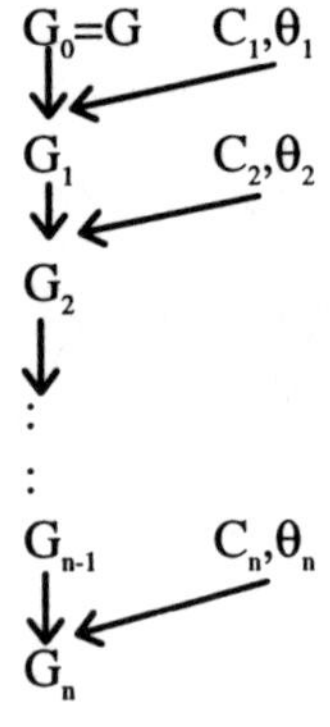

Fig. 8.1: SLD Derivation

[7] The acronym SLD stands for linear resolution with a selection function for definite clauses

SLD derivation is finite if the corresponding sequence of goals is finite and otherwise infinite. If an SLD derivation of $P \cup \{G\}$ via BR is finite and it ends in G_n then we write:

$$P \cup \{G\} \vdash_R G_n$$

For example, given the following logic program:

A_1 $p(a)$:-
A_2 $p(b)$:-
A_2 $p(a)$:- $q(a)$.
A_4 $q(X)$:- $p(X)$.

the query:

G_0 :- $q(a),p(b)$.

and the calculation rule:

BR: chose the left literal in the goal

The SLD derivation for the program given, for the query and selection rule is therefore:

G_0 :- $q(a),p(b)$
C_0 $q(X)$:-$p(X)$. ; with A_4
θ_0 $\{x/a\}$

G_1 is the resolvent of G_0 and the clause K_0 with θ_0 as unifier.
G_1 :- $p(a),p(b)$.
C_1 $p(a)$. ; with A_1
θ_1 { }
G_2 is the resolvent of G_1 and clause C_1 with θ_1 as unifier.
G_2 :-$p(b)$.
C_2 $p(b)$. ; with A_2
θ_2 { }

G_3 is an empty clause. The resolvent of the query G_2 and the clause C_2 with the unifier
G_3 []

The series
G_0 :-$q(a),p(b)$.
G_1 :-$p(a),p(b)$.
G_2 :-$p(b)$.
G_3 []

is thus the SLD derivation with respect to the given facts, selection rule and the query.

Three possibilities arise in SLD derivation:

1. SLD refutation
   An SLD refutation of $P \cup \{G\}$ with respect to BR is a *finite* SLD derivation which ends with the empty clause or whose last clause is the empty clause:
   $$P \cup \{G\} \vdash_R []$$
   SLD refutation is also known as successful SLD derivation.
2. Failed SLD derivation
   An SLD derivation whose last goal is G_n and not an empty clause and which can not be resolved with a clause from *P*.
3. Infinite SLD derivation
   Derivations which do not end with the empty clause and do not end. For example:

p(*a*):-
p(*b*):-
p(*a*):-*q*(*a*).
q(*x*):- *p*(*x*).

1. G_0 :-*q*(*a*),*p*(*b*). ; leads to success
2. G_0 :-*p*(*c*). ; does not lead to success
3. G_0 :-*q*(*a*). ; leads to an infinite derivation (without *p*(*a*)).

Remarks

- In SLD resolution the variables of the program clause C_i are renamed in order to enable them to be searched by the query G_i.
- The success set *SP* of a program *P* is defined as follows:
  $SP := \{A \in HB(P) | P \cup \{\leftarrow A \vdash_{BR} [], BR$ any desired calculation rule$\}$
- In infinite SLD resolution
  $$G=G_0, G_1, ..., G_n$$
  the composition θ_i of the first single unifiers $\theta_i := \theta_1, \theta_2, ... \theta_n$ $1 \leq i \leq n$, the actual substitution of which is shown for goal G_i as *BR calculated substitution.*
- The substitution restricted to the variables of *G* $\sigma = \theta_n$ *means BR calculated answer substitution* for $P \cup \{G\}$.

For example P is a slowsort program with the query:
```
:- sort(7.5.11.10.nil,y).
```
and BR is a given calculation rule, therefore $\theta = \{y/5.7.10.11.nil\}$ a BR answer substitution.

For example: P is a logic program:
p(X,Y):q(X,Z),r(Z,Y).
q(X,Y):-r(Y,X).
r(a,b).

A possible SLD derivation of the goal :- p(b,X).
G_0 :-p(*b*,*X*).

C_1 $p(X_0,Y_0)$:-$q(X_0,Z_0)$,r(Z_0,Y_0)
θ_0 $\{X_0/b,X/Y_0\}$

G_1 :-$q(b,Z_0),r(Z_0,Y_0)$.
C_1 $q(X_1,Y_1)$:- $r(Y_1,X_1)$.
θ_1 $\{X_1/b,Z_0/Y_1\}$

G_2 :-$r(Y_1,b),r(Y_1,Y_0)$.
C_2 $r(a,b)$.
θ_2 $\{Y_1/a\}$

G_3 :-$r(a,Y_0)$.
C_3 $r(a,b)$.
θ_3 $\{Y_0/b\}$

G_4 []

The composition of the most general unifer or the calculated substitution by this SLD derivation is then:

$\theta_0\theta_1\theta_2\theta_3=\{X_0 b,X/b,X_1/b,Z_0/a,Y_1/a,Y_0/b\}$

17.1 SLD Unsatisfiability

With the aid of the notion of SLD refutation we can now formulate the procedural counterpart for the smallest Herbrand model of a logic program.

SLD resolution is, therefore, a special case of (general) resolution, correct, of course, and, as a special variant (linear-input resolution) suited to Horn clause logic, it is also complete.

The following sentence is therefore true:

Theorem: given a program *P*, a goal *G* and a calculation rule BR.
$P \cup \{G\}$ is unsatisfiable if and only if a SLD refutation exists (cf. Herbrand refutation).

This theorem also means that: if $P \cup \{G\}$ is unsatisfiable then there is a calculation rule BR with:

$$P \cup \{G\} \vdash_R []$$

As a consequence of this result the agreement of the smallest Herbrand model *HM(P)* with the success set *SP* necessarily follows for a given program *P*:
HM(P)=SP

Example:
A_1 $p(X,Z)$:-$p(Y,Z),q(X,Y)$.
A_2 $pp(X,X)$:-

A_3	$q(a,b)$:-
G_0	:-$p(S,b)$
BR	"Select the right literal of the goal"

First Attempt

G_1	:-$p(Y,b),q(S,Y)$	G_0 and A_1 with $\theta_1=\{X/S,Z/b\}$
G_2	:-$p(b,b)$	G_1 and A_3 with $\theta_2=\{S/a,Y/b\}$
G_3	:-$p(Y,b),q(b,Y)$	G_2 and A_1 with $\theta_3=\{X/b,Z/b\}$
G_4	$q(b,Y)$	Failure

Second Attempt

G_1	:-$p(Y,b),q(S,Y)$	G_0 and A_1 with $\theta_1=\{X/S,Z/b\}$
G_2	:-$p(b,b)$	G_1 and A_3 with $\theta_2=\{S/a,Y/b\}$
G_3	:-[]	G_2 and A_2 with answer $S=a$

Theorem: Correctness of SLD resolution
If P is a program, θ an answer substitution for a goal G: :-$A_1, A_2, ..., A_m$ via a calculation rule BR. Then:

1. If every BR calculated answer-substitution is a correct answer substitution,
2. there is a calculation rule BR for every correct answer substitution θ,
3. if $\forall(A_1, A_2, ..., A_m)\theta$ is a logical consequence of the program.

$$P \models \forall(A_1, A_2, ..., A_m)\theta$$

This theorem does not apply if occurs check does not take place in the unification algorithm.

Example:
f-construct($f(T,Y),T$).
bizarre(X):- *f*-construct(X,X).
crazy(X):- bizarre($f(Y,X)$).

G_0	:-crazy(X)
C_0	crazy(X_0):- bizarre($f(Y_0,X_0)$).
θ_0	$\{X_0/X\}$

G_1	:-bizarre($f(Y_0,X)$).
C_1	bizarre(X_1):- *f*-construct(X_1,X_1).
θ_1	$\{X_1/f(Y_0,X)\}$

G_2	:-*f*-construct($f(Y_0,X),f(Y_0,X)$)
C_2	*f*-construct($f(T_1,Y_2),T_1$).
θ_2	$\{f(T_1,Y_2)/f(Y_0,X),T_1/f(Y_0,X)\}$

Unifications algorithms with occurs check report an error.
Unification algorithms without occurs check return "yes".

G_3 []

The answer substitution:
$\theta = \theta_0 \theta_1 \theta_2$
$\theta = \{X_0/X\}\{X_1/f(Y_0,X)\}\{f(T_1,Y_2)/f(Y_0,X),T_1/f(Y_0,X)\}$
$\theta = \{X/Y_2\}$

i.e., every term is crazy as long as it is not true in this model and, therefore, not a logical consequence of the program.

Theorem: Completeness of SLD resolution
If P is a program, G is a goal and BR, like BR' are calculation rules. Then the following is true:

1. If $P \cup \{G\} \vdash_{BR} []$ then $P \cup \{G\} \vdash_{BR'} []$.
2. If σ and σ' employ the calculation rules BR and BR' respectively for calculating answer substitutions then $G\sigma$ is a variant of $G\sigma$'.

This result is immediately obvious as the order in which the subgoals (joined with commutative logical conjunction) of the composite goals are repeatedly reduced to subgoals should be logically unimportant. The only and ultimately important factor is that they combine with a unifier to form a composite goal. Therefore:

$$P \cup \{G\} \vdash_{BR} G_0$$

is written simply as

$$P \cup \{G\} \vdash G_0$$

if the calculation rule BR is either irrelevant or obvious from the context in which the proposition occurs.

With this simplification, the completeness result which has just been mentioned can be heightened:

$$SP = \{A \in HB(P) \mid P \cup \{\leftarrow A\} \vdash_{BR} []\}$$

Although all the correct answers can not be derived, all the correct answers can be produced from the most general unifier. For example:

:-$p(X)$.
$p(f(y))$.
$q(a)$

$\{X/f(a)\}$ is an answer which can not be derived although it is a logical consequence of the program.

$\{p(f(y)),q(a)\} \models p(f(a))$
However, the answer $\{x/f(a)\}$ can be produced from the most general unifier:
$\sigma = \theta\gamma = \{X/f(Y_0)\}\{Y_0/a\} = \{X/f(a)\}$

17.2 SLD Tree

The SLD tree is a structure for a program *P*, a goal *G* and a calculation rule BR; it makes it possible to search all SLD derivations. The SLD tree is inductively defined as follows:

- the root node of the tree is *G*,
- every node of the SLD tree is a (possibly empty) goal,
- if *K* is a node of the tree which shows the query, G_0 and G_1, ..., G_n are the possible resolvents of query G_0 with the program clauses of *P* then the node *K* has exactly *n* successors which are indicated by G_1, ..., G_n.
- nodes with the empty goal [] have no successors,
- the numbers of the clauses which are used in order to produce the resolution stand on the side of the SLD tree.

Each (root) path of the SLD tree therefore corresponds to a derivation from $P \cup G$. We separate these paths into three possible SLD derivations:

A successful branch is one which must be passed through when following a path from the root to a leaf, indicated by an empty clause. These successful branches are SLD refutations. If $P \cup \{G\}$ is unsatisfiable then there is at least one successful branch in the corresponding SLD tree.

The path which does not end at an empty clause is known as a failure path. A never-ending path is that which does not end at a leaf when traced from its root to a great depth.

Although the SLD trees induced for $P \cup \{G\}$ by the various calculation rules have a different nature due to their completely different nature they must agree on the success paths due to theorems about the completeness of SLD resolution.

Example: An SLD tree

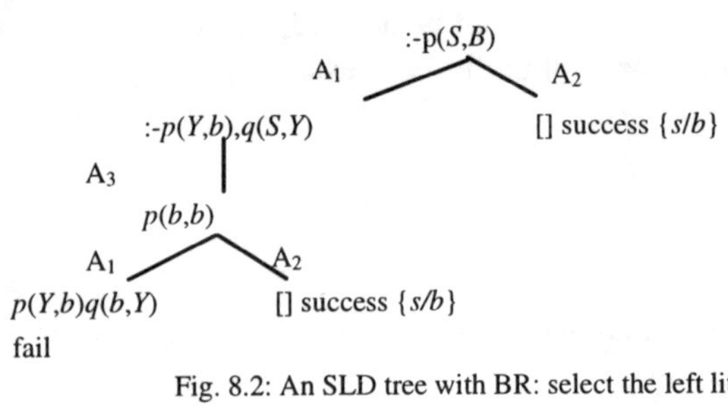

Fig. 8.2: An SLD tree with BR: select the left literal

A_1	$p(X,Z)$:-$p(Y,Z),q(X,Y)$.
A_2	$p(X,X)$:-
A_3	$q(a,b)$:-

G_0 $:\!-p(S,b)$

BR: select the right literal

17.3 Search Rule SR

In order to search for successful paths in a SLD tree, a SLD refutation procedure uses just one particular *search strategy*. In the search rule the order of the execution of the clauses is clearly laid down. A concrete SLD refutation procedure is therefore determined by two parameters: a calculation rule BR and a search strategy for the SLD trees induced by BR.

Example: Given the clauses:

A_1 $p(X,Z):\!-q(X,Z).$

A_2 $p(X,Z):\!-q(X,Y),p(Y,Z).$

A_3 $q(a,b).$

A_4 $q(b,c).$

The query: G_0 $:\!-p(a,z).$

The selection rule BR: "select the left literal",

and the search rule SR: "select the clauses as per their order in the text".

The SLD tree has the following structure:

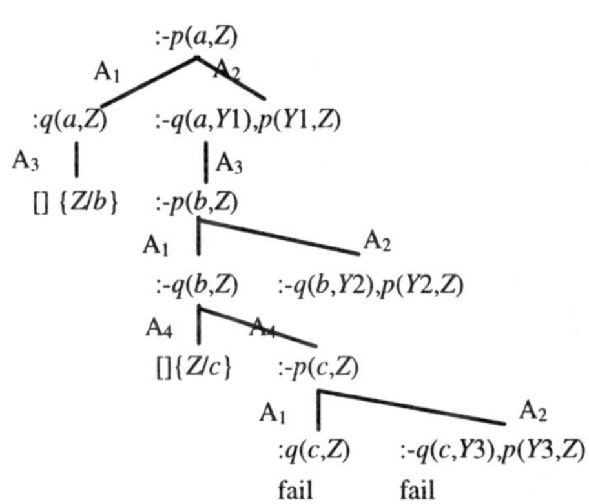

Fig. 8.3: An SLD tree with BR: select the left literal

If, for the above program, instead of using the calculation rule "select the left literal", the rule "select the right literal" is used then the corresponding SLD tree is noticeably different from the previous tree:

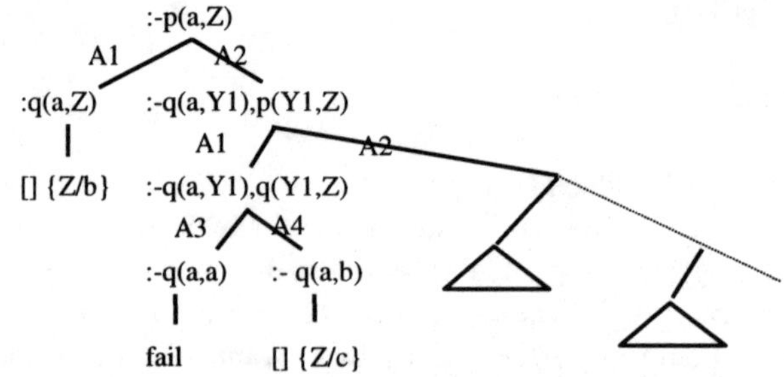

Fig. 8.4: SLD Tree with BR: select the right literal

If clauses A_1 and A_2 are swapped so that the search rule given differs in its selection of clauses from the first example, the following SLD tree is produced:

A_1	*p(X,Z):- q(X,Y),p(Y,Z).*
A_2	*p(X,Z):- q(X,Z).*
A_3	*q(a,b).*
A_4	*q(b,c).*
G_0	*p(a,Z).*

BR: Select the left literal
SR: Select the clauses as per the order in the text

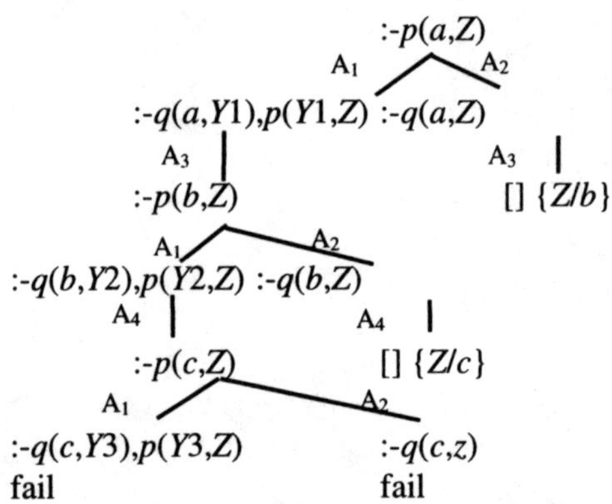

Fig. 8.5: An SLD tree with prescribed SR

Theorem: *P* is a program, *G* a query

- If $P \cup \{G\}$ is unsatisfiable then the SLD tree contains at least one success branch.
- Either every SLD tree for $P \cup \{G\}$ contains infinitely many success branches or every SLD tree contains the same number of success branches **independently** of BR.

The question is, therefore: How are success branches found? This is the reason why we look at search strategies in the next topic.

17.4 Exercises for the Topic

1. Given the following program

```
A1  p(a,b)
A2  p(b,a):- q(a,b).
A3  q(Y,X):- p(X,Y).
```

and the selection rule "select the last literal".

Give the SLD derivations with resolvents and unifiers for the following queries.

```
a.  :-p(a,b),q(b,a).
b.  :-q(a,b).
c.  :-q(b,b).
```

2. Given the program

```
A1  p(a,b).
A2  p(c,b).
A3  p(X,Z):-p(X,Y),p(Y,Z).
A4  p(X,Y):-p(Y,X).
```

the query

```
G   :-p(a,c).
```

a. Give an SLD refutation for $P \cup \{G\}$.

b. Give the composition of the most general unifiers (mgus) with respect to the calculated substitution after SLD refutation.

3. Given the following program

```
ones-and-zeroes(X):- ones(X), zeroes(X).
ones(nil).
ones(1.u.Y):- ones(Y).
zeroes(nil).
zeroes(U.O.Y):- zeroes(Y).
```

a. Show the SLD proof for query G

```
:- ones-and-zeroes(1.0.1.0.nil)
```

and the calculation rule "select the left literal in the goal". Would the proof for "select the right literal" be more efficient?

b. Which of the selection rules is more efficient for the query `ones-and-zeroes(1.2.1.0.nil).`

c. An interpreter can search the arguments of a query. Which calculation rule would you suggest so that both queries can be efficiently processed?

4. A simple program for the reversing the order of a list is:

```
reverse(nil,nil).
reverse(U.X,Y):- reverse(X,W),append(W,U.nil,Y).
append(nil,Z,Z).
append(V.X,Y,V.Z):- append(X,Y,Z).
```

Determine which calculation rule is better for the following query: "select the left literal of the goal" or "select the right literal of the goal".

a. `:-reverse(a.b.c.nil,Y).`
b. `:-reverse(X,c.b.a.nil).`
c. `:-reverse(a.b.c.nil,c.b.a.nil).`

5. For the following programs, use:
BR: "select the right literal in the goal"
SR: "select the clauses as per their order in the text"
Draw the SLD tree for:

a.
```
:-p(a,Z).
p(X,Z):- q(X,Y),p(Y,Z).
p(X,Z):- q(X,Z).
q(a,b).
q(b,c).
```
b.
```
:-p(X).
p(X):- q(X),r(X).q(A).
r(X):-r1(X).
r1(a).
```

6. Given the following program:
```
p(X,Z):-q(X,Y),p(Y,Z).
p(X,X).
q(a,b).
:-p(X,b).
```
Show the SLD tree for the calculation rule:
a. "Select the first left literal in the goal"
b. "Select the first right literal in the goal"
SR: "Select the clauses according to their order in the text"

7. Given the following program with:
BR: "Select the left literal in the goal"
SR: "Select the clauses according to their order in the text"
```
p(Y):-q(X,Y),r(Y).
p(X):-q(X,X).
q(X,X):-s(X).
r(b).
s(b).
:-p(X).
```
Draw the SLD tree.

8. Show a program, a goal and two calculation rules. For one calculation rule the SLD tree should be infinite and for the other finite.

9. *P* is the following program:
```
p(a,b).
```

```
p(c,b).
p(X,Z):-p(X,Y),p(Y,Z).
p(X,Y):-p(Y,X).
```

and the goal `:-p(a,c).`

Show that $P \cup \{G\}$ has no refutation if a clause is dropped regardless of the calculation rule.

To be or not to be, that is
the question.
- William Shakespeare -

9 NEGATION IN LOGIC PROGRAMMING

Definition: Definite clauses and definite program
A definite clause is a clause with exactly one positive literal and null or more negative clauses.

$\forall x(B \lor \neg A_1 \lor A_2, ..., \neg A_n)$

is, for example, a definite clause. These clauses are also called contingent clauses or Horn clauses.

A definite program is a finite set of definite clauses. All other programs are *non-definite programs.*

$P1{:}\ \neg A_1 \lor A_2 \ldots \neg A_n$

is, for example, a non-definite program, consisting of a single non-definite clause.

Definite programs deliver just positive knowledge. This sentence can be explained technically. The knowledge that is contained in the program can be seen as the set of all atomic logical consequences of the program. The simplest example of negative knowledge would be a negated atomic formula (negative literal), e.g., "Joanna does not like Henry". Because of the restricted syntax of definite programming the example can not be expressed in a corresponding program. There is, therefore, no negative literal which is a consequence of the definite program. The reason for this is that the Herbrand basis of a definite programs is always one of program models. This makes for a less interesting model, as all the predicates are inter-related. All negative literals are "untrue" in this model; it can, therefore not be a logical consequence of the program. (A logical consequence of the program is a formula which is true in every model).

Analogously to relational databases, it seems natural to take on board that the relationship between individuals can only hold if they can be derived by the program. This is known as the *closed-world assumption* (CWA) [37] and can be seen as a special class of models. However, not all models of the program are dealt with by this.

Negative information can be represented with the cut operator. Here is an example:

```
if_then_else(p,q,r):- p,!,q.
if_then_else(p,q,r):- r.
```

procedurally, the semantics of this Prolog program is the well-known conditional formula:
if_then_else(p,q,r) iff $(P\wedge q)\vee(\neg p\vee r)$.

Not, however, the declarative:
if_then_else(p,q,r) iff $(p\wedge q)\vee r$.

In conjunction with the fail operator, the combination can also be used as a restricted form of negation, which is characterised by *negation-by-failure*:

The negation *not(q)* of a literal *q* is seen to be proved if *q* is not proved.

The clause then has the form:

P:- ... , *not*(*q*), ...

Obviously only negated tail literals, but not negated head literals, can be treated in this way. It is also evident that the establishment of a closed world assumption based on this form of negation is not allowed.

Clark showed that negation by failure does not have the full power of negation in standard logic. Due to the undecidability of logic, no theorem prover can recognise all the situations in which failure can occur. The deductive power of negation by failure can be strengthened by extending the program.

We shall look at this method in the next topic.

Topic 18

The not Procedure

Both the built-in procedures `cut` and `fail` provide the programmer with a number of possibilities when they are used in combination. Both predicates take no arguments, that is, the success of the goals for `cut` and `fail` is independent of the value of any variables. The `fail` predicate is defined so that it can never be fulfilled as a goal and therefore initiates backtracking. If fail appears after the cut, the backtracking effect is modified by the cut.

With the cut fail combination negation can be represented in a limited form, e.g., if we want to say that "susie likes all animals apart from snakes".

```
likes(susie,X):- snakes(X),!,fail.
likes(susie,X):- animal(X).
```

This combination leads to the definition of the not procedure.

not(Goal) is successfully proved only
 if the Goal subgoal ultimately fails

This definition can be written in Prolog as:

```
not(P):- call(P),!,fail.
not(P).
```

In this definition, the argument *P* is called with the help of the built-in predicate call. The predicate call treats the *P* as a goal and attempts to prove it. If the goal *call(P)* fails then Prolog finds the fact *not(P)* which is always true. Thus the goal *not(P)* is fulfilled if *P* is not provable.

As an example we shall consider a knowledge base in which there is just one fact `test(a)` with queries. The functioning of the not predicate is illustrated by means of the trace protocol:

```
not(P):- call(P),!,fail.
not(P).
test(a).
```

a) Query: `:- not(test(a)).`
Answer: no

```
:- not(test(a)).
      not(test(a))          call; prove not(test(a))
      test(a)               test(a) is a fact
      test(a)               exit; test(a) is in the
                            knowledge base
      cut in not(test(a))       no backtracking
                                of the fail
```

```
        fail            fail, as a main goal,
                        does not succeed
```

b) Query: `:-not(test(b)).`

```
:- not(test(b))
        not(test(b))        call; prove not(test(b))
        test(b)             fail; test(b) is not
                            in the knowledge base
        not(test(b))        call; second rule
        not(test(b))        proof successful
```

The Susie example can also be defined in this way; in it the cut fail combination is replaced by the not predicate:

```
likes(susie,X):- animal(X),not(snake(X)).
```

Remarks on the not predicate

The proof of `not(P)` can lead to false results if `P` contains variables. Let us consider the following knowledge base:

```
smoker(smith).
smoker(miller).
tennisplayer(jones).
notsmoker(X):- not(smoker(X)).
```

and the query about a tennis-playing non-smoker:

```
:- tennisplayer(X), notsmoker(X).
```

produces the expected answer from Prolog, "yes" with "X=jones".

The query about a non-smoking tennis player:

```
:- nonsmoker(X), tennisplayer(X).
```

confuses Prolog returning the answer "no". The goal fails when it is attempted to prove `not`. But it is successful if it is called first, when X is already instantiated. The desired semantics of `not(smoker(X))` is $\exists X \neg smoker(X)$. Instead of this, Prolog calculates $\exists X smoker(X)$. It checks to see if an X exists which is a smoker and negates the result. This results in $\neg\exists X \neg smoker(X)$ or $\neg\forall X \neg smoker(X)$.

If this form of negation is used then careful attention has to be paid to employing *not* only when the variable is already instantiated.

Note what "the goal finally fails" means, in the definition of the not procedure. It means that the SLD tree for the proof of *Goal* must have *a finite depth and breadth* and that all nodes must terminate with failure. The tree should, at least, have one or more failing terminal nodes (*finite failure tree*).

In addition, if the evaluation of Goal is neither successful nor fails, the same applies to the evaluation of not(Goal). In order to show this we shall look at the following facts in the Prolog database.

```
person(chris).
person(bernie).
person(eric).
child-of(bernie, chris).
child-of(eric,chris).
```

For the query

```
:- person(X)., not(child-of(X,chris)).
```

Prolog first performs the `call person(X)` and finds that `X=chris`. This reduces the query to:

```
:-not(child-of(chris,chris)).
```

The sub-call

```
child-of(chris,chris).
```

fails and therefore

```
not(child-of(chris,chris))
```

is proven. Execution terminates with success. After backtracking, we get the second solution `X=bernie` from the sub-call `person(X)` and the query reduces to:

```
:- not(child-of(bernie,chris)).
```

The sub-call `child-of(bernie,chris)` is successfully proven and the call `not(child-of(bernie,chris)` fails. The third solution also fails.

In general, calling not without variables (ground call) poses no problems. If we, for example, begin with the call:

Q `:-not(child-of(X,chris)).`

we must be clear about what we are asking. Here, we are asking if there is an `X` such that `child-of(X,chris)` ultimately fails. The finite-failure rule first formulates the sub-call:

Q'   `:-child-of(X,chris).`

and searches for all `X` for which `child-of(X,chris)` is true. This query delivers two answers. The query *Q* is therefore rendered totally false and we get no answer, although there is an `X`, i.e., `X=chris`. The finite failure rule is, therefore, incomplete if it is used in queries with uninstantiated variables. In the following section we shall look at these problems in more detail.

18.1 Exercises on the topic

1. Why can free variables not appear in "not".

2. Given the following program:

```
likes(Who,What):- not hates(Who,What).
likes(susie,cats).
hates(susie,snakes).
```

   What are the answers to the following queries?

   a. `:-likes(susie,snakes).`
   b. `:-likes(susie,cats).`
   c. `:-likes(Who,cats).`
   d. `:-likes(Who,snakes).`
   e. `:-likes(susie,What).`

Topic 19

Closed World Assumption

A program P contains a certain set of propositions. As in relational databases, it seems natural to assume that the relationship between individuals can hold only if it can be derived from the program. From this, it follows that every declaration q about such a relation is true if and only if p implies q, otherwise q is false. This is known as the closed world assumption (abbreviated to CWA, below) which means that a closed world is assumed and that this world relates to the database. Under the CWA some answers are produced whose opposite can not be proved. If no positive literal can be found for the query then it is assumed that its corresponding negation is true. The database is, as it were, extended to include the negation of all literals which do not appear.

The CWA rule can be represented as an inference rule:

$$\frac{P \not\models A}{\neg A}$$

If it can be concluded that A does not follow from P then $\neg A$ is true - in which A is a ground atom. It should be noted that the CWA is not an inference rule in the traditional sense and that P $\not\models$ A is not a formula of the object language but of the meta-language.

Reasoning with the closed-world assumption is also known as *default inference* and may be seen to be reasoning in the face of unknowns. There are many situations in everyday life as well as in special circumstances, in which reasoning with unknowns is necessary. It serves to extend deductive inference.

As far as logic programming is concerned the main interest lies with the atoms of the Herbrand basis. Let us look at a simple program made up of just a single clause:

```
P1     A:-B.
```

We assume, in addition, that $HB(P)$ is exactly $\{A,B\}$. By the closed world assumption we can conclude that $\neg q$ is true for every atom $q \in HB(P)$ which is not contained in P. That is, a general conclusion because of default inference: we conclude $\neg q$ since nothing allows us to conclude that q is contained in P.

This should be considered from two points of view:

1. We assume that P is free of contradiction else P would necessarily contain q and $\neg q$.
2. We consider the case that q exists as an atom otherwise if in P neither r nor $\neg r$ was implied it would be necessary to conclude $\neg r$ and $\neg\neg r$ by default inference which would, once again, be a contradiction.

Back to the program `P1`, above. As *P* clearly exists it must be free of contradiction and may not imply either *A* or *B*. By this the CWA allows us to conclude ¬*A* and ¬*B*. Generally, the combination of *P* with default inference as *CWA*(*P*) is defined as:

$$CWA(P)=P\cup\{q\in HB(P) \text{ and } not\ P \models q\}$$

For the program `P1` means:

$$CWA(P1)=\{A\text{:-}B,\neg A,\neg B\}$$

Figure 9.1 shows how *CWA*(*P*) is composed of its components *P* and *HB*(*P*).

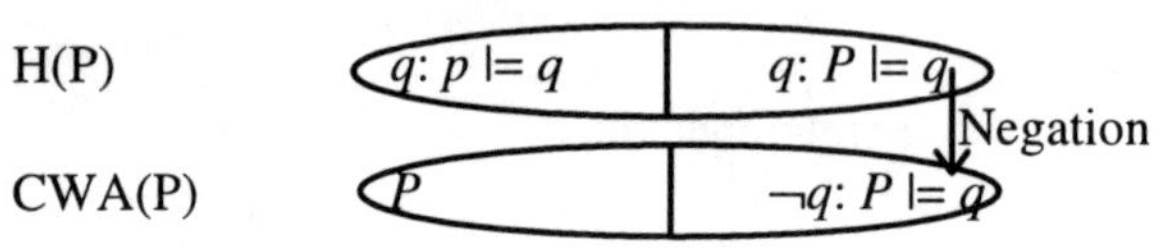

Fig. 9.1 Use of the closed world assumption

After defining the expression "closed world assumption", attention is now paid to the correctness and completeness of the proof procedure with respect to negative information.

Assuming we wish to create and query a database P, with entries for all the tenants of a house "h" (which are known) - "miller" and "smith". The simplest way to record the information is:

```
tenant(h1,miller).
tenant(h1,smith).
```

In the open world assumption there is no reason to conclude that, for example, "jones" is not a tenant of *h*1. Nothing is stated to exclude this possibility. However, in the closed world assumption the database specifies fully who is and who is not a tenant and it is possible to conclude: ¬tenant(*h*1,jones).

Relational databases are restricted. It is, therefore, always possible to check, in finite time, whether or not a given tuple is contained in the database. In the case of unambiguous programs the Herbrand basis can be infinite. It can be proved that the problem of whether or not a given atomic formula is a logical consequence of the program is decidable. In other words there are no general algorithms which for any given unambiguous program and atom can answer the question in a limited amount of time.

The question is then how soundness can be formulated with respect to logical consequence. Soundness for the derivation of positive inferences in *the open world assumption* (*OWA*) can be formulated as follows:

$$\forall q \in HB(P), P \models q \text{ if } P \vdash_{OWA} q$$

Here soundness of $\vdash_{OWA}$ (derived from) with respect to program *P* is shown. Which logical construct can the soundness of negative inferences in the closed world assumption be related to? One possibility is the CWA(*P*).

$$\forall q \in HB(P),\ CWA(P) \models \neg q \text{ if } p \vdash_{CWA} \neg q$$

A particular problem is: if *P* is given, it is not possible for the CWA(*P*) be immediately produced since it is not possible to determine which particular negative facts $\neg q$ are contained in it - they must all be derived. A further problem is the fact that CWA(*P*) is free of contradiction if *P* is infinite otherwise it is very likely to be contradictory.

Let us consider a program *P* which consists of just one clause:

```
A or B
```

In this case CWA(*P*)={*A* or *B*,¬*A*,¬*B*} which is contradictory. For this reason the CWA can not be used under all circumstances. In the following we shall use default inference in an indefinite program and derive the satisfiability criteria.

19.1 Exercises on the Topic

1. Construct the CWA(P) for each of the sets of clauses *P* and determine whether or not they are consistent. Assume HB(*P*)={derek,chris}.
   a. likes(chris,*X*):- likes(derek,*X*).
   b. likes(chris,*X*):- likes(*X*,chris).
   c. likes(derek,*X*):- likes(*X*,chris).
   d. likes(derek,*X*).
   likes(*X*,chris).
   e. ¬likes(derek,derek).
   likes(*X*,derek):- likes(chris,*X*).
   likes(chris,*X*).

Topic 20

Negation as Failure

The closed world assumption is not valid in all cases. A solution lies in a weakening of the applicability of the CWA. In practice, this means restricting the CWA to those formulae F of the Herbrand basis HB(P) of a definite program, for which the proof search with SLD resolution can be seen to have failed after a finite number of steps.

Definition: P is a definite program and G a goal. If the SLD tree $T(P,G)$ for $P \cup \{G\}$ satisfies the two following conditions:

1. $T(P,G)$ contains only finite paths and
2. none of the nodes of $T(P,G)$ is the empty clause []

then we call the SLD derivation for $P \cup \{G\}$ "finite failure" and write:

$$P \cup G \;|\!\!-\!/_{\text{SLD}}\; []$$

The finite failure set $FF(P)$ of P is thus the following set of goals:

$$FF(P) := \{A \in HB(P) \mid P \cup \{\leftarrow A\} \;|\!\!-\!/_{\text{SLD}}\; []\}$$

Due to the completeness and soundness of SLD resolution the following is obviously true for a given program P and every formula $A \in HB(P) \cap FF(P)$:

- $P \models\!\!\!\!/\; A$ and
- the SLD tree for $P \cup \{A\}$ contains only finite or failed branches.

The above also applies to all SLD trees of $P \cup \{A\}$and is, therefore, independent of the concrete calculation rule. The actual investigation as to whether the given formula $A \in HB(P)$ is a logical consequence of P occurs when the prover attempts the goal $\leftarrow A$. Two cases can, therefore, be distinguished:

1. $A \in FF(P)$ in which case the SLD tree for A can be read off, a failed SLD derivation took place, "no" was given as an answer and by the CWA $\neg A$ was concluded or
2. all the SLD trees contain at least one infinite branch which was being searched through by the system at that time.

Example: The loves Program

```
loves(X,Y):- mother(X), child-of(Y,X).
loves(john,tom).
loves(maria,john).
mother(maria).
```

```
child-of(tom,maria).
```

From this program `loves(john,maria)` can not be derived. The SLD tree for the query `:- loves(john,maria)` is infinite and does not constitute a successful path. It follows, from the completeness of SLD resolution, that `loves(john,maria)` is not a logical consequence of the program. Therefore, the atom is not in the Herbrand model and it is, therefore, possible to conclude ¬`loves(john,maria)` by the CWA rule.

For the query `:-loves(X,maria)` the answer "yes" is produced. In other words: "no one loves Maria".

For the goal `:-loves(X,john)` the goal `:-loves(X,john)` leads to success with the answer `X=maria`. However, this is insufficient to be able to conclude that there is no one whom John does not love, for example, Thomas does not love John.

The process sketched out is the well-known negation by failure rule (abbreviated to NF-rule below). It is a modified form of CWA for definite programs. This rule leads to queries which contain negative literals. Such a query is called a *normal goal,* as it is in the logic programming literature. Similarly, a logic program which contains negative literals as clause premises is known as a *normal program.*

The NF- rule can be summarised as an inference rule:

$$\frac{:\text{-}\ A_1, \ldots\ A_{i\text{-}1}, \neg A_i, \ldots\ A_{i+1} A_n \qquad\qquad :\text{-}\ A_i\ \textit{ultimately fails with P}}{:\text{-}\ A_1, \ldots\ A_{i\text{-}1}, A_{i+1}, \ldots\ A_n}$$

As for the CWA-rule it is really a meta-inference rule. In the special case (n=1) it has the effect of deriving ¬*A* from the program *P*, although no negative literals are a logical consequence of a definite program. This moves the problem of logical meaning to the NF-rule.

Informally, the rule states the following; if a path of an SLD tree which proves a ground clause A is finite and leads to a fail then ¬*A* is valid. This rule provides the basis for negation in logic programming. It can be proved: if a definite program *P* implies ¬*A* then ¬*A* can be derived from a program *P** which is the completion of *P*. *P** is the Clark completed program and is indicated with *comp*(*P*). In general terms *comp*(*P*) is produced from *P* by replacing "implication" → by "bi-implication" ↔.

The NF-rule is not always valid. If we assume that *P* means "either *A* or *B* is true", i.e., $P=\{A \vee B\}$ The query ¬*A* can not be proved in *P*. All the possible branches which prove *A* are finite and lead to an untrue "fail". Therefore ¬*A* is true. Similarly ¬*B* can not be proved. But, the set $\{A \vee B, \neg A, \neg B\}$ is inconsistent.

This raises the problem of the soundness of the NF-rule, which will be treated later.

20.1 Completion of a Definite Program

With the help of the NF-rule, the negations of a normal program (a program with negative literals in the clause premise) can be processed. In this way, it is always possible to make conclusions about absent information but not however about negative information itself. The reason for this is, of course, that definite programs (programs with Horn clauses) contain no bi-implication. In order to be able to give the NF-rule a logical meaning too then the definite program must be completed.

An alternative suggestion for formalising the CWA was proposed by K. Clark. The definite program P is extended to a theory P* = comp(*P*) in which the conditions given by the definite program as *necessary* for the satisfiability of the predicates concerned are transformed into *adequate* conditions. The inferences of the NF-rule are then logical consequences of comp(*P*).

In the following, we show the transformation in propositional and predicate logic.

Program Completion in Propositional Logic

In the case of propositional logic the construction is especially easy.

1. Given the program *P* which consists of a set of clauses of the form $q \leftarrow body$.
2. For every *q* which occurs in the body but is not defined in *P* then construct $\neg q$.
3. Transform all *q* of the form below which are defined in *P*:
   $q \leftarrow \text{body}_1$
   .
   .
   .
   $q \leftarrow \text{body}_n$
   to the sentence
   $q \leftrightarrow (\text{body}_1 \vee \ldots \vee \text{body}_n)$

The resultant *comp*(*P*) exactly contains the completed forms of all the defined relations in *P*.

For example: *P* is a program:

$A \leftarrow B$

The comp(*P*) consists of the sentences:

$\neg B$

$A \leftrightarrow B$

The program P implies neither A nor B. The comp(P) however implies both $\neg A$ and $\neg B$, which corresponds exactly to the result which we would have obtained from the CWA. For CWA(P), however, we must define $\neg A$ explicitly, but not in comp(P).

In certain cases both constructions produce different results.

For example: P is the program:

$A \leftarrow A$

in which CWA(P) implies $\neg A$ whilst comp(P) does not.

Example: P is the program:

$A \leftarrow \neg B$

The CWA(P) implies both $\neg A$ and $\neg B$ and is therefore inconsistent whilst *comp*(P) is consistent and implies $\neg B$ but not $\neg A$.

Example: P is the program:

$A \leftarrow \neg A$

The CWA(P) is consistent and implies no negative fact whilst *comp*(P) is consistent and implies everything.

Program Completion in Predicate Logic

The construction of *comp*(P) for a definite program P is somewhat more difficult in predicate logic.

P is an n-place predicate of the normal program P.

1. Firstly n *new* variables $x_1, \ldots, x_n$ are introduced. With the help of these variables and an equality relation (still to be specified) "=" all of the clauses belonging to the predicate
   $p(t_1, \ldots, t_n) \leftarrow L_1, \ldots, L_m$
   are transformed into a (predicate logic) formula
   $p(x_{1,} \ldots, x_n) \leftarrow \exists y_1, \ldots, \exists y_{yd}((x_1 = t_1), \ldots, (x_n = t_n), \ L_1, \ldots, L_m)$
   in which $y_1, \ldots, y_d$ signify the variables of the original clause.
2. All K-clauses for the predicate p are used in the form
   $p(x_1, \ldots, x_n) \leftarrow B_1$
   .
   .

$p(x_1 ..., x_n) \leftarrow B_k$
in which B_1 is of the pattern
$\exists y_1, ..., \exists y_d((x_1=t_1), ..., (x_n=t_n), L_1, ..., L_m)$

3. In this formula implication is replaced by bi-implication and combined into a single formula.
   $\forall x_1, ..., \forall x_n(p(x_1 ..., x_n) \leftrightarrow B_1 \vee ...\vee B_1 \vee ...\vee B_k)$
4. If a predicate q appears in the clause premises which is not defined by a clause then the formula
   $\forall x_1, ..., \forall x_n \neg q(x_1, ..., x_n)$
   should be incorporated.

If all the predicates of *P* are treated in the manner indicated the conversion to a predicate logic theory comp(*P*) is, in principle, complete and only the "=" relation remains to be defined.

For example: *P* is a definite program:
loves(x,y)←mother(x),child_of(y,x)
loves(john,thomas)
loves(maria,john)
mother(maria)
child_of(thomas,maria)

1. Introduction of new variables for the predicate loves:
   loves(x_1,x_2)←$\exists x \exists y$mother(x_x=x,x_2=y,mother(x),child_of(y,x)
   loves(x_1,x_2)←x_1=john,x_2=thomas
   loves(x_1,x_2)←x_1=maria,x_2=john
2. Combining into a single formula
   loves(x,y)←[$\exists x \exists y$(x_1=x,x_2=y,mother(x),child_of(y,x))∨x_1=john,x_2=thomas,∨x_1 =maria,x_2=john]
3. Replacement of ← with ↔:
   loves(x,y) ↔ [...]
4. Steps 1 .. 3 for the other predicates
   mother(x_1,)↔x_1=maria
   child_of(x_1,x_2)↔x_1=maria,x_2=thomas

The predicate symbol "=" now needs to be defined and identity theory formulated. It is sufficient to refer to the Herbrand universe. The Herbrand universe is infinite in many cases and, therefore, the corresponding definition of "=" is also. We prefer a finite definition. Clark used a set of axioms which are known as *Clark's equality theory* (*CET*) and are defined as:

1. $c \neq c'$ — for constants c, c'
2. $f(x_1, ... x_n) \neq g(y_1, ... y_m)$ — for functors f, g
3. $f(x_1, ... x_n) \neq c$
4. $f(..., x, ...) \neq x$

5. $f(x_1, ..., x_n) \neq f(y_1, ..., y_m) \rightarrow x_i \neq y_i$
6. $f(x_1, ... x_m) = f(y_1 ... y_m) \rightarrow x_1 = y_1 \wedge ... x_m = y_m$
7. $x=x$
8. $x=y \rightarrow y=x$
9. $(x=y) \wedge (y=z) \rightarrow (x=z)$
10. $p(x_1, ..., x_m) \rightarrow p(y_1, ..., y_m) \wedge x_1 = y_1 \wedge ... \wedge x_m = y_m$

These definitions can be understood as follows:

1. Different constants relate to different objects.
2. Different functions produce different objects.
3-4. Datastructures always produce new objects.
5-6. Constructed objects are equal if the are made up of (un)equal components.
7-10. Standard equivalence axioms.

These definitions also define the basis of the unification algorithm. In sentences 1-3 the non-unifiability of constants and functions symbols, due to mismatch, are treated. Sentence 4 corresponds to non-unifiability due to occurs check failure. Sentence 5 corresponds to the non-unifiability of terms if some components can not be unified. Sentences 6-10 correspond to the conditions under which terms are unifiable.

The completion of a program *P* over a given Herbrand universe is defined as a unification of the completed definitions with the associated equivalence theory:

$$\text{comp}(P) := \text{IFF}(P) \cup \text{Eq}(HU, P)$$

such that the definite program *P* is transformed into a new set of axioms comp(*P*) with a different semantics (different class of models). The justification for this construction is the psychological argument that the programmer really means “if and only if” (iff) when using “if “ in a program. Even if this is not so nothing is changed, as long as the goals do not contain negative literals.

The completion of a definite program *P* retains “positive knowledge” represented by *P*. From the construct IFF(*P*) and eq(*P*) it follows that comp(*P*) $\models$ *P* so that if *A* is a logical consequence of *P* then it is also a logical consequence of comp(*P*). According to the soundness of SLD resolution, the computed answer for θ for a definite goal $\leftarrow B$ is also a logical consequence $B\theta$ of comp(*P*). In other words: the computed answers are also sound for the iff version of the definite program.

20.2 Soundness of the NF-rule

Our general discussions of the CWA and NF rules hint that the use of these rules can soon lead to inconsistencies. For this reason, it is necessary to be clear about the use of the not predicate, in order to avoid inconsistency. As a normal goal[8] is treated differently by a definite program, from a normal program we treat this separately. The difference lies in the fact that the resolution of normal programs can produce new negative subgoals.

Theorem: *Soundness of the NF rule*
P is a definite program, *G* a definite goal of the form $\leftarrow A_1, A_2, ..., A_m$ and a calculation rule BR.

- If the SLD system eventually fails when proving *G* with BR then the negation of *G* can be deduced from comp(*P*):
  comp(*P*) $\vdash \forall\neg(A_1, ... A_m)$
- If the system produces a proof with the answer σ then this answer is sound with respect to comp(*P*), i.e.:
  comp(*P*) $\vdash \forall(G\sigma)$

This theory is especially important for *m*=1, as it makes the composition of SLD resolution possible with the NF rule. The subgoal L_k selected by the calculation rule BR from a normal goal $\leftarrow L_1, ... L_k, ... L_n$ is treated as follows:

- if L_k is a positive literal then standard resolution is used.
- if L_k is a negative literal of the form $\neg A$ and $\leftarrow A$ eventually fails then $\neg A$ is proved and the next goal of the sequence is $\leftarrow L_1, ... L_{k-1}, L_{k+1}, ... L_n$.

Let us consider the loves program and the goal:
```
:- loves(X,Y),¬mother(X).
```

The Prolog system produces the answer `X=john, Y=thomas`. Since the NF rule is sound the answer is sound, i.e.:

comp(*p*) |= loves(john,thomas) ∧ ¬mother(john).

Note that we have not suggested a method to check whether or not the SLD tree for a given goal is finite. We have also said nothing about the nature of the calculation rule which gives us sound answers. In the above example the selection of "first literal on the left" as employed in Prolog systems, will suffice for this purpose. This is not sufficient, however, in all cases in which the SLD tree for a goal fails with one calculation rule in finite time and in infinite time with another. In theory, the problem can be solved by a restriction on the calculation rule. The most widely known constraints on the calculation rule are the *safe calculation rule* and the *fair calculation rule*.

---

[8] That is a conjunction of a finite number of possibly negative literals formulated with the vocabulary induced in *P*.

The inclusion of *finite failure* in the SLD proof procedure under the assumption of the safe and fair calculation rules is called the *SLDNF inference system* (SLD extended with the NF rule).

The Safe Calculation Rule

The safe calculation rule ensures that the NF rule behaves correctly. The constraints are:

- all global variables of *L* must be instantiated before the evaluation of `not(L)` (with the help of positive conditions).
- an instantiated `not(L)` which has been selected must be fully evaluated before a further goal from the literal can be selected.
- the proof of `not(L)` can not instantiate any variables of L (as a side effect).

Example: the Person Program

```
person(chris).
person(bernie).
person(eric).
child_of(bernie,chris).
child_of(eric,chris).
```

The query `:-person(X),¬child_of(X,chris)` fails with the answer `X=chris, X=bernie, X=eric.`

In this query `person(X)` is placed `before ¬child_of(X,chris).` Thus as the negative literal is instantiated before its call, it fails.

The query `:-¬child_of(X,chris)` fails, eventually, but without an answer. This indicates that the inference system is *not complete*. We can eliminate incompleteness by adding the negative literal to the program as a clausal premise.

Let us assume that we add the definition of `parents_of` and `childless` to the program:

```
parents_of(Y):- ¬childless(Y).
childless(Y):- ¬child_of(X,Y).
```

and begin the query `:-parents_of(Y).` We receive the answer "yes" without any binding for Y, i.e., the answer is *false* and the NF rule is sound. In fact, the answer is not false but the intuitive interpretation of the query is not correct. The semantics of not is obviously:

- $p(x) \leftarrow \neg q(x)$ means $\forall x p(x) \leftarrow \neg q(x)$
- $p(x) \leftarrow \neg q(y)$ means $\forall x p(x) \leftarrow \neg \exists y q(y)$
  $\equiv \forall y \forall x p(X) \leftarrow \neg q(y)$

$\equiv \forall x p(x) \leftarrow \exists y \neg q(y)$

Let us see what occurs when we start the query `:-child_of(X,chris),person(X).`
Using the safe calculation rule only `person(X)` can be selected which produces the correct answer `X/chris`. By backtracking, we get two correct answers and an eventual failure. If we had originally chosen `child_of(X,chris)` then we would not have had an answer at all.

Let us once more consider the query `:-parents_of(Y)` but, this time, with a safe calculation rule. The execution produces an uninstantiated, negative subgoal `:-¬childless(Y)`, from which no further subgoal can be selected. In this situation, we say that the execution *floundered*. The execution must be terminated without any explanation of the answer. At the least this result prevents us from computing incorrect answers.

Soundness is also eventually violated in that only solutions for the negated literal produce variable bindings in the goal clause. However, as no proof for a goal can be found in which all variables are quantified, there is also no logical justification for the fact that failure does not arise.

Example: For the Persons program the query: `child_of(X,Y),person(Y)`
would appear as the SLDNF tree in Fig. 9.2 under a secure calculation rule:

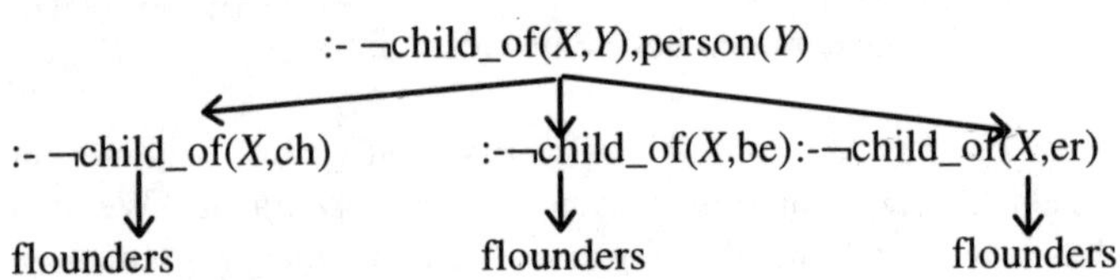

Fig. 9.2: An SLDNF Tree

Note: The calculation rule here is "secure first literal on the left", i.e., only secure subgoals are selected and then, of these, the first literal on the left. In the step given, the rule jumps over ¬call and selects the person literal. For the strict interpretation of "first literal on the left", the calculation always results in floundering.

Secure calculation rules are not easy to implement, as the variable bindings of the candidates must be monitored, in order to decide whether or not they may be selected. Few Prolog systems implement the secure condition. Instead of this, they leave it to the programmer to order the calls, so that they are ideally suited for the standard calculation rule.

The Fair Calculation Rule

Fairness means that all the literals of a goal (or subgoal) are selected within a given amount of time. If a goal has a finitely failed SLD tree for a calculation rule then every fair calculation rule also has a finitely failed SLD tree.

The Prolog calculation rule is obviously not fair. The atom selected is searched by a depth-first search method and other goals are not selected until the goal chosen is fully computed. If a subgoal runs into an infinite loop then no other goals are ever selected.

A simple example program is a one-clause program:

```
q:- r,q.
```

The query `:- q` fails finitely under the standard Prolog rule, whereas under the "right literal" it gets stuck in a loop and fails *ad infinitum.*

In practice, serious efficiency problems are caused by the implementation of the fair calculation rule. On the other hand, using the unfair calculation rule does not result in any great danger of producing incorrect answers. Calculations with unfair rules can get stuck in loops, whilst a fair rule terminates. A looping calculation produces no answer. A program which is in an endless loop can be transformed into an equivalent program which terminates under the Prolog calculation rule.

20.3 Completeness of the SLDNF Rule

Completeness means that every correct answer can be found. *P* is a definite program :- *A* is a normal goal and θ a substitution such that *A*θ is a logical consequence of comp(*P*). The question is if θ can always be produced by SLDNF resolution. The answer is no, as the following example will show:

```
teacher(john).
student(tom).
enrols_lectures(X):- student(X).
```

The completion of this program describes the situation only if students enrol for lectures. The question if there are any people who enrol for lectures, can not be answered by SLDNF resolution. Let us consider the goal `:-` `¬select_lectures(Y)`. As it contains a negative literal we consider the goal `:- select_lectures(Y)`. This goal is successful, with the answer `Y=thomas` such that `:-¬select_lectures(Y)` produces no answer. On the other hand the answer `Y=john` is correct as `:-select_lectures(Y)` is successful and indicates that `¬select_lectures(Y)` is the logical consequence of comp(P). The reason lies in the fact that the NF rule is really just a test. It is not resolution in the classical sense. The rule checks to see if a negated literal is a logical consequence of the completed program. As this checking refers to a predicate, the other predicates can not be tested.

20.4 Normal Programs with Normal Goals

In real world formulations, negation does not just occur in the query but also in the clause premises. The construction of an answer is more problematic than for Horn clause programs. The reason for this is that the processing of a negative goal can lead to the production of negative subgoals. This can lead to nested negation whose semantics are lost. Let us consider the following program:

```
p(a,b).
p(x,y)←¬p(y,x)
```

A program with such a rule is called a normal program. Stated more precisely a normal clause is a clause of the form $q \leftarrow L_1, \ldots L_n$ in which $n \geq 0$, q is an atom and $L_1, \ldots L_n$ are positive or negative literals. A normal program is a finite set of such clauses.

Unfortunately the completion of a normal program can be inconsistent, i.e., it is possible for the completion to have no model, as in the case of this program. The completion of this program:

$a \neq b$ (unique name assumption)
$\forall u, v(p(u,v) \leftrightarrow (u=a \wedge v=b) \vee \neg p(v,u))$

is inconsistent as for $u=v=a$ the contradiction
$p(a,a) \leftrightarrow \neg p(a,a)$ follows.
A program which contains a negation is not a construct of classical logic. However, there are suggestions in the literature for handling this problem.

The problem arises if we investigate the soundness of the SLDNF. We would like the following:

$\forall q \in HB(P)$:-q successful under SLDNF if comp(P) $\models q$
:- q successful under SLDNF if comp(P) $\models \neg q$

This result is actually correct if P is a definite program. Unfortunately, it is not generally correct if P is a normal program. Even this idealised requirement is insufficient, for two reasons. Firstly, it is possible that comp(P) is inconsistent in itself. In this case it is not relevant what we derive (everything is derivable). Secondly, in order to be able to declare that it is successful under SLDNF, we must state under which safe calculation rule. We are not in a position to specify this rule. A fair rule is also difficult to come by. Therefore, the mathematical treatment of SLDNF is not as expressive as is the case for SLD.

One method for securing consistency is to insist on the fact that *P* has the so-called *call-consistent* characteristic. The simplest way to define this is by means of a *dependency graph.* It is a directed graph of the following form:

- the nodes on the graph are the predicate symbols of *P*.
- for every clause in *P* of the form *p*:- ..., *q*, ... the graph has an arc annotated with "+" from node *p* to node *q*.
- for every clause in *P* of the form *p*:- ,¬*q*, ... the graph has an arc annotated with "-" from node *p* to node *q*.

P is call consistent if and only if its dependency graph has no loops with uneven numbers of "-" nodes. This characteristic actually guarantees that no predicate symbol *p* and ¬*p* are directly or indirectly defined in *P* which, furthermore, guarantees the consistency of *comp*(*P*). In practice, this restriction is always appropriate.

Example: The dependency graph of two programs:

```
a)      p(X):- ¬q(X)                b)      p(X):- q(X).
        p(X):- q(X), r(X), p(X).            q(X):-¬p(X).
        r(X).                               q(X):- q(X).
```

is shown schematically in Fig. 9.3. The first graph is, clearly, call-consistent and the second is not.

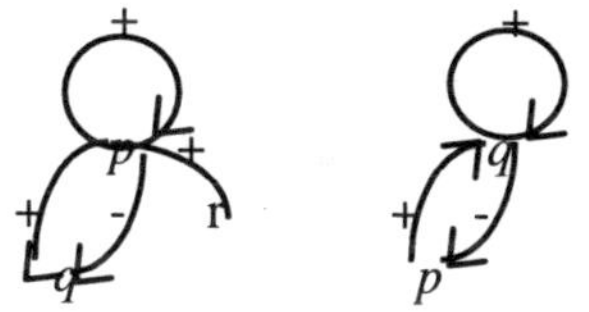

Fig. 9.3: Dependency Graph

It is also useful to restrict the class of permitted queries. We do not permit queries which prove a predicate *y*(...) and ¬*y*(...). We formalise the class of permitted queries as follows. Presume that the dependency graph contains a path of nodes *x* to *y*. If this path has an even number of "-" then we say that: "*x* depends positively on *y*" otherwise "*x* depends negatively on *y*". If *Q* is a query then we say: *P* is *strictly* related to *Q* if and only if

- *Q* does not contain a call for *y*(...) and ¬*y*(...);
- *Q* contains the call for either *x*(...) or ¬*x*(...), in which case there are no nodes in the dependency graphs *y* such that *x* positively and negatively depends on *y*.

Example: *P* is a program:

```
p:- ¬q,t.
q:- r.
r:- p.
```

and Q the query :-r. P is not strictly related to Q as r is both positively and negatively dependent on q.

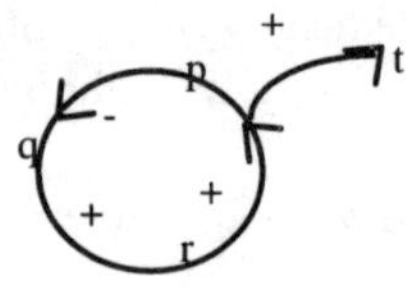

Fig. 9.4: A Program which is not call consistent

Presuming call consistency and strictness, we can make some statements about the soundness of SLDNF for normal programs, in which a further structural constraint is required. For such structurally limited programs we have:

$\forall q\ q \in HB(P)$:- q succeeds under SLDNF if comp(P) $\models q$
:- q succeeds under SLDNF if comp(P) $\models \neg q$

The most well-known structural constraints are the so-called admissible programs. A program is admissible if and only if for every clause in the program all variables which occur in a clause occur in at least one non-negative literal - by these means floundering becomes impossible. The above proposition is then valid.

Let us summarise soundness and completeness in SLDNF: if a program is admissible, call consistent and strict with respect to :-Q then:

- :- Q is successful with answer substitution θ if and only if comp(P) $\models \forall Q\theta$,
- :- Q eventually fails if and only if comp(P) $\models \neg\exists Q$.

Example: consider the following program P:

```
parents_of(Y):- ¬childless(Y).
childless(Y):- has_child(Y).
has_child(Y):- child(X,Y).
child_of(bernie,chris).
child_of(eric,chris).
```

and the query Q:

```
:- child_of(U,V).¬parent_of(V).
```

P is both call consistent and strict, with respect to Q, but not admissible (as the variables Y in both first clauses do not occur with a positive literal). Although the variables in the `child_of` call are not instantiated we get a flounder-free execution under SLDNF, as shown in the figure. The ultimate failing of the execution has implications for the correct answer: no one can have children and not be a parent.

comp(P) $\models \neg\exists U \exists V$child_of($U,V$),$\neg$parent_of($V$).

In contrast to this the query `:-child_of(U,V), parent_of(V)` succeeds with two substitutions:
θ_1={U/bernie,V/chris}
θ_2={U/eric, V/chris}

That means:
comp(*P*) |= (child_of(bernie,chris),parents_of(chris)
and comp(*P*) |= (child_of(eric,chris),parents_of(chris))

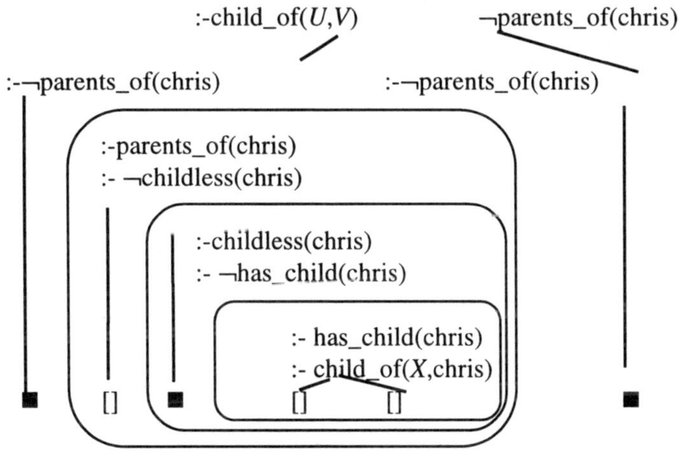

Fig. 9.4: SLDNF execution of a normal program with a normal goal

It is time for some remarks about the use of negation in Prolog:

Most Prolog systems do not implement the correct version of SLDNF resolution. If a Prolog system finds the occurrence of a negative literal ¬*q* in the goal it attempts to prove *q*. If this goal can be proved then ¬*q* fails. As explained this does not give rise to problems as long as the answer calculated for q is *empty*. However, most Prolog systems do not carry out this test, as it is relatively ineffective. As a consequence, calculations with nested negations can produce false answers. The responsibility for ensuring that this situation does not arise is left with the programmer. It is good practice to ensure that in negation in Prolog the negative literals are positioned at a place where they will have to be instantiated: the calculated answer substitution is empty and the problem mentioned above does not occur. The use of negation which leads to the selection of a non-instantiated negative literal is called *the insecure use of negation*. The insecure use of negation can also lead to a misunderstanding, e.g., it is usual to write:

```
orphan(X):- ¬parents_of(Y,X).
```

and interpret it as: X is an orphan if there is no Y such that Y are the parents of X. However, the normal meaning of this clause can be seen by considering the universal quantifier, namely:
$\forall X \forall Y$(orphan(X):-¬parents_of(Y,X))

which is equivalent to:
$\forall X$(orphan(X):- $\exists Y$¬parent_of(Y,X))

and is read as: X is an orphan if Y is someone who is not a parent of X,. Which is something completely different from what we wanted to express.

20.5 Exercises on the topic of NAF

1. Construct comp(P) for the following programs:
   a. $A \leftarrow B$
      $A \leftarrow \neg C$
      B
   b. $A \leftarrow \neg B \wedge C$
      $B \leftarrow C$
      C
   c. $A \leftarrow A \wedge C$
   d. $A \leftarrow B$
   e. $C \leftarrow \neg B$

2. a. Give an example of a non-definite program whose *comp*(*P*) has only one *HB*.
   b. Give another example of a non-definite program whose *comp*(*P*) has only one *HB*.

3. Construct the completion of the following programs:
   a. num(0)
      num($s(x)$)←num(x)
   b. dup($u.x$)←$u \in x$
      dup($v.x$)←dup(x)
   c. knows(frank,y)←computers(y)∧aspects(x,y)
      knows(chris,y)←*says*(frank,y,chris)
   d. $p(y) \leftarrow q(x,y), r(x)$
      $p(x) \leftarrow r(x)$
      $q(f(x),y) \leftarrow q(x,y)$
      $r(b)$

4. Draw the SLDNF tree for the persons program in the topic for the following queries under a secure calculation rule which selects the first left literal.
   a. `:-person(Y),¬child_of(X,y).`
   b. `:-person(Y),¬person(y).`
   c. `:-child_of(X,X).`

5. Give a clause of the form:
   `p:- ¬q(X), others ...`
   in which X is the local variable in `¬q(X)`. Under the secure calculation rule the execution will flounder. This floundering can be eliminated by transforming this clause into two clauses.

   a. What is the clause?
   b. Compare the execution for the persons program of the queries:
   `:-childless(bernie).`
   `:-childless(chris).`

i. using the clause `childless(Y):-¬child_of(X,Y).`
ii. using the transformation

c. How does the transformation behave for the query `:-childless(Y)` and what is a simple help.

6. Find a fair calculation rule for the following goal and program:
```
:-p(X),q(X,Y).
p(f(X)):-p(X).
q(X,Y):-p(Y),s(X<a).
s(X,X).
```

7. Prove whether or not the comp(*P*) of the following programs is consistent:
$p \leftarrow \neg q, t$
$q \leftarrow r$
$r \leftarrow p$

8. Draw the dependency graphs for every program *P* and investigate call consistency. Then construct comp(*P*) and investigate consistency.

a. $p \leftarrow q$
$q \leftarrow \neg p, r$
$r \leftarrow q$

b. $p \leftarrow q$
$p \leftarrow r$
$q \leftarrow t$
$r \leftarrow \neg t$

c. $p \leftarrow \neg q$
$q \leftarrow t$
$t \leftarrow p$

d. $p(a) \leftarrow q$
$q \leftarrow t$
$t \leftarrow p(b)$

9. Produce the normal program *P* and *HU*(*P*)={maria,susie, fred,john}:
```
C1: likes(maria,susie).
C2: likes(fred,susie).
C3: likes(john,maria).
C4: likes(maria,X)←¬likes(X,maria).
```
Write all the ground atoms $q \in HB(P)$ for which $p \models q$.

10. Which of the following programs are call consistent?

a. $p(x) \leftarrow q(x), r(x)$
$p(x) \leftarrow \neg r(x)$
$q(x) \leftarrow \neg r(x), s(x)$
$r(x) \leftarrow \neg s(x)$

b. $p(x) \leftarrow p(x), s(x)$
$s(x) \leftarrow r(x)$
$r(x) \leftarrow \neg p(x)$
$r(a)$

c. $p(x) \leftarrow \neg q(x), r(x)$
$r(x) \leftarrow q(x)$
$q(x) \leftarrow \neg s(x)$

d. $p(x) \leftarrow r(x), p(x)$
$r(x) \leftarrow \neg p(x)$
$r(x) \leftarrow r(x)$

11. Construct the completion of the normal program:

$p(a) \leftrightarrow \neg q(b)$

and show that $\{p(a), a=a, b=b\}$ is a Herbrand model of the completion. Show that the model is minimal.

The best is the deep silence in which,
against the world, I live, grow and gain ...
-Johann Wolfgang von Goethe -

10 SEARCH

Logic programs are non-deterministic, i.e., there may be more than one possibility at every step of computation. This makes the search for the correct solution more difficult.

So that non-deterministic problems can be solved by the computer, highly efficient search strategies must be developed. Search strategies establish the order in which the non-deterministic steps of computation are executed.

Before we study the derivation of search strategies and their use, we should firstly recap Prolog's proof algorithm and search method, using the terminology introduced.

In order to execute a goal the first clause whose head is unifiable with the goal is searched for. The unification process (hopefully with occurs check to guarantee the soundness of derivations) produces the most general instance of both Prolog terms. If the clause heads and the goal are unifiable then the clause in question is activated, i.e., activated according to the order of the subgoals specified in its tail - and indeed in the order of their occurrence.

If the system finds no suitable clause for a subgoal then backtracking commences and the most recently activated one is rejected (in that all substitutions arising from pattern matching with it are undone).

Finally, the goal which activated the backtracked clause is inspected anew and an alternative conclusion clause is sought, which can also be made to match the (sub)goal.

Execution is seen to be terminated as soon as no more subgoals need to be executed.

At the end of the proof procedure the system notes either the unprovability (with respect to the given Prolog program and Prolog implementation) of the given goal or it delivers a true instance of the original goal with respect to the declarative semantics of the program. By means of user-initiated backtracking, further attempts to prove the goal in question can be made.

If we now try to describe Prolog with our terminological apparatus from SLD resolution then we can see the following:

- The procedural semantics of Prolog are largely SLD resolution.

The typical Prolog calculation rule BR is:
$BR(\leftarrow A_1, ..., A_n) := A_1$

- Prolog's search strategy for a given SLD tree is *depth-first* from left to right.

From this, a simplified presentation of the refutation procedure emerges, which uses a stack, on which the currently investigated root of the SLD tree is processed:

- On climbing the SLD tree each goal found is placed on the stack.
- As soon as a leaf *G* is reached there are two possibilities:
  a. *G* is an empty goal []. In this case success is reported and, after a subsequently initiated user command, backtracking is initiated, in all cases, in order to find the next solution.
  b. *G* is not an empty clause: in this case the root path on the stack corresponds to a failed derivation and backtracking is initiated in order to find solutions in the next path.
  c. The stack always holds exactly one root path of the SLD tree.

This implementation of such a refutation procedure has, on the one hand, a low memory resource requirement and, on the other, also concretises backtracking and leads to the repeated computation of subgoals which may often be required several times in a complex proof.

Our discussion demonstrates the importance of the search procedure in Prolog systems. Indeed, solutions to many real-world problems can be solved by search. There are two standard search strategies: breadth-first search and depth-first search. We shall study these methods in the following and shall use them in an example.

Topic 21

Search Strategies

21.1 Breadth-First Search

In breadth-first search, all the nodes of one level are produced before all the nodes of the next level are produced. It is clear that a successful calculation will be found after a finite number of search steps. In other words the breadth-first evaluation strategy is complete. The disadvantage of this evaluation strategy is the great need for memory and processing time: in order to arrive at the nodes of level t of the tree, breadth-first search needs an exponential (in t) number of processing steps (provided that the tree does not consist of a single path). The following tree is therefore searched in the order 1, 2, 3, 4, 5, 6, 7, 8, 9, breadth-first. A further disadvantage of breadth-first search leads to the incompleteness of the SLD tree, if the tree is infinite.

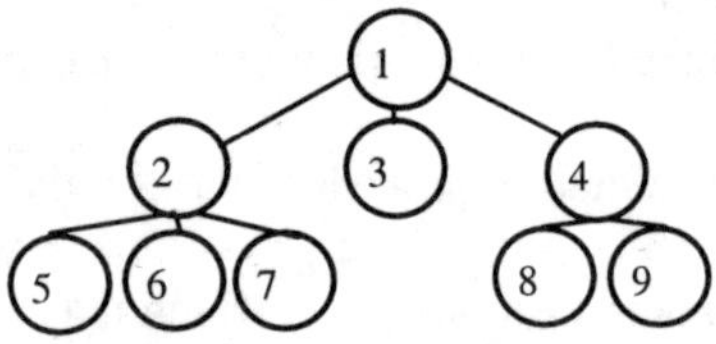

Fig.: 10.1 The breadth first strategy

21.2 Depth-First Search

This method searches the subtrees in a given order (from left to right) recursively from the root. In contrast to breadth-first search, it dives deeply into the tree. If a failure arises then the search can not proceed and the search returns to a parent node (backtracking). From there it attempts to continue with another configuration of conclusions.

The depth algorithm

1. Each node of the tree is
   either an empty query [];
   or a non-empty query with a direct successor;
   or a query with one or more successors.
   The first two cases are called terminal nodes,
   the third case is a non-terminal node.
2. For every non-terminal node the direct successors are given a priority.
3. The search begins with the creation of root nodes.
4. A **search step** at a non-terminal node: the successor nodes with the higher priority are found. The next search step proceeds from the successor nodes.
5. A search step at a terminal node: the direct predecessor is identified. The next search step is from the predecessor node. If there is no predecessor node then the whole tree is produced.

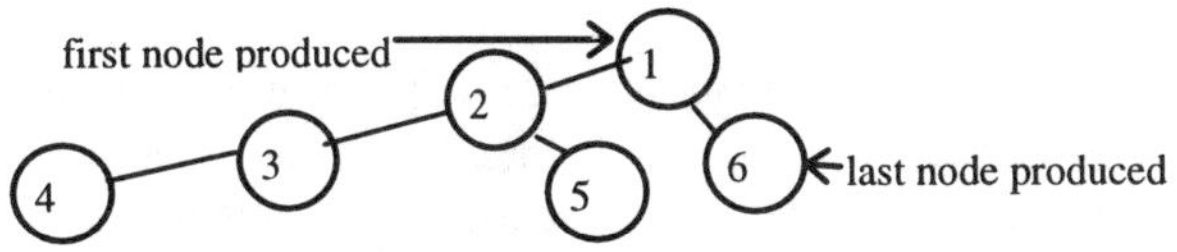

Fig. 10.2 The depth first search strategy

Advantages of this procedure can be listed as:

- every possible solution is found in finite time. This leads to the realisation of SLD completeness.
- optimal memory utilisation, if the tree is finite.

Disadvantages of this procedure are:

- if an infinite branch exists on the left of a successful branch then depth-first search is at least as inefficient as breadth-first search.

Due to the efficiency advantages which depth-first strategies can bring, most Prolog implementations keep to this incomplete evaluation strategy. The problem is, as it were, handed over to the Prolog programmer. He must be clear about the Prolog evaluation procedure and, therefore, plan the order of the program clauses with care. This however stands in contrast to the ideal conception of logic programming as just formal problem specification. In the ideal situation the programmer would just have to tell the system "What is the problem?" rather than "How is the problem to be solved?".

Kowalski [38] introduced the equation:

algorithm=logic + control

in the sense that algorithms always have two implicit components: a logic component, which specifies the knowledge about the problem to be solved, and a control component, which provides the solution strategy for the problem. Whilst both components are closely intertwined and can barely be separated, logic programs should - at least in the ideal case - just include the logic component, whilst the control component remains the domain of the system, that is the evaluation mechanism for the program.

This ideal situation has clearly not been achieved with existing Prolog systems with the depth-first search strategy. The breadth-first strategy is, indeed, complete but inefficient. A compromise must therefore be struck between the ideal situation of logic programming (the complete separation of logic and control components) and efficiency.

21.3 Derivation of the Breadth-First Search Strategy

For many problems of the real world the following Prolog relations can be written:

```
action(current,next)
```

This relation specifies all possible actions from the current position to a position that will be reached after the action, that is the next position. The search procedure uses this relation in order to find the consequence of an action which must be carried out in order to progress from the current to the desired position. In a directed graph, this collection of actions corresponds to the solution path. It would be ideal if the search procedure required the minimum computational and memory resources for this.

We define the relation:

```
depth_first(Goal, Processed, Answer)
```

as a recursive procedure with two inputs, `Goal` and `Processed`, and an output, `Answer`. The variable `Answer` contains the solution path, i.e., `Answer` is a list of nodes which must be passed through in order to get from the initial situation (start node) to a goal situation (end node). The variable `Goal` represents a situation which should be reached by given actions. In the variable `Processed`, the nodes which have already been passed through are stored. This has the advantage that it is possible to check if a node has already been visited. This approach makes it possible to avoid getting into an endless loop. The variable `Processed` stores, as its head, the current situation or start node and the variable `Answer` contains the desired situation or goal node, at the start of the program. The search procedure can be defined in two rules:

```
depth_first(Goal,[Goal|_],[Goal]).
depth_first(Goal,[Current|Previous],[Current|After]):-
        action(Current,Next),
        not(element(Next,Previous)),
        depth_first(Goal,[Next|[Current|Previous]],After).
```

The first rule means: if the goal situation is identical to the current situation (the head of the list `Processed`) then the problem is solved. The list `Answer` then contains just one element the goal state. The first rule corresponds to the termination condition of recursion. The second rule uses "|", in order to split the list `Processed` into the list head `Current` and the rest of the list `Previous`. The rest of the list `Processed` consists of the predecessor nodes of `Current`. The third parameter is the output parameter `[Current|After]`. It consists of the nodes which must still be visited. The tail of the rule consists of three relations. The first relation is called `action`, which performs the operation of moving from one state to the next. The test `not(element)` establishes whether or not the nodes are `Next` elements of the list `previous`. If this is the case then the nodes of `Next` are not immediately visited. The last relation `depth_first` is the recursive call of the search procedure with the node `Next` as head of the list `Processed`.

21.4 The Farmer Problem

In the following example, we shall implement the farmer problem in Prolog. The farmer would like to cross a river with his fox, goose and grain. The boat which he wishes to use can only carry one item plus himself. How can the farmer cross the river without leaving the fox alone with the goose or the goose with the grain.

Before writing the Prolog rules a suitable datastructure needs to be found. In the farmer problem the locations of the individual objects constitute the situation or nodes.

In this we can ignore the location of the boat, as it is always the same as the location of the farmer. The locations can be stored in the following datastructure:

```
location(Farmer, Fox, Goose, Grain).
```

The variables `Farmer`, `Fox`, `Goose`, `Grain` represent the locations of the individual objects. The Prolog datastructure, therefore, has a function name with four variables.

Next, a predicate `action(Current, Next)` is defined, i.e., in our case `move(Current, Next)`. This relation represents the possible moves from a current situation `Current` to a following situation `Next`. The first rule for the definition of move says that the farmer may move from one location to another, if the two locations are different and neither the goose is left alone with the fox nor the grain with the goose.

```
move(location(Farmer, Fox, Goose, Grain),
location(Farmer2, Fox, Goose, Grain):-
      different(Farmer,Farmer2),
      safe(location(Farmer2,Fox,Goose,Grain).
```

In the relation `move`, two further predicates occur, `different` and `secure`. The relation `different` checks if the locations of `Farmer` and `Farmer2` are different. The predicate `secure` determines if the goose or the grain are secure.

Apart from the first move there are three further moves:
- the farmer crosses the river with the fox,
- the farmer crosses the river with the goose and,
- the farmer crosses the river with the grain.

These can be written in Prolog as:

```
move(location(Farmer, Farmer, Goose, Grain),
location(Farmer2, Farmer2, Goose, Grain):-
      different(Farmer,Farmer2),
      safe(location(Farmer2,Farmer2,Goose,Grain).
move(location(Farmer, Fox, Goose, Grain),
location(Farmer2, Fox, Farmer2, Grain):-
      different(Farmer,Farmer2),
      safe(location(Farmer2,Fox,Farmer2,Grain).
move(location(Farmer, Fox, Goose, Grain),
location(Farmer2, Fox, Goose, Farmer2):-
      different(Farmer,Farmer2),
      safe(location(Farmer2,Fox,Goose,Farmer2).
```

The predicate `different` can be defined with two facts:

```
different(east,west).
different(west,east).
```

Whether or nor the situation is safe depends on the critical object "Goose". The goose can either eat the grain or be eaten by the fox. The next two rules define that a situation is safe if either the farmer and the goose are on the same side or the goose is completely alone on one side.

```
safe(location(Farmer,Fox,Farmer,Grain)).
safe(location(Farmer,Farmer,Goose,Farmer)):-
different(Farmer,Goose).
```

With these rules the farmer problem is completely defined. What we now need is a search procedure which finds the solution path from a given initial situation, i.e., a start node to the desired goal situation, i.e., a goal node.

Start node: `location(west,west,west,west).`
Goal node: `location(east,east,east,east).`

The search procedure is defined as above:

```
depth_first(Goal,[Goal|_],[Goal]).
depth_first(Goal,[Current|Previous],[Current|After]):-
       action(Current,Next),
       not(element(Next,Previous)),
       depth_first(Goal,[Next|[Current|Previous]],After).
```

If the farmer would like to get from the west to the east side of the river, the goal situation is:

```
location(east,east,east,east).
```

and the list processed is initialised to the initial situation:

```
location(west,west,west,west).
```

The `Program` call is therefore:

```
depth_first(location(east,east,east,east),[location(w
est,west,west,west)|_],Answer).
```

For this goal the breadth-first search strategy would generate the following list:

```
[location(west,west,west,west),location(east,west,
east,west),location(west,west,east,west),location(
east,east,east,east),location(west,east,west,west),
location(east,east,west,east),location(west,east,west
,east),location(east,east,east,east)].
```

In the list the first situation is the starting situation and the last the goal situation. The farmer problem is implemented in Prolog in the appendix.

21.5 Exercises for the Topic

1. Define a scheme for sequential breadth-first search which produces each level of the tree in sequence.

There is nothing good apart from having a go.
- Erich Kästner -

APPENDIX A
Solutions to the exercises
Solutions to Topic 2

1. Family Problem

a. i. NO
ii. Person=ollie
Person=freda
iii. NO
iv. Person_1=susie
Person_2=gayle

b. i. `?-parent(Person,peter).`
ii. `?-parent(anne,Child).`
iii. `?-parent(P_1,thomas), parent(P_2,P_1).`

c. i. `happy(Person):- parent(Person,Child).`
ii.
```
two_children(Person):-
parent(Person,Child_1),
                    parent(Person,Child_2),
                    female(Child_2).
```

d. i.
```
grandchild(Child,Pers_1):-
parent(Pers_2,Child),
                    parent(Pers_1,Pers_2).
```
ii.
```
aunt(Pers_1,Pers_2):- parent(Pers_3,Pers_2),
                    sister(Pers_1,Pers_3).
```

2. Company Problem

a.
```
/* Facts */
/* board(A,Z1,Z2,F) means A was from Z1 to Z2 */
/* in board and had the function F */
board(henry,1990,1992,department_head).
board(ollie,1988,1990,department_head).
board(will,1992,1993,department_head).
board(henry,1990,1992,apprentice_supervisor).
board(freda,1988,1990,apprentice_supervisor).
board(harry,1990,1992,treasurer).
board(harry,1990,1992,organising_committee).
```

b.
```
successor_rule(P):-
        board(P,From,To,department_head),
        board(P,From,To,apprentice_supervisor).
```

c. i. `?-board(henry,From,To,apprentice_supervisor).`
ii.
```
?-board(henry,From,To,_),
board(ollie,From,To,_).
```

3. Flight network problem

a.
```
/*flight(A,B) means flight from A to B */
flight(hamburg,bremerhaven).
flight(bremerhaven,newyork).
flight(bremerhaven,paris).
flight(hamburg,frankfurt).
flight(frankfurt,paris).
flight(paris,london).
flight(newyork,london).
```

b.
```
?- flight(hamburg,paris).
```

c.
```
?-flight(Town1,Town2),flight(Town2,Town3).
/* flight from several towns */
/* flight_connection(A,B) means: */
/* a flight connection from A to B */
flight_connection(Town1,Town2):- flight(Town1,Town2).
flight_connection(Town1,Town2):- flight(Town1,Town),
                  flight_connection(Town,Town2).
```

d.
```
?- flight(Town1,paris), flight(Town2,paris),
Town1 \== Town2.
/* Town is flown to from several towns */
several_flights(Town):-      flight(Town1,Town),
                  flight(Town2,Town),
                  Town1 \== Town2.
```

Solutions to Topic 3

1. a. variables

b. atom

c. atom

d. variable

e. atom

f. structure

g. number

h. syntactically false

i. structure

j. structure

2. a. yes

b. no

c. no

d. D=2, E=2

e. P1=point(-1,0),P2=point(1,0),P3=point(0,Y)

3. a. segment(point(5,Y1),point(5,Y2)).

b. regular(rightangle(point(X1,Y1),point(X2,Y1),point(X1,Y2),point(X2,Y2))).

```
4. uncle(X,Y):- brother(X,Z), parents(Z,Y);
               wife(W,X),sister(W,Z),parents(Z,X).
parents(X,Y):- child(Y,X).
wife(X,a):- married(X,a),male(a).
husband(X,b):- married(X,b),female(b).
aunt(X,Y):- parents(Z,Y),sister(X,Z).
```

Solutions to Topic 4

```
1. fib(0,1).
fib(1,1).
fib(N,Result):-   N > 1,
               Nminus1 is N-1,
               fib(Nminus1,E1),
               Nminus2 is N-2,
               fib(Nminus2,E2),
               Result is E1 + E2.
?- fib(7,X).
X=21

?- fib(7,21).
yes
```

```
2. nat(0).
nat(N):- nat(M),N is M+1.
?- nat(0).
yes

nat(2).
yes
```

3. Exercise for the reader.

Solutions to Topic 5

1. *a*. .(*a*.(*b*,[]))
b. .(*a*,*b*)
c. .(*a*.,(*b*.,(*c*,[])),.(*d*,[])))
d. .(*a*,.(*b*,*X*))
e. .(*a*,.(*b*,.(*c*,[])))
f. .(*a*,.(*b*,[]))
g. .([],[])
h. .(*a*,.(*b*,*c*[])))

2. *a*. *X*=*a*,*Y*=[*b*]
b. *X*=*a*,*Y*=*b*,*Z*=[[*c*,*d*]]
c. not possible

d. *X*=1
e. *X*=[2,3]

3. a. _1=*a*,*x*=*b*,_2=*c*
b. *Y*=*a*
c. *Y*=*c*
d. *Y*=[*b*,*c*],*Y*= [], ...
e. yes

4. a. no
b. *X*=*a*
X=*b*
X=*c*
no
By backtracking all elements of the list can be produced.

5. Exercise for the reader

6.
```
sum([],0).
sum[Head|Tail],Rest):-
      sum(Tail,Rest1),
      Rest is Head + Rest1.
run:-       write('Input list: '),nl,
      read(List),
      sum(List,Result),
      write('Sum of elements in a list: '),
      write(Result).
```

7.
```
last(Element,[Element]).
last(Element,[_|Tail]):- last(Element,Tail).
run:-       write('Input list: '),nl,
      read(List),
      last(Element,List),
      write('Last element: '),
      write(Element).
```

8.
```
nextto(Element1,Element2,[Element1,Element2|_]).
nextto(Element1,Element2,[_|Tail]):-
nextto(Element1,Element2,Tail).
run:-       write('Input list: '),nl,
      read(List),
      write('Input the first element: '),nl,
      read(Element1),
      write('Input the second element: '),nl,
      read(Element2),
      nextto(Element1,Element2,List),
```

```
      write('The elements are neighbours'),nl.
run:- write('The elements are not neighbours'),nl.

9. difference([],Set,[]).
difference([Value|Tail],Set,Difference):-
      element(Value,Set),!,
      difference(Tail,Set,Difference).
difference([Value|Tail],Set,[Value|Difference]):-
      difference(Tail,Set,Difference).
element(Value,[Value|_]).
element(Value,[_Tail]):- element(Value,Tail).

10.   a. last(Element,List):-
            append(_,[Element],List).
      b. last(Element,[Element]).
       last(Element,[First|Rest]):-
            last(Element,Rest).

11. length([],0).
length([X|Y],N):- length(Y,M),N is M+1.

12. even_length([]).
even_length([First|Rest]):-
      uneven_length(Rest).
uneven_length([_]).
uneven_length([First|Rest]):-
      even_length(Rest).

13. reverse([],[]).
reverse([First,Rest],Reversed):-
      reverse(Rest,Reversed_rest),
      append(Reversed_rest,[First],Reversed).

14. palindrome(List):-
      reverse(List,List).
reverse([],[]).
reverse([First|Rest],Reversed):-
      reverse(Rest,Reversed_rest),
      append(Reversed_rest,[First],Reversed).

15. rotate([First|Rest],Rotated):-
      append(Rest,[First],Rotated).

16. subset([],[]).
subset([First|Rest],[First|Part]):-
      subset(Rest,Part).
```

```
subset([First|Rest],Part):-
       subset(Rest,Part).
```

17.
```
split_list([],[],[]).
split_list([X],[X],[]).
split_list([X,Y|List],[X|List1],[Y|List2]):-
       split_list(List,List1,List2).
```

18.
```
element(X,[X|_]).
element(X,[_|List]):-
       element(X,List).
sublist([],_).
sublist([X|Tail],List):-
       element(X,List),
       sublist(Tail,List).
```

19.
```
mix([],List,List).
mix([X|List],[],[X|List]).
mix([X|List1],[Y|List2],[X,Y|List3]):-
       mix(List1,List2,List3).
```

20.
```
ggt(X,X,X).
ggt(X,Y,T):-
       X < Y,
       Y1 is Y-X,
       ggt(X,Y1,T).
ggt(X,Y,T):-
       Y < X,
       ggt(Y,X,T).
```

21.
```
msort([],[]).
msort([X],[X]).
msort(List,Sorted_list):-
       split(List,List1,List2),
       msort(List1,Sorted1),
       msort(List2,Sorted2),
       mix(Sorted1,Sorted2,Sorted_list).
split([X],[X],[]).
split[X,Y|List],[X|List1],[Y|List2]):-
       split(List,List1,List2).
```

22.
```
ordered([X]).
ordered([X,Y|Tail]):- X < Y,
       ordered([Y|Tail]).
```

Solutions to Topic 6

```
1. action(1):- !,write('You typed one').
action(2):- !,write('You typed two').
action(3):- !,write('You typed three').
action(X):- X =\= 1,X=\=2, X=\=3,
     write('I do not recognise this number').
:- write('Enter a number from 1 to 3'),
read(Choice),action(Choice).
```

2. a.,b.

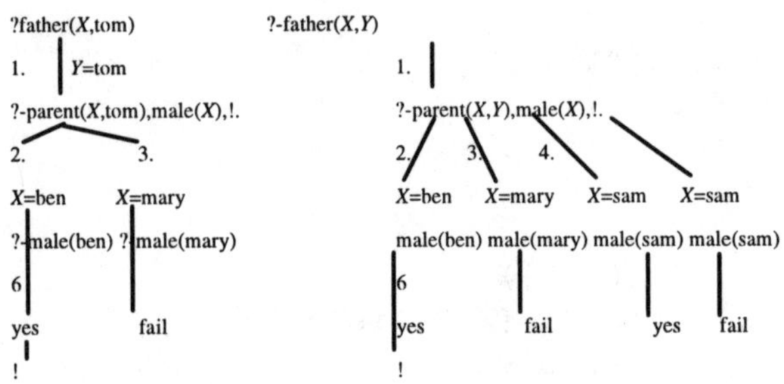

3. a., b.

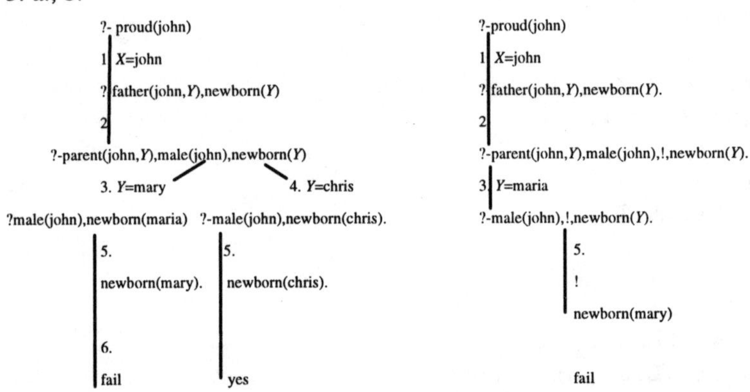

4. a., b.

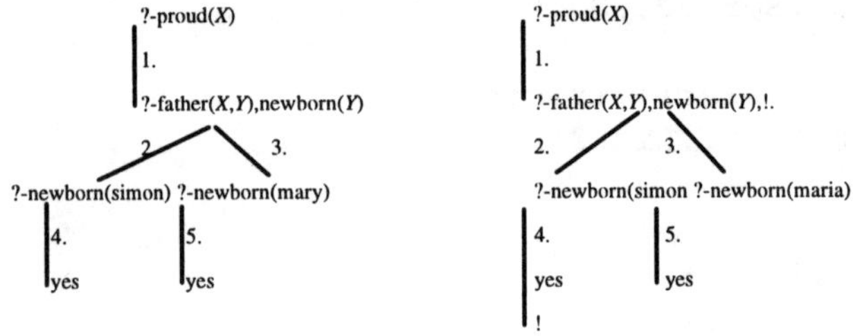

5.

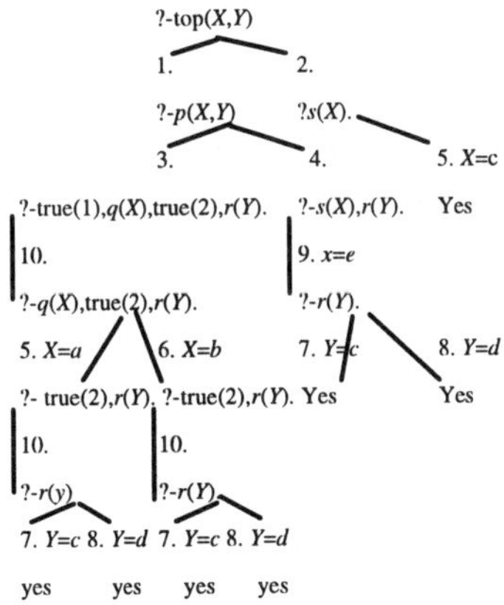

a., b.

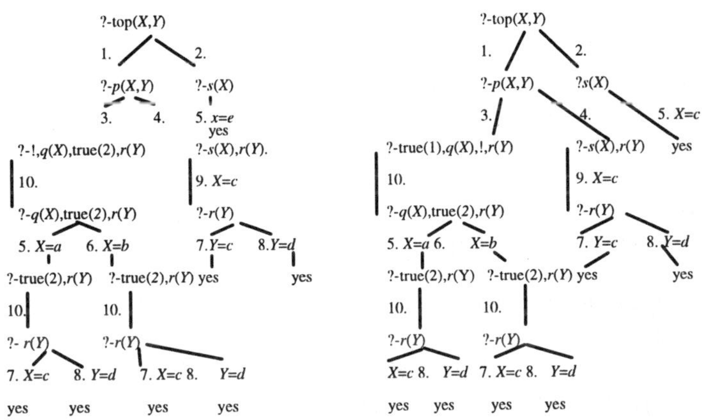

Solutions to Topic 7

1. Determining possible permutations by the n-over-k calculation.

```
newk(N,1,N).
newk(No1,No2,Result):-
        No2 > 0,
        Quotient is No1 / No2,
        Help1 is No -1,
        Help2 is No2 -1,
        newk(Help1,Help2,Temp),
        Result is *(Quotient, Temp).
```

2. Fibonacci numbers

```
fibno(Number,Result):- fib(Number,Result, 1,0,2,1).
fib(Number,Result,Number,Result,_,_).
fib(Number,Result,_,_,Number,Result).
```

```
fib(Number,Result,Nhelp1,Rhelp1,Nhelp1,Rhelp2):-
       Nhelp11 is Nelp1+1,
       Nhelp22 is Nhelp2+1,
       Rhelp11 is Rhelp2,
       Rhelp22 is Rhelp1+Rhelp2,
       fib(Number,Result,Nhelp11,Rhelp11,Nhelp22,Rhelp
22),!.
```

Solutions to Topic 9

1.a. 1. → Elimination

$\neg[P\to Q]\vee[\neg R\to[S\wedge T]]$

$\neg[\neg P\vee Q]\vee[\neg R\to[S\wedge T]]$

$\neg[\neg P\vee Q]\vee[\neg\neg R\vee[S\wedge T]]$

2. ¬ Reduction

$[\neg\neg P\wedge\neg Q]\vee[\neg\neg R\vee[S\wedge T]]$

$[P\wedge\neg Q]\vee[R\vee[S\wedge T]]$

$[P\wedge\neg Q]\vee[R\vee[S\wedge T]]$

3. Use of Distribution

$[P\wedge\neg Q]\vee[[R\vee S]\wedge[R\vee T]]$

$[P\vee[(R\vee S)\wedge(R\vee T)]]\wedge[\neg Q\vee[(R\vee S)\wedge(R\vee T)]]$

$[[P\vee(R\vee S)\wedge[P\vee(R\vee T)]]\wedge[[\neg Q\vee(R\vee S)]\wedge[\neg Q\vee(R\vee T)]]$

$(P\vee R\vee S)\wedge(P\vee R\vee T)\wedge(\neg Q\vee R\vee S)\wedge(\neg Q\vee R\vee T)$

b. 1. →Elimination

$(\neg\neg P\vee R)\vee\{[\neg(P\wedge\neg Q)\vee R]\wedge[\neg R\vee(P\wedge Q)]\}$

2. ¬Reduction

$(P\vee R)\vee[(\neg P\vee Q)\vee R]\wedge[\neg R\vee(P\wedge\neg Q)]$

3. Use of Distribution

$\{(P\vee R)[(\neg P\vee Q)\vee R]\}\wedge\{(P\vee R)\vee[\neg R\vee(P\wedge\neg Q)]\}$

$\{(P\vee R)[(\neg P\vee Q)\vee R]\}\wedge\{(P\vee R)\vee[\neg(R\vee P)\wedge(\neg R\vee Q)]\}$

$\{(P\vee R)[(\neg P\vee Q)\vee R]\}\wedge\{[(P\vee R)\vee(\neg R\vee P)]\wedge[(P\vee R)\vee(\neg R\vee Q)]\}$

$[P\vee R\vee\neg P\vee Q\vee R]\wedge[(P\vee R\vee\neg R\vee P]\wedge[P\vee R\vee\neg R\vee Q]$

2. $w\to[f\wedge[[w\vee f]\to[w\leftrightarrow w]]]$

since $w\vee f=w$ and $w\leftrightarrow w=$w

$w\to[f\wedge[w\to w]]$

since $w\to w=w$

$w\to[f\wedge w]$

since $f\wedge w=f$

$w\to f$

$f\Rightarrow$ the formula is false for this interpretation

3. $\{A:=f;B:=w;C:=*\}$

$\{A:=w;C:=f;B:=*\}$

4. $\neg(A\to B)\wedge\neg(C\to\neg B)\to(A\to\neg C)$

$=\neg[\neg(A\to B)\wedge(\neg C\to\neg B)]\vee(A\to\neg C)$
$=(\neg B\to\neg A)\vee(\neg\neg B\to\neg C)\vee(A\to\neg C)$
$=(\neg B\to\neg A)\vee(B\to\neg C)\vee(A\to\neg C)$
$=(B\vee\neg A)\vee(\neg B\vee\neg C)\vee(\neg A\vee\neg C)$
$=(B\vee\neg B)\vee(\neg C\vee\neg C)\vee(\neg A\vee\neg A)$
$=$true $\vee(\neg C)\vee(\neg A)$
$=$true

5. On line 3 it can be seen: where P→Q and P∨Q and ¬P are true then Q is also true.

P	Q	P→Q	P∨Q	¬P
t	t	t	t	f
t	f	f	t	f
f	t	t	t	t
f	f	t	f	t

Solutions to Topic 10

1. A	$1=1\times 1$
$A\to B$	$[1=1\times 1]\to[\log 1=\log(1\times 1)]$
B	$\log 1=\log(1\times 1)$
$B\to C$	$[\log 1=\log(1\times 1)]\to[\log 1=2\log 1]$
C	$\log 1=2\log 1$
$C\to D$	$[\log 1=2\log 1]\to[0=\log 1]$
D	$\log 1=0$

2. it rains ∨ it snows ∨ it is dry
↓ $\neg A\to B\leftrightarrow A\vee B$
¬ it rain → [it snows ∨ it is dry]
↓ Pa3 and Modus Ponens
it snows ∨ it is dry
↓ $A\vee B\leftrightarrow\neg A\to B$
¬ it snows → it is dry
↓ Pa4 and Modus Ponens
it is dry

3. $<D,C,A>$ is the proof for A and
$<D,C,B,\neg A>$ is the proof for $\neg A$
hence inconsistent

4.

P	Q	R	$P\wedge R$	$P\vee(Q\wedge R)$	$P\vee Q$	$P\vee R$	$(P\vee Q)\wedge(P\vee R)$
t	t	t	t	t	t	t	t
t	t	f	f	t	t	t	t

t	f	t	f	t	t	t	t
t	f	f	f	t	t	t	t
f	t	t	t	t	t	t	t
f	t	f	f	f	t	f	f
f	f	t	f	f	f	t	f
f	f	f	f	f	f	f	f

5.

P	*Q*	¬*P*	¬*P*→*Q*	*P*	¬*Q*	Model?
t	t	f	t	t	f	
t	f	f	t	t	t	yes
f	t	t	f	f	f	
f	f	t	f	f	t	

6.

P	*Q*	*R*	¬*Q*	¬*R*	*P*→¬*Q*	¬*R*→*P*	*Q*	*R*	Model?
t	t	t	f	f	f	t	t	t	
t	t	f	f	t	f	t	t	f	
t	f	t	t	f	t	t	f	t	
t	f	f	t	t	t	t	f	f	
f	t	t	f	f	t	t	t	t	yes
f	t	f	f	t	t	f	t	f	
f	f	t	t	f	t	f	f	t	
f	f	f	t	t	t	t	f	f	

7. The opposite of the proposition is assumed.

¬*B*	log1=0
A→*B*	[log(*a*/*a*)=log *a* - log *a*]→[log 1/1=0]
¬*A*	log(*a*/*a*)≠0
C→*A*	[log(*a*/*b*)=log *a*-log *b*]→[log 1/1=0]
¬*C*	log(*a*/*b*) ≠ log *a* - log *b*

This is a contradiction of the premise thus log 1≠0 is false, i.e., log 1 is true.

8. The opposite of the proposition is assumed and added to the theory. We get:
Th'={(*P*→*Q*),¬*Q*,*P*}

We use modus tollens and get:

¬*Q*
P→*Q*
¬*P*

¬*P* is a contradiction of the premise, i.e., ¬*P* is a theorem of the theory.

9. Assuming that the first clause has m positive literals and the second clause n positive literals then the resolvent $(m+n-1)$ must have positive literals as a positive literal is eliminated.
If both clauses are Horn clauses then we have $m \leq 1$ and $n \leq 1$, in this case $(m+n-1) \leq 1$ is true and it follows from this that the resolvent is a Horn clause.

10. From a) and b) the following resolvent follows:
male(*X*):- parent(*X*), not mother(*X*).

11. Pa1: $P \leftrightarrow Q \equiv \neg P \vee Q \wedge \neg Q \vee P$
Pa2: Q

We add the negation of the axioms ¬P to the theory and transform the theory into clausal form.

S={[¬P,Q],[¬Q,P],[Q],[¬P]}
[¬Q] is a resolvent of [¬Q,P] and [¬P], add it to
S'={[¬P,Q],[¬Q,P],[Q],[¬P],[¬Q]}
The resolvent of [Q] and [¬Q] is []. Add it to S'
S''=S'∪[]
S'' is unsatisfiable; P must be a theorem of the theory.

12. An exercise for the reader.

Solutions to Topic 11

1. a. *A*∨¬*A*; in which *A*: it rains
b. ∀*x*((student(*x*)∧assigned(*x*,info)→
∃y(range(*y*)∧(studies(*x*,*y*)∧¬equal(*y*,sport))))
c.∀*x*(number(*x*)∧¬equal(*x*,0)→∃*y* equal(*x*,succ(*y*)))
d. ∀*x*(∃*y* parent(*x*,*y*)←parent(*x*)∨mother(*x*))
e.∀*x*∃*y* mother(*x*,*y*)←parent(*x*)∧female(*x*)
f. ∃*y* child(*y*) ← ∀*x* parent(*x*)

2. a. ¬∀*x* gleams(*x*) → gold(*x*)
b. endswell(*x*)→allswell(*x*)
c. purpose(*x*) ∧ means(*y*,*x*) → justifies(*x*,*y*)
d. likes(harry,harry)
¬(*x*=harry)→¬likes(harry,*x*) or ¬likes(harry,*y*) ∧ *y*= ¬harry
c. ∀*x*∃*y* (nat(*x*) ∧ ¬equal(*x*,0) →smaller(*y*,*x*))

3. a. *p*(*X*) ← *q*(*X*).
b. *p*(*X*) ← *q*(*X*,*Y*),*r*(*X*).
c. *r*(*X*) ←*p*(*X*),*q*(*X*).
d. *p*(*X*) ←*q*(*X*),*r*(*X*).

4. a.∀*x*(*F*(*x*) →*G*)≡∀*x*(¬*F*(*x*)∨*G*)

$\equiv \forall x \neg F(x) \vee G$
$\equiv \neg \exists x F(x) \vee G)$
$\equiv \exists x F(x) \rightarrow G$

b. $\exists x(F(x) \rightarrow G(x)) \equiv \exists x(\neg(F(x) \vee G(x))$
$\equiv \exists x \neg F(x) \vee \exists x G(x)$
$\equiv \neg \forall x F(x) \vee \exists x G(x)$
$\equiv \forall x F(\mathrm{x}) \rightarrow \exists x G(x)$
$\equiv \forall y F(y) \rightarrow \exists x G(x)$

c. $(F \vee G) \wedge (\neg F \vee H) \models (\neg\neg G \vee F) \wedge (\neg F \vee H)$
$\models (\neg G \rightarrow F) \wedge (F \rightarrow H)$
$\models (\neg G \rightarrow H)$
$\models (G \vee H)$

d. $F \rightarrow (G \leftrightarrow H)$ $\models F \rightarrow ((H \rightarrow G) \wedge (G \rightarrow H))$
$\models F \rightarrow ((G \rightarrow H) \wedge (H \rightarrow G))$
$\models (F \rightarrow (G \rightarrow H)) \wedge (F \rightarrow (H \rightarrow G))$
$\models F \rightarrow (G \rightarrow H)$
$\models (F \wedge G) \rightarrow H$

5.

1. $\forall x(a \wedge b) \rightarrow a \wedge b$	axiom
2. $a \wedge b \rightarrow a$	axiom
3. $\forall x(a \wedge b) \rightarrow a$	1., 2., transitivity
4. $\forall x(a \wedge b) \rightarrow \forall x a$	3. universal quantifier introduction
5. $a \wedge b \rightarrow b$	axiom
6. $\forall x(a \wedge b) \rightarrow b$	1., 5., transitivity
7. $\forall x(a \wedge b) \rightarrow \forall x b$	6. universal quantifier introduction
8. $\forall x(a \wedge b) \rightarrow \forall x(a) \wedge \forall x(b)$	4., 7., conjunction rule

Solutions to Topic 12

1. a. There is an x that is not a secretary.
Skolem form: ¬*secretary*(*skolem*)
b. For all x if x is a person then there is an entity y such that y is the father of x.
Skolem form: *person*(x)→*has_father*(*x*,*father_of*(*x*))
c. For all x if x is a teacher then there is an entity y such that x teaches y and y is a student.
Skolem form: *teacher*(*x*)→[*teaches*(*x*,*student_of*(*x*))]∧*student*(*student_of*(*x*))]

2. *a*. likes(harry,*y*)
b. likes(harry,skolem)
c. likes(*x*,*y*)
d. likes(*x*,skolem(*x*))
e. likes(skolem,*y*)
f. likes(skolem1, skolem2)
g. ¬likes(skolem(*x*),harry)
h. ¬likes(*x*,skolem(*x*))
i. ¬likes(*x*, skolem(*x*))

j. $\neg\text{likes}(x,y)$

3.

a. Initial: $\forall x[p(x)\rightarrow[\forall y p(y)\rightarrow p(f(x,y))\wedge\neg\forall y[q(x,y)\rightarrow p(y)]]]$
Step 1 : $\forall x[\neg p(x)\vee[\neg\forall y p(y)\vee p(f(x,y))\wedge\neg\forall y[\neg q(x,y)\vee p(y)]]]$
Step 2: $\forall x[\neg p(x)\vee[\exists y\neg p(y)\vee p(f(x,y))\wedge\exists y[q(x,y)\wedge\neg p(y)]]]$
Step 3: $\forall x[\neg p(x)\vee[\exists y[\neg p(y)\vee p(f(\mathrm{x},y))]\wedge\exists y[q(x,y)\wedge\neg p(y)]]]$
Step 4: $\forall x[\neg p(x)\vee[\exists y[\neg p(y)\vee p(f(x,y))]\wedge\exists z[q(x,z)\wedge\neg p(z)]]]$
Step 5: $\forall x[\neg p(x)\vee[[\neg(g(x)\vee p(f(x,g(x)))]\wedge[q(x,h(x))\wedge\neg p(h(x))]]]$
Step 6: $[\neg p(x)\vee[[\neg(g(x)\vee p(f(x,g(x)))]\wedge[q(x,h(x))\wedge\neg p(h(x))]]]$
Step 7:
$[[\neg p(x)\vee[\neg p(g(\mathrm{x})\vee p(f(x,g(x)))\vee p(f(x,g(x))]]\wedge[\neg p(x)\vee[q(x,h(x))\wedge\neg p(h(x))]]]$
$[[\neg p(x)\vee\neg p(g(x)\vee p(f(x,g(x)]\wedge[[\neg p(x)\vee q(x,h(x))]\wedge[\neg p(h(x))]]]$
Step 8: $\{\{\neg p(x),\neg p(g(x)),p(f(x,g(x)))\}\wedge\{\neg p(x),q(x,h(\mathrm{x}))\}\wedge\{\neg p(h(x))\}\}$
Step 9:
$\{\{\neg p(x1),\neg p(g(x1)),p(f(x1,g(x1)))\}\wedge\{\neg p(x2),q(x2,h(x2))\}\wedge\{\neg p(x3),\neg p(h(x3))\}$
$\}$

b. Initial: $\forall x\forall y[q(x,y)\leftrightarrow\forall u(p(g,u)\vee\neg p(x,u))]$
Step 1:
$\forall x\forall y[[q(x,y)\vee\neg\forall u(p(y,u)\vee\neg p(x,u)\vee\neg p(x,u))]\wedge[\neg q(x,y)\vee\forall u(p(y,u)\vee\neg p(x,u))]]]$
Step 2: $\forall x\forall y[[q(x,y)\vee\exists u(\neg p(y,u\wedge p(x,u))]\wedge[\neg q(x,y)\vee\forall u(p(g,u)\vee\neg p(x,u))]]$
Step 3: $\forall x\forall y[[\exists u(q(x,y)\vee(\neg p(y,u)\wedge p(y,u)))]\wedge[\forall u(\neg q(x,u)\vee(p(y,u)\vee\neg p(x,u))]]$
$\forall x\forall y[\exists u(q(x,y)\vee(\neg p(y,u)\wedge p(x,u)))]\wedge\forall x\forall y\forall u[\neg q(x,y)\vee p(y,\mathrm{u})\vee\neg p(x,u)]$
Step 4:
$\forall \mathrm{x}_1\forall \mathrm{y}_1[\exists \mathrm{u} q(x_1,y_1)\vee(\neg p(y_1,u)\wedge p(x_1,u)))]\wedge\forall x_2\forall y_2\forall u[\neg q(x_2,y_2)\vee p(y_2,u)\vee p(x_2,u)]$
Step 5: $\forall x_1\forall y_1[q(x_1,y_1)\vee(\neg p(y_1 f(x_1,y_1))\wedge p(x_1 f(x_1,y))))]$
$\wedge\forall x_2\forall y_2\forall u[\neg q(x_2,y_2)\vee p(y_2,u)\vee p(x_2,u)]$
Step 6: $[q(x_1,y_1)\vee(\neg p(y_1,f(x_1,y_1))\wedge p(y_1,f(x_1,y_1)))]\wedge[\neg q(x_2,y_2)\vee p(y_2,u)\vee\neg p(x_2,u)]$
Step 7:
$[(q(x_1,y_1)\vee\neg p(y_1,f(x_1,y_1))\wedge(q(x_1,y_1)\vee p(x_1,f(x_1,\mathrm{y}_1)))]\wedge[\neg q(x_2,y_2)\vee p(y_2,u)\vee\neg p(x_2,u)]$
Step 8: $\{\{q(x_1,y_1\vee\neg p(y_1,f(x_1,y_1))\},$
$\{q(x_1,y_1\vee p(x_1,f(x_1,y_1))\},$
$\{\neg q(x_2,y_2)\vee p(y_2,u)\vee\neg p(x_2,u)\}\}$

c. $p(x,y)\leftarrow(q(y)\leftarrow\neg g(x))$
$p(x,y)\rightarrow(g(y)\leftarrow g(x))$

$p(x,y)\leftarrow q(y)\vee g(x)$
$p(x,y)\leftarrow g(y)\vee\neg g(x)$

$p(x,y)\vee)\neg g(y)\wedge g(x)$
$\neg p(x,y)\vee g(y)\vee\neg g(x)$

$(p(x,y)\vee(\neg g(y)\wedge(p(x,y)\vee g(x))$
$\neg p(x,y)\vee g(y)\vee\neg g(x)$

d. $(p(x,y)\lor\neg g(y))\land(p(x,y)\lor g(x))$
$\neg p(x,y)\lor g(y)\lor\neg g(x)$

$p(x,y)\lor\neg g(y)$
$p(x,y)\lor g(x)$
$\neg p(x,y)\lor g(y)\lor\neg g(x)$

e. Exercise for the reader.
f. Exercise for the reader.
g. Exercise for the reader.

Solutions to Topic 13

1. a. $HU=\{a,f(a),g(a),f(f(a)),f(g(a)),g(f(a)),g(g(a)), \ldots$
$b(f(b),g(b),f(f(b)),f(g(b)),g(g(b)), \ldots\}$
b. $HU=\{a,f(a,a),f(f(a,a),a),f(a,f(a,a)),f(f(a,a),f(a,a)), \ldots\}$
c. $HU=\{a,f(a),f(f(a)),f(f(f(a))), \ldots\}$

2. Initial: $\forall x\exists y$ has_father$(x,y)\land\exists x\forall y$ $\neg$has_father(y,x)
1. Renaming of variables
$\forall x\exists y$ has_father(x,y) $\land$ $\exists w\forall z$ has_father(z,w)
2. Elimination of $\exists$
$\forall x$ has_father(x,f(x) $\land$ $\forall z\neg$has_father(z,a)
in which: f-skolem functionl a=skolem constant
3. Skolem normal form
has_father$(x,f(x)$ $\land$ $\neg$has_father(z,a)
4. $HU=\{a,f(a),f(f(a)),f(f(f(a))), \ldots$ etc$\}$
5. HB=\{has_father$(a,f(a))\land\neg$has_father(a,a),
has_father$(f(a),f(f(a)))\land\neg$has_father(a,a),has_father$(a,f(a))\land\neg$\{has_father$(f(a),a$
), ...}}

3. a. HU=\{chris,this-book, you\}
HB=\{likes(chris,chris),buys(chris,chris)
likes(chris,you),buys(chris,you)
likes(chris,this-book),buys(chris,this-book)

likes(you,chris),buys(you,chris)
likes(you,you),buys(you,you)
likes(you,this-book),buys(you,this-book)

likes(this-book,chris),buys(this-book,chris)
likes(this-book,you),buys(this-book,you)
likes(this-book,this-book),buys(this-book,this-book)

sensible(chris)
sensible(you)

sensible(this-book)

b. $HU_0=\{a,b\}$
$HU_{i+1}=\{f(x)|x\in U_i\}\cup\{g(x)|x\in U_i\}$
$HU(\mathrm{P})=U^{\infty}_{i=0}\ U_i$
$HB(P)=\{q(x,y)|x,y\in U_p\}\cup\{p(x)|x\in U_p\}$
c. $HU(P)=\{0,s(0),s(s(0)), ...\}$
$HB(P)=\{p(x,y,z)|x,y,z\in U_p\}$

4. Formulae b,c and e.

5. a. There are 39 ground clauses in GP(P $\cup\neg$C) which are listed below:
g_1 : ¬path(a,c)
g_2 : link(a,b)
g_3 : link(b,c)
g_4 : path(a,a):- link(a,a).
g_5 : path(a,b):- link(a,b).
g_6 : path(a,c):- link(a,c).
g_7 : path(b,a):- link(b,a).
g_8 : path(b,b):- link(b,b).
g_9 : path(b,c):- link(b,c).
:
g_{13} : path(a,a):- link(a,a), path(a,a).
:
g_{20}: path(a,c):- link(a,b),path(b,c).
:
g_{39} : path(c,c):- link(c,c),path(c,c).

b. For k=1,2, ... we test to see if $\{g_1, ... g_k\}$ is satisfiable. The test is not successful up to k=20 and is thereafter unsatisfable. This is due to the clause: g_1, g_2, g_3, g_9, g_{20}.

Solutions to Topic 14

1. a. $F\theta$=likes(mum(y),dad(chris))
b. $F\theta$=likes(mum(chris,father(chris))
c. $F\theta=g(t(t(u,u),t(u,u)))$
d. $F\theta=\exists x$ wife(x,y)←husband(y)&married(y,elizabeth)
x is wife(x,y) it is not replaced as it is bound.

2.
a. legal, but not idempotent
b. legal and it is known as the identity substitution
c. legal and it is known as the null-substitution
d. not legal
e. a variable in the list can only appear once

f. legal, but not idempotent
g. illegal
h. illegal - only variables can be replaced

3.
a. $\sigma^*=\{w/f(a,b),x/a,y/b,z/c\}$
b. $\sigma^*=\{x/f(b),y/b,z/y\}$
c. $\sigma^*=\{x/f(a,b),w/f(u,z),y/b,v/c\}$
$p(v,x,w)\ \sigma^*=p(c,f(a,b),f(u,z))$
$p(v,x,y,w)\ \sigma^*=p(v,f(a,y),y,f(u,z))$
$(p(v,x,y,w)\ \sigma_1)\sigma_2=p(c,f(a,b),b,f(u,z))$

4. Just c.

Solutions to Topic 15
1. a. m.g.u. $=\{y/a,x/b\}$; no l.g.u.
b. m.g.u. $=\{x/y,z/x\}$; l.g.u. $=\{x/a,\ y/a,z/a\}$
c. m.g.u. $=\{x/y_1,y/x_1\}$ l.g.u. $=\{x/a,y_1/a,y/b,x_1/b\}$
Note that variables are renamed so that no two atoms have the same variables.
d. m.g.u. $=\{x/a,z/t(a,b)\}$; no l.g.u.
e. no m.g.u.
f. mgu$=\{x/f(y_1),x_1/f(y)\}$; l.g.u. $=\{x/f(a),x_1/f(b),y_1/a,y/b\}$
Note that variables are renamed so that no two atoms have the same variables.
g. no m.g.u.
h. not unifiable - why?

2. a. $S=\{p(f(y),w,g(z)),p(u,u,v)\}$
$D_0=<f(y),u>\sigma_0$
$\sigma_1=\{u/f(y)\}$
$D_1=<w,f(y)>\sigma_1=<w,f(y)>$
$\sigma_2=\{u/f(y),w/f(y)\}$
$D_2=<g(z),v>\sigma_2=<g(z),v>$
$\sigma_3=\{u/f(y),w/f(y),v/g(z)\}=$ m.g.u.

b. $S=\{p(f(y),w,g(z)),p(u,u,v)\}$
$D_0=<f(y),u>\sigma_0$
$\sigma_1=\{u/f(y)\}$
$\mathrm{D}_1=<w,f(y)>\sigma_1$
$\sigma_2=\{u/f(y),w/f(y)\}$
$\mathrm{D}_2=<g(z),v>\sigma_2$
$\sigma_3=\{u/f(y),w/v,v/g(z)=$ m.g.u.

c. $S=\{p(a,x,f(g(y)),p(z,h(z,w),f(w)\}$
$D_0=<a,z>$
$\sigma_1=\{z/a\}$
$D_1=<x,h(z,w)>\sigma_1=<x,h(a,w)>$

$\sigma_2=\{z/a,x/h(a,w)\}$
$D_2=<f(g(y)),f(w)>\sigma_2=<f(g(y((,f(w)>$
$\sigma_3=\{z/a,x/h(a,g(y)),w/g(y)\}=$ m.g.u.

d. $S=\{p(a,x),f(g(y)),p(z,f(z),f(a)\}$
$\sigma_0=\{\}$
$D_0=<a,z>$
$\sigma_1=\{a,z\}$
$D_1=<x,f(a)>\sigma_1=<x,f(a)>$
$\sigma_2=\{z/a,x/f(a)\}$
$D_2=<f(g(y)),f(a)>$ not unifiable

e. $S=\{p(\text{john},x,f(g(y))),p(z,f(z),f(w))\}$
$D_0=<\text{john},z>$
$\sigma_1=\{z/\text{john}\}$
$D_1=<x,f(z)>\sigma_1=<x,f(\text{john})>$
$\sigma_2=\{z/\text{john},x/\text{f(john)}\}$
$D_2=<f(g(y)),f(w)>\sigma_2=<f(g(y)),f(w)>$
$\sigma_3=\{z/\text{john},x/\text{f(john)},w/g(y)\}=$ m.g.u.

f. $S=\{p(f(a),g(x),p(y,y)\}$
$D_0=<f(a),y>$
$\sigma_1=\{y/f(a)\}$
$D_1=<g(x),f(a)>\sigma_1$ not unifiable

g. $S=\{p(a,x,h(g(z))),p(z,h(y),h(y))\}$
$D_0=<a,z>$
$\sigma_1=<z/a>$
$D_1=<x,h(y)>\sigma_1=<x,h(y)>$
$\sigma_2=\{z/a,x/h(y)\}$
$D_2=<y,g(z)>\sigma_2=<y,g(a)>$
$\sigma_3=\{z/a,x/h(g(a)),y/g(a)\}=$ m.g.u.

Solutions to Topic 16

1. a. $\neg\forall x(p(x)\rightarrow p(x))$
$\neg\exists x(\neg p(x)\wedge p(x))$=false
b. Hint - transform into clausal form!

2. Transformation of the first and second, using the resolution method:
1. $\neg p(x)\vee\neg q(y)\vee t(x)$
2. $\neg r(y)\vee\neg q(y,x)\vee t(x)$
3. $p(a)$
4. $q(b,c)$
5. $t(a)$
6. $r(b)$
7. $\neg t(z)$ negation of theorem

8. $\neg q(b,x) \vee t(x)$ $\{y/b\}$ by 2 and 6
9. $t(c)$ $\{x/c\}$ by 8 and 4
10. [] $\{z/c\}$ by 9 and 7

3. Transform 1. into clausal form

$p(x,y) \leftarrow (q(y) \leftarrow q(x))$
$p(x,y) \rightarrow (q(y) \leftarrow q(x))$

$p(x,y) \leftarrow q(y) \vee \neg q(x))$
$p(x,y) \rightarrow (q(y) \vee \neg q(x))$

$p(x,y) \vee (\neg q(y) \& q(x))$
$\neg p(x,y) \vee q(y) \vee \neg q(x)$

$(p(x,y) \vee (\neg q(y)) \& (p(x,y) \vee q(x))$
$\neg p(x,y) \vee q(y) \vee \neg q(x)$

1. $p(x,y) \vee \neg q(y)$
2. $p(x,y) \vee q(x)$
3. $\neg p(x,y) \vee q(y) \vee \neg q(x)$
4. $q(c) \vee \neg q(b)$
5. $q(b) \vee \neg q(a)$
6. $\neg p(a,c)$
7. $\neg q(c)$ by 1 and 6
8. $\neg q(b)$ by 4 and 7
9. $\neg q(a)$ by 5 and 8
10. $p(a,c)$ by 2 and 9
11. [] by 6 and 10

Solutions to Topic 17

1. a. G_0: :-$p(a,b),q(b,a)$
C_0: $q(Y,X)$:- $p(X,Y)$. with A_3
θ_0: $\{Y/b, X/a\}$

G_1: :-$p(a,b),q(a,b)$.
C_1: $q(a,b)$ with A_1
θ_1: { }

G_2: :-$p(a,b)$.
C_2: $p(a,b)$.
θ_2: { }

G_3: { }

b.
G_0: :-$q(a,b)$.

C_0: $q(Y,X)$:- $p(X,Y)$. with A_3
θ_0: $\{Y/a.X/b\}$

G_1: :-$p(b,a)$.
C_1: $p(b,a)$:- $q(a,b)$. with A_2
θ_1: $\{\}$

G_2: :-$q(a,b)$.
etc., infinite SLD resolution.

c.
G_0: :-$q(b,b)$.
C_0: $q(Y,X)$:- $p(X,Y)$. with A_3
θ_0: $\{Y/a,x/b\}$

G_1: :-$p(b,b)$
failed SLD resolution - there are no clauses for $p(b,b)$.

2.
a.
G_0: :-$p(a,c)$.
C_0: $p(X,Z)$:- $p(X,Y),p(Y,Z)$. with A_3
θ_0: $\{X/a,Z/c\}$

G_1: :-$p(a,Y),p(Y,c)$.
C_1: $p(a,b)$. with A_1
θ_1: $\{Y/b\}$

G_2: :-$p(b,c)$.
C_2: $p(X2,Y2)$:-$p(Y2,X2)$. with A_4
θ_2: $\{X2/b,Y/c\}$

G_3: :-$p(b,c)$.
C_3: $p(c,b)$. with A_4
θ_3: $\{\}$

G_4: $\{\}$

b. The composition of the most general unifiers (m.g.u.s) or the calculated substitution is according to this SLD refutation:
$\theta_0 \circ \theta_1 \circ \theta_2 \circ \theta_3 = \{X/a, Z/c, Y/b, X_2/b, Y_2/c\}$

3.
a.
G_0: :-ones-and-zeros(1.0.1.0.nil)

C_0: ones-and-zeros(X_0):- ones(X_0), zeros(X_0).
θ_0: {X_0/1.0.1.nil}

G_1: :- ones(1.0.1.0.nil),zeros(1.0.1.0.nil).
C_1: ones(1.U.1.Y_1):- ones(Y_1).
θ_1: {U_1.Y_1/0.1.0.nil}

G_2: :-ones(1.0.nil),zeros(1.0.1.0.nil).
C_2: ones(1.U_2.Y_2):- ones(Y_2).
θ_2: {U_2.Y_2/0.nil}

G_3: :-ones(nil),zeros(1.0.1.0.nil).
C_3: ones(nil).
θ_3: { }

G_4: :-zeros(1.0.10.0.nil)
C_4: zeros(U_4.O.Y_4):- zeros(Y_4)
θ_4: {U_4.O.Y_4/1.0.1.0.nil}

G_5: :-zeros(1.0.nil)
C_5: zeroes(U_5.O.Y_5):- zeros(Y_5).
θ_5: {U_5.0.Y_5/1.0.nil}

G_6: :- zeros(nil).
C_6: zeros(nil).
θ_6: { }

G_7: []

b.
G_0: ones-and-zeros(1.2.1.0.nil).
BR: "choose the right literal"
G_1: :-ones(1.2.1.0.nil),zeros(1.2.1.0.nil).
G_2: fail
Execution ends without evaluating further goals.

c. The calculation rule is: choose the left literal in the goal, if the second element in the list is 0 else select the right literal in the goal.

4.
a. "select the left literal" otherwise the tree is infinite.
b. "select the right literal" otherwise the tree is infinite.
c. There is no difference. In both cases the answer is obtained after 10 steps, the selection of the left literal is generally shorter and leads to better memory utilisation.

5.

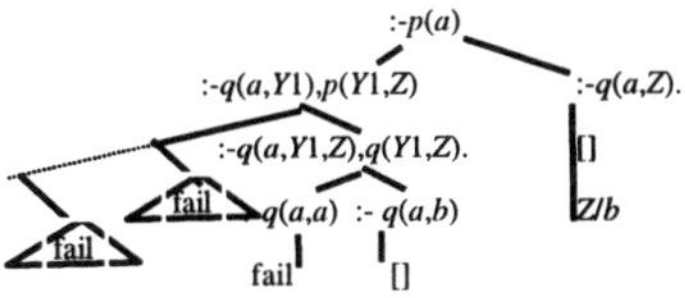

6. a., b.

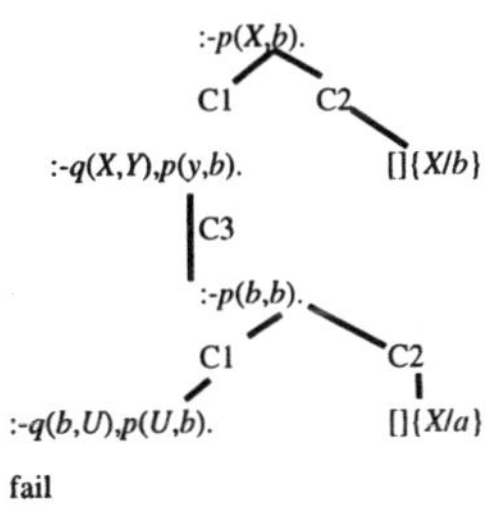

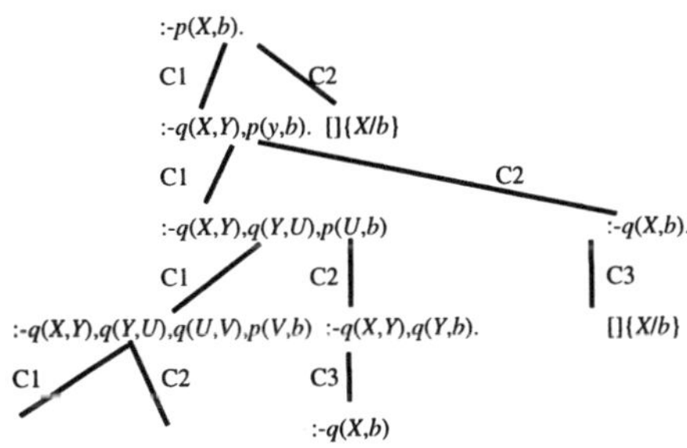

7. {*X*/*b*} is produced twice and {*X*/*b*} once.

8. :-*p*(*a*).
p(*X*):-*p*(*X*),*q*(X).
BR: First left literal leads to an infinite tree.
BR: First right literal leads to an infinite tree.

9. Exercise for the reader.

Solutions to Topic 18

1. "not" is always satisfiable if its argument (as a goal fails) returns the value FALSE. This is the case if the variables of the goal are bound from the start.

2. a. no
b. yes
c. Who=susie
d. Who=no
e. Who=cat

Solutions to Topic 19

1. Using the abbreviation CD, DC, ... etc.
a. *P*∪{¬CD,¬CC,¬DC,¬DD} consistent
b. *P*∪{¬CD,¬DC,¬DD} inconsistent
c. *P*∪{¬CD,¬CC,¬DC,¬DD} inconsistent

d. $P \cup \{\neg \mathrm{CD}\}$ consistent
e. $P \cup \{\neg \mathrm{DC}\}$ inconsistent

Solutions to Topic 20

1. a. $A \leftrightarrow (B \vee C)$
$\neg C$
B

b. $A \leftrightarrow (\neg B \wedge C)$
$B \leftrightarrow C$
C

c. $A \leftrightarrow ((A \wedge C) \vee B)$
$C \leftrightarrow \neg B$
$\neg B$

2. a. $A \leftarrow \neg B$
comp(P) has only one model $\{A\}$

b. $A \leftarrow \neg B$
$B \leftarrow B$
comp(P) has two models $\{A\}$ and $\{B\}$

3. a. $\mathrm{num}(y) \leftrightarrow y=0 \vee \exists x(y=s(x) \wedge \mathrm{num}(x))$

b. $\mathrm{dup}(y) \leftrightarrow \exists u \exists x(y=u.x \wedge u \in x) \vee \exists v \exists x(y=v.x \wedge \mathrm{dup}(x))$

c. $\mathrm{knows}(w,y) \leftrightarrow (w=\mathrm{frank} \wedge \exists x\ \mathrm{computer}(x) \wedge \mathrm{aspects}(x,y))) \vee$
$(w=\mathrm{chris} \wedge \mathrm{says}(\mathrm{frank},y,\mathrm{chris}))$

Informally, Frank knows everything about computer; Chris knows everything which Frank has told him; neither of them knows anything else and no one else knows anything at all.

d. $p(x_1) \leftrightarrow \exists xy(x_1=y,q(x,y),r(x)) \vee \exists x(x_1=x,r(x))$
$q(x_1,x_2) \leftrightarrow \exists x,y(X_1=f(x),x_2=y,q(x,y))$
$r(x_1) \leftrightarrow x_1=b$
and corresponding parts of the Equation.

4. a.

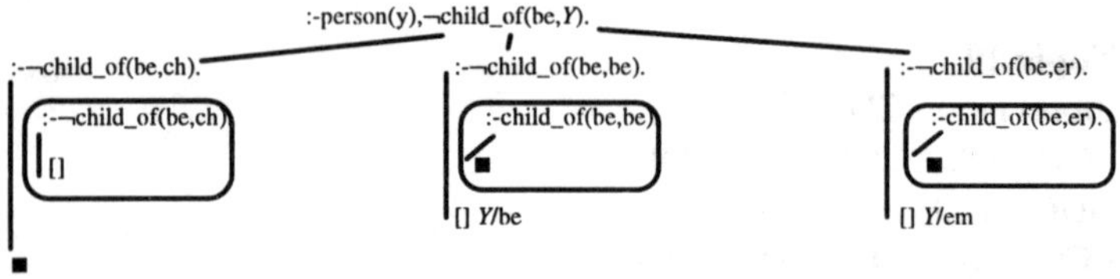

b.

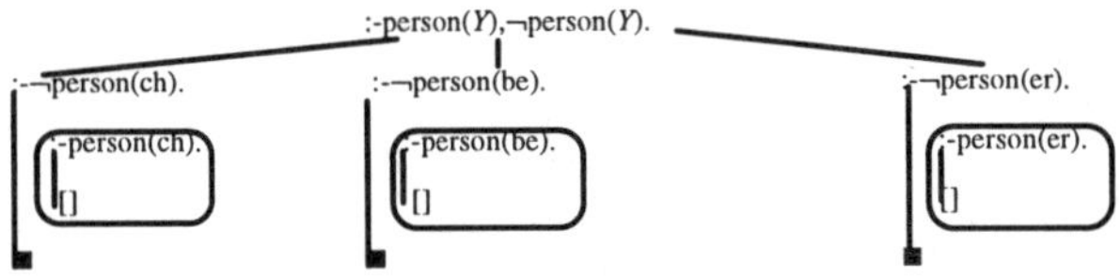

c.

:- children_of(X,X).

|

|

flounders

5. a. p:- ¬r., various

r:- $q(X)$.

Introduction of an atom r which must be instantiated if ¬r is called.

b.

i) :-childless(be)	:-childless(ch)
|	|
:-¬child_of(X,be)	:-child_of(X,ch).
|	|
flounders	flounders

ii) The transformation of the clauses is:
childless(*Y*):- ¬*r*(*Y*).
r(*Y*):- child_of(*X*,*Y*).

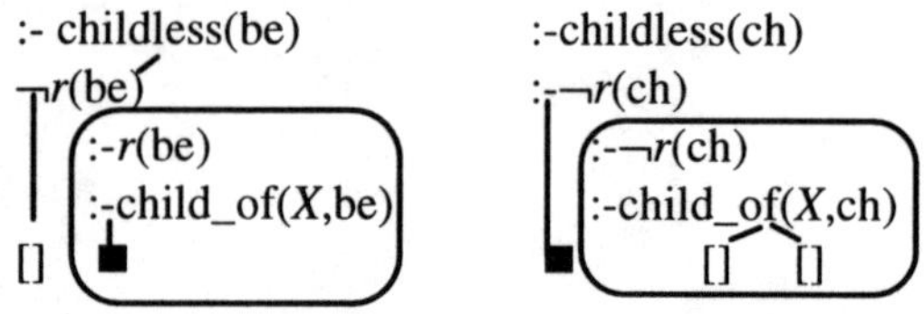

c. childess(*Y*)
|
:-¬*r*(*Y*)
|
flounders

The simplest aid for this *special example* is the first clause transformation to:
childless(*Y*):- person(*Y*),¬*r*(*Y*). modified.

6. A calculation rule which selects the first left and the first right literal in sequence.

7. A set of sentences is consistent because as the loop *q*→*r*→ has a "-" arc.

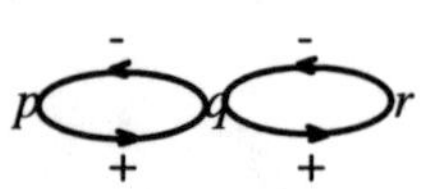

The completion is call consistent because of the model {p,r}
p↔¬*q*
q↔¬*p*,*r*
r↔¬*q*

b. This program is call consistent as there are no loops in the graph.

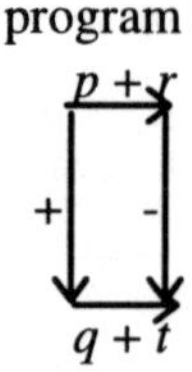

The completion of the program is consistent because of the model {*p*,*q*,*t*}.

c. This program is not call consistent as there is a loop $p \to q \to t \to p$ which has three "-".

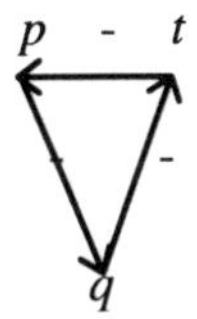

The completion is consistent. It implies $p \leftrightarrow q$, which is untrue and is therefore not a model.

$p \leftrightarrow \neg q$
$q \leftrightarrow \neg t$
$t \leftrightarrow \neg p$

d. This program is not call consistent as the graph is identical to that of c. However the completion does have a model: $\{p(a), t, a=a, b=b\}$.

$p(x) \leftrightarrow X=a, \neg q$
$q \leftrightarrow \neg t$
$t \leftrightarrow \neg p(b)$
Along with Eq(HB,P) in which $HB=a,b$.

9. Using abbreviations for ground atoms, e.g., ms for maria likes susie.
P implies ms, fs and jm, as can be seen from the clauses C_1-C_3. The instantiation of clause C_4 with the elements of the HU results in:
mm ∨ nm
ms ∨ sm
mf ∨ fm
mj ∨ jm
Of these clauses only nm ∨ nm implies a ground atom, namely nm. Therefore the atoms q, for $p \models q$ are: ms, fs, jm, mm.

10. Only a and c.

11. The comp(P) consists of:
$p(x_1) \leftrightarrow x_1=a, \neg q(b)$
$q(x_1) \leftrightarrow []$
and some equivalences including $a=a$, $b=b$.

Solutions to Topic 21

1. Every node on the tree is
either an empty query []
or a non-empty query with no direct successors
or a query with one or more successors.
First and last instances are known as terminals;

third case non-terminals.

2. The search begins by producing the root node which represents the first level of the tree.

3. A search step to a non-terminal results in a successor node which has not yet been produced.

4. A level step comprises all possible search steps from non-terminals in the current level.

5. If the current level does not contain any further non-terminals then the whole tree is produced; otherwise a further level is produced.

For all the great the first step is courage.
- Johann Wolfgang von Goethe -

APPENDIX B

Program Code for the Examples

The programs for the exercises are written in the Quintus Prolog 2.4 language.

a. The family program

```
parent(caron,peter).
parent(harry,peter).
parent(ollie,susie).
parent(freda,susie).
parent(peter,anne).
parent(peter,gayle).
parent(susie,anne).
parent(susie,gayle).
parent(susie,thomas).
parent(peter,thomas).
parent(gayle,carl).

female(caron).
female(freda).
female(susie).
female(anne).
female(gayle).
male(harry).
male(ollie).
male(peter).
male(thomas).
male(carl).

grandparent(Pers1,Pers2):-parent(Pers1,Child),
                          parent(Child,Pers2).
mother(Person,Child):- parent(Person,Child),
                          female(Person).
unequal(Person1,Person2):- Person1 \== Person2.
sister(Pers1,Pers2):- parent(Parent,Pers1),
            parent(Parent,Pers2),
            female(Pers1),
            unequal(Pers1,Pers2).
descendant(Pers1,Pers2):- parent(Pers2,Pers1).
descendant(Pers1,Pers2):- parent(Pers2,Child),
            descendant(Pers1,Child).
predecessor(Pers1,Pers2):- parent(Pers1,Pers2).
predecessor(Pers1,Pers2):- parent(Pers1,Child),
                          predecessor(Child,Pers2).
```

b. The Company Program

```
/* board(A,Z1,Z2,F) means A was from Z1 to Z2 */
/* in board and had the function F */
board(henry,1990,1992,department_head).
board(ollie,1988,1990,department_head).
```

```
board(will,1992,1993,department_head).
board(henry,1990,1992,apprentice_supervisor).
board(freda,1988,1990,apprentice_supervisor).
board(harry,1990,1992,treasurer).
board(harry,1990,1992,organising_committee).

successor_rule(P):-
      board(P,From,To,department_head),
      board(P,From,To,apprentice_supervisor).
```

c. The Flight Link Program

```
/*flight(A,B) means flight from A to B */
flight(hamburg,bremerhaven).
flight(bremerhaven,newyork).
flight(bremerhaven,paris).
flight(hamburg,frankfurt).
flight(frankfurt,paris).
flight(paris,london).
flight(newyork,london).
```

b. ?- flight(hamburg,paris).

c. ?-flight(Town1,Town2),flight(Town2,Town3).

```
/* flight from several towns */
/* flight_connection(A,B) means: */
/* a flight connection from A to B */
flight_connection(Town1,Town2):-flight(Town1,Town2).
flight_connection(Town1,Town2):- flight(Town1,Town),
                  flight_connection(Town,Town2).

/* Town is flown to from several towns */
several_flights(Town):-
                  flight(Town1,Town),
                  flight(Town2,Town),
                  Town1 \== Town2.
```

d. The Farmer Program

```
element(X,[X|_]).
element(X,[_|Y]):- element(X,Y).
different(east,west).
different(west,east).
safe([Farmer,_,Farmer,_]).
safe([Farmer,Farmer,Goose,Farmer]):-
      different(Farmer,Goose).
move([Farmer, Fox, Goose, Grain], [Farmer2, Fox,
Goose, Grain]):-
      different(Farmer,Farmer2),
      safe([Farmer2,Fox,Goose,Grain]).
```

```
move([Farmer,   Farmer,   Goose,   Grain],   [Farmer2,
Farmer, Goose, Grain]):-
      different(Farmer,Farmer2),
      safe([Farmer2,Farmer2,Goose,Grain]).
move([Farmer,  Fox,  Farmer,  Grain],  [Farmer2,  Fox,
Farmer2, Grain]):-
      different(Farmer,Farmer2),
      safe([Farmer2,Fox,Farmer2,Grain]).
move([Farmer,  Fox,  Goose,  Farmer],  [Farmer,  Fox,
Goose, Farmer2]):-
      different(Farmer,Farmer2),
      safe([Farmer2,Fox,Goose,Farmer2]).

depth_first(Goal,[Goal|_],[Goal]).
depth_first(Goal,[Current|Previous],[Current|After]):
-
      action(Current,Next),
      not(element(Next,Previous)),
      depth_first(Goal,[Next|[Current|Previous]],Afte
r).
```

Call:
depth_first([east,east,east,east],[[west,west,west,west]],Answer).

Solution:
Answer=[[west,west,west,west],
[east,west,east,west],
[west,west,east,west],
[east,east,east,west],
[west,east,west,west],
[east,east,west,east],
[west,east,west,east],
[east,east,east,east]]

Answer=[[west,west,west,west],
[east,west,east,west],
[west,west,east,west],
[west,west,east,east],
[east,east,east,east]]
Two solutions

BIBLIOGRAPHY

[1] K. Apt, R. Boll, Logic Programming and Negation, *Logic Programming*, 19(20), 9-71, 1994

[2] C. Beckstein, *Zur Logic der Logik-Programmierung*, Springer Verlag, 1987

[3] F. Belli, *Einführung in die logische Programmierung mit Prolog*, BI-Wissenschaftsverlag, 1988

[4] W. Bibel, *Deduktion, Automatisierung der Logic*, Oldenburg Verlag, 1992

[5] B. Boehringer, C. Chiopris, I. Futo, *Wissensbasierte Systeme mit Prolog*, Addison Wesley, 1988

[6] F. Bogdan, *Prolog User's Handbook*, Ellis Horwood, 1988

[7] P. Bothner, *Programmierung in Prolog, eine umfassende and praxisgerichtete Einführung*, Vieweg Verlag, 1991

[8] I. Bratko, *Prolog Programming for Artificial Intelligence* (2nd. ed.), Addison Wesley, 1990

[9] A. Bundy, *The Computer Modeling of Mathematical Reasoning*, Academic, 1983

[10] Burnham and Hal, *Prolog Programming and Applications*, Macmillan 1985

[11] K. L. Clark, Negation as failure, in H. Gallaire and J. Minker (eds), *Logic and Databases*, 293-322, Plenum Press, 1978

[12] K. L. Clark, F. G. McCabe, *Micro-Prolog: Programming in Logic*, Prentice Hall, 1984

[13] W. F. Clocksin, C. M. Mellish, *Programming in Prolog*, Springer Verlag, 1987

[14] W. F. Clocksin, C. M. Mellish, *Programming in Prolog*, Springer Verlag, 1989

[15] H. Coelho, J. C. Cotta, *Prolog by Example: How to Learn, Teach and Use It*, Springer Verlag, 1988

[16] A. Colmerauer, Opening the Prolog iii universe, *Byte Magazin*, 177-182, 1987

[17] T. Conlon, *Start Problem Solving with Prolog*, Addison Wesley, 1985

[18] Cordes, Kurso, Labgendoerfer, Rust, *Prolog eine methodische Einführung*, Vieweg Verlag, 1987

[19] D. Crookes, *Introduction to Programming in Logic*, Prentice Hall, 1988

[20] Doores, Reiblin, Varda, *Prolog Programming for Tomorrow*, Sigma, 1987

[21] Dowsing, *A first Course in Logic with Computer Science Application*, Blackwell Scientific, 1986

[22] A. W. Ertl, *Prolog verstehen und anwenden*, IWT Verlag, 1988

[23] N. E. Fuchs, *Kurs in logischer Programmierung*, Springer Verlag, 1990

[24] J. H. Gallaier, *Logic for Computer Science, Foundation of Automatic Theorem Proving*, John Wiley, 1986

[25] M. R. Genesareth, N. J. Nilsson, *Logical Foundations of Artificial Intelligence,* Morgan Kaufmann, 1989

[26] F. Giannesini, H. Kanoui, R. Pasero, *Prolog*, Addison Wesley, 1988

[27] P. Gochet, E. Gregorie, *From Standard Logic to Logic Programming*, John Wiley, 1988

[28] S. Gregory, *Parallel Logic Programming in Prolog: The Language and its Implementation*, Addison Wesley, 1987

[29] Heinmann and Weihrauch, *Logic für Informatik*, B. G. Teubner Verlag, 1991

[30] J. Herbrand, Investigation into proof theory, in J van Jeijenoort (ed), *From Frege to Gödel: A Survey Book in Mathematical Logic*, 1879-1931, 525-581, Harvard University Press, 1967

[31] J. Jaffar, M. Mahr, Constraint logic programming, *Logic Programming*, 19(20):503-581, 1994

[32] A. Janson, *Die Programmiersprache Turbo Prolog*, Franzis Verlag, 1988

[33] A. Johansson, A. Eriksson, A. Erdman, *Prolog Versus You: An Introduction to Logic Programming*, Springer Verlag, 1989

[34] H. Klein-Büning, Schmitgen, *Prolog*, B. G. Teubner Verlag, 1988

[35] F.Kluzniak, S. Szpakowiez, J. Bien, *Prolog for Programmers*, Academic, 1985

[36] I. Kononeko, Lavrac, *Prolog through Examples: A Practical Programming Guide*, Sigma, 1988

[37] R. Kowalski, Closed World Assumption, in H. Gallaire, J. Minker, (eds), *Logic and Databases*, Plenum, 1978

[38] R. Kowalski, *Algorithm=logic+control*, CACM, 22(7): 424-36, 1979

[39] R. Kowalski, *Logic for problem solving*, North Holland, 1979

[40] R. Kowalski, D. Kuehner, Linear Resolution with selection function, *Artificial Intelligence*, 2, 227-60, 1992

[41] W. Kreutzner, B. McKenzie, *Programming for Artificial Intelligence, Methods, Tools and Applications*, Addison Wesley, 1990

[42] C. Lehner, *Prolog and Linguistik*, Oldenburg Verlag, 1990

[43] J. W. Lloyd, *Foundation of logic Programming*, 2nd ed., Springer Verlag, 1987

[44] G. F. Luger, W.A. Stubblefield, *Artificial Intelligence, Structures and Strategies for Complex Problem Solving*, 2nd ed., 1993

[45] D. Maier, D. S. Warren, *Computing with Logic*, Benjamin Cummings, 1988

[46] J. Malpas, *Prolog: A Relational Language and its Application*, Prentice Hall, 1987

[47] U. Niloson, J. Maluszynski, *Logic Programming and Prolog*, John Wiley, 1990

[48] J. A. Robinson, *A Machine-oriented Logic Based on the Resolution Principle*, ACM, 12, pp. 23-14, 1965

[49] P. Ross, *Advanced Prolog Techniques and Examples*, Addison Wesley, 1989

[50] P. H. Schmidt, *Theorie der logischen Programmierung eine elementare Einführung*, Springer Verlag, 1992

[51] U. Schöning, *Logic für Informatiker*, BI Wissenschaft, 1989

[52] V. Sperschneider, G. Antoniou, *Logic: A Foundation for Computer Science*, Addison Wesley, 1991

[53] L. Sterling, E. Shapiro, *Prolog*, Addison Wesley, 1988

[54] L. Sterling, E. Shapiro, *The Art of Prolog*, MIT press, 1986

[55] D. S. Touretzky, *LISP - A Gentle Introduction to Symbolic Computation*, Harper & Row, 1984

[56] E. J. Yannakoudakis, *The architectural Logic of Database Systems*, Springer Verlag, 1986

INDEX

— - —

-, 99

— * —

*, 99

— / —

/, 100

— + —

+, 99

— < —

<, 100

— = —

=, 101, 108
=<, 101
==, 108

— > —

>, 100
>=, 101

— A —

abolish, 102
admissible programs, 230
alphabet, 113
AND-OR tree, 77
anonymous variable, 30
arity, 36, 144
asserta, 102
assertz, 102
atom, 121, 144
atom(X), 107
atomic(X), 107
atoms, 36
axiom system, 115, 153

— B —

backtracking, 31
Begriffsschrift, 11
breadth-first search, 239
bubblesort, 60
built-in predicates, 91

— C —

calculation rule, 196
calculus, 113
call-consistent, 229
CET, 222
Clark's equality theory, 222
clausal form, 14
clause, 121, 145
closed world assumption, 215
compare, 109
complementary pair, 183
completeness, 16, 153, 154
completion of a definite program, 223
conjunctions, 119
conjunctive normal form, 122
consistency checking with resolution, 188
consistent, 154
cut operator, 80
CWA, 215

— D —

decidability, 155
decidable, 156
default inference, 215
definite clauses, 208
definite program, 208
dependency graph, 229
depth first search, 240
display(Term), 92
divergent pair, 184

— E —

entity resolution, 194
equivalence, 130
extensionality principle, 120

— F —

fact, 26
fair calculation rule, 227
finite failure, 227
finite failure tree, 212
floundered, 226
formal logic, 13
formula
  consistency, 127
  interpretation, 146
  model, 126
  satisfiability, 127
functor, 36

— G —

generally valid, 148
get(Char), 92
goal, 28

— H —

Herbrand basis, 166
Herbrand domain, 164
Herbrand interpretation, 167
Herbrand model, 168
Herbrand proof procedure, 162
Herbrand theorem, 169
Herbrand universe, 11, 166
Horn clauses, 15, 121

— I —

inconsistency, 155
instantiation, 31
integer(X), 107
interpretation, 146
introduction rules, 152
is, 98

— L —

linear resolution, 194
list
  adding an element, 50
  bracket notation, 50
  dot notation, 50
  functor notation, 51
  membership, 52
  reverse, 58
  sublist, 57
listing, 103
literal, 121, 145
logic
  foundations, 112
logical equivalence, 151
logic programming systems, 10

— M —

matching, 28, 39
mathematical logic, 13
matrix method, 123
merge sort, 66
mod, 100
model, 148
model theory, 114
modus barbara, 132
modus ponens, 131
modus tollens, 132, 137
most general unifier, 183

— N —

N_1 resolution, 193
naïve sort (slowsort), 69
negation by failure rule, 209, 219
nl, 92
nonvar(X), 107
normal goal, 219, 228
normal program, 219, 228
not procedure, 210

— O —

occurs check, 186

— P —

P_1 and N_1 resolution, 193
predicate logic, 14
predicates, 14
Prolog, 24
proof by contradiction, 136
proof theory, 114
propositional logic, 118
  axiom systems, 121
  inference rules, 131
  syntax, 121
put(Number), 93

— Q —

quantifier, 145
queries, 28
quicksort, 62

— R —

read(Term), 92
recursive rules, 42
replacement rule, 152
resolution, 15, 132, 138
resolution methods, 176
resolution strategies, 192
retract, 103

— S —

safe calculation rule, 215
satisfiable, 148
search, 236
search rule, 203
search strategy, 203
see(File), 95
seeing(X), 96
semantic methods, 136
semantic trees, 169
semantics, 112
semi-decidable, 156
skolemisation, 158
SLD derivation, 196, 198
SLD refutation, 196, 198
SLD resolution, 196
SLD tree, 202
SLD unsatisfiability, 199
SLDNF inference system, 225
sorting by insertion, 64
sound, 154
soundness, 16, 132
standard predicates, 91
strict program, 230
  idempotent, 179
subsumes, 194
subsumption resolution, 194
syntactic methods, 135
syntax, 112

— T —

tautology, 128
tell(file), 95
telling(X), 95
term, 38, 144
  ground, 38, 144
theorem, 114, 155
theory, 128, 155
  completeness, 155
  consistent, 128
  decidable, 155
  inconsistent, 128, 155
  model, 128
  theorems, 128

— U —

unification, 182
unifier, 182
unsatisfiable, 127

— V —

var(X), 108
variables, 36

— W —

write(Term), 92